SECURING RESPECT

Behavioural expectations and anti-social behaviour in the UK

Edited by Andrew Millie

This edition published in Great Britain in 2009 by

The Policy Press
University of Bristol
Fourth Floor
Beacon House
Queen's Road
Bristol BS8 1QU
UK

Tel +44 (0)117 331 4054
Fax +44 (0)117 331 4093
e-mail tpp-info@bristol.ac.uk
www.policypress.org.uk

North American office:
The Policy Press
c/o International Specialized Books Services (ISBS)
920 NE 58th Avenue, Suite 300
Portland, OR 97213-3786, USA
Tel +1 503 287 3093
Fax +1 503 280 8832
e-mail info@isbs.com

© The Policy Press 2009

British Library Cataloguing in Publication Data
A catalogue record for this book is available from the British Library.

Library of Congress Cataloging-in-Publication Data
A catalog record for this book has been requested.

ISBN 978 1 84742 093 0 paperback
ISBN 978 1 84742 094 7 hardcover

The right of Andrew Millie to be identified as editor of this work has been asserted by him in accordance with the 1988 Copyright, Designs and Patents Act.

The statements and opinions contained within this publication are solely those of the contributors and editor authors and not of The University of Bristol or The Policy Press. The University of Bristol and The Policy Press disclaim responsibility for any injury to persons or property resulting from any material published in this publication.

The Policy Press works to counter discrimination on grounds of gender, race, disability, age and sexuality.

Cover design by The Policy Press.
Front cover: image kindly supplied by Jef Aérosol.
Printed and bound in Great Britain by TJ International, Padstow.

Lack of respect, though less aggressive than an outright insult, can take an equally wounding form. No insult is offered another person, but neither is recognition extended; he or she is not *seen* – as a full human being whose presence matters. (Richard Sennett, 2003)

Once you leave behind such class concerns as how to balance the peas on the back of a fork, all the important rules surely boil down to one: *remember you are with other people; show some consideration.* (Lynne Truss, 2005)

... preventing crime for me also means all of us as a community setting boundaries between what is acceptable and unacceptable behaviour – with clear penalties for stepping over the line. Boundaries that reflect the words I was taught when I was young – words upon which we all know strong communities are founded: discipline, respect, responsibility. (Gordon Brown, 2007)

There was no respect for youth when I was young, and now that I am old, there is no respect for age – I missed it coming and going. (Attributed to J.B. Priestley)

Contents

List of figures and tables   vi
Acknowledgements   vii
Notes on contributors   viii

Introduction   I
Andrew Millie

Part One: Respect in context
one   Respect and the politics of behaviour   23
        Elizabeth Burney
two   'A Jekyll in the classroom, a Hyde in the street':   41
        Queen Victoria's hooligans
        Geoffrey Pearson

Part Two: Respectful young people and children
three   Giving respect: the 'new' responsibilities of youth in   75
        the transition towards citizenship
        Alan France and Jo Meredith
four   Every child matters in public open spaces   97
        Helen Woolley

Part Three: Respectful communities and families
five   Disciplining women: anti-social behaviour and the   119
        governance of conduct
        Judy Nixon and Caroline Hunter
six   'The feeling's mutual': respect as the basis for   139
        cooperative interaction
        Peter Somerville

Part Four: Respectful city living
seven   Tolerance, respect and civility amid changing cities   171
        Jon Bannister and Ade Kearns
eight   Respect and city living: contest or cosmopolitanism?   193
        Andrew Millie

Part Five: Respect, identities and values
nine   Civilising offensives: education, football and 'eradicating'   219
        sectarianism in Scotland
        John Flint and Ryan Powell
ten   'You lookin' at me?' Discourses of respect and disrespect,   239
        identity and violence
        Peter Squires
eleven   Conclusions: promoting mutual respect and empathy   267
        Andrew Millie

Index   277

List of figures and tables

Figures

7.1   The foundations of tolerance   178

Tables

1.1   The government's Respect Agenda   12
6.1   Realms of interaction   146
7.1   The objects of tolerance   175
7.2   Tolerant assessments (of unfavoured behaviours)   176
7.3   Tolerant responses   177

Acknowledgements

As with any book a lot of people need to be thanked for their help and guidance. Firstly, I am hugely indebted to the authors who contributed to this volume. They come from a number of disciplinary backgrounds, yet I believe their contributions have formed a coherent whole. I'd also like to thank Adam Crawford, Mike Hough and Nick Tilley, who agreed to be referees for my initial proposal to The Policy Press. And of course I am very grateful to The Policy Press for agreeing to publish! At The Policy Press I particularly want to thank Karen Bowler, Leila Ebrahimi, Jessica Hughes, Jo Morton and Emily Watt. Thanks are due also to the anonymous reviewers.

Chapter 2, by Geoffrey Pearson, is an updated version of a paper included in a collection edited by David Downes: many thanks to David Downes and to Palgrave Macmillan for permitting its reproduction here. The original reference is: Pearson, G. (1989) '"A Jekyll in the classroom, a Hyde in the street": Queen Victoria's hooligans', in D. Downes (ed) *Crime and the City: Essays in Memory of John Barron Mays*, Basingstoke: Macmillan, reproduced with permission.

Finally, many thanks to the artist Jef Aérosol for allowing me to use his painting for the front cover. I came across his work at Banksy's 'Cans Festival' held in London in 2008. Jef's work can be found at www.myspace.com/jefaerosol, http://jefaerosol.free.fr and elsewhere.

Notes on contributors

Jon Bannister is Senior Lecturer in the Department of Urban Studies, University of Glasgow. He is also the 'Communities and Crimes' Network leader of the Scottish Centre for Crime and Justice Research, as well as managing editor of the journal *Urban Studies*. His current research interests concern: the interplay between civility and disorder in the urban realm; territoriality and youth 'gangs'.

Elizabeth Burney is an honorary senior fellow at the Institute of Criminology, University of Cambridge, an author of books in the criminal justice field and formerly a staff writer on *The Economist*. She has written extensively about the policy, practice and politics surrounding anti-social behaviour. Elizabeth is the author of *Making People Behave: Anti-social Behaviour, Politics and Policy* (Willan, 2005).

John Flint is Professor of Housing and Urban Governance in the Centre for Regional Economic and Social Research (CRESR) at Sheffield Hallam University. He has conducted research in the areas of housing, regeneration, anti-social behaviour and urban governance. John is the editor of the book *Housing, Urban Governance and Anti-social Behaviour* (The Policy Press, 2006).

Alan France is Professor of Social Policy Research and Director of the Centre for Research in Social Policy (CRSP) at Loughborough University. He is the author of a range of publications relating to pathways into crime, youth, children and communities. With Ross Homel he co-authored the book *Pathways and Crime Prevention* (Willan, 2007).

Caroline Hunter is a barrister and Professor in the Law School, University of York. She has written extensively on housing law and on the response of social landlords to anti-social behaviour. She also has particular research interests in the role of the courts in the eviction of tenants.

Ade Kearns is Professor of Urban Studies at the University of Glasgow. He has conducted policy-related research into a wide range of housing and urban issues. His current research interests include: community mix, neighbourhood quality and social cohesion; patterns and impacts of ethnic residential segregation; neighbourhood change, health and well-being; and the impacts of residential turnover.

Jo Meredith is a research assistant at the Centre for Research in Social Policy (CRSP) at Loughborough University. Her research interests include youth policy, drug and alcohol policies and social exclusion.

Andrew Millie (editor) is a lecturer in Criminology and Social Policy in the Department of Social Sciences, Loughborough University. Andrew has published on a range of topics, including anti-social behaviour, crime and the city, policing, sentencing, and crime prevention. Over the last few years his main focus has been anti-social behaviour. He is author of *Anti-social Behaviour* (Open University Press, 2009), and co-author of *Anti-social Behaviour Strategies: A Need for Balance* (The Policy Press, 2005).

Judy Nixon is a principal lecturer in Urban Governance at Sheffield Hallam University. She has experience in the fields of housing policy and sociolegal issues. Her areas of interest include responses to domestic violence, housing management and evictions. For several years she has been specialising in work around anti-social behaviour.

Geoffrey Pearson is Professor of Criminology in the Department of Professional and Community Education (PACE) at Goldsmiths College, University of London. His research interests concern crime, drugs, youth studies and historical criminology. From 1998 to 2006 he was Editor-in-Chief of the *British Journal of Criminology*. He is the author of *Hooligan: A History of Respectable Fears* (Macmillan, 1983).

Ryan Powell is a research fellow at the Centre for Regional Economic and Social Research (CRESR) at Sheffield Hallam University. He has a broad range of research experience in the geographies of exclusion and urban sociology. Specific interests include housing market change and inequalities, housing and identity, nomadism, local labour markets and the sociology of Norbert Elias.

Peter Somerville is Professor of Social Policy in the Department of Policy Studies, University of Lincoln. Peter has a background in housing practice and in research on housing and social policy. He has published widely on participation, empowerment and social exclusion and has been responsible for numerous research projects in the field of housing need, particularly the needs of black and minority ethnic groups, and for surveys of resident opinion, including on issues of crime and the fear of crime. He is the author of *Social Relations and Social Exclusion* (Routledge, 2000) and he edited the book *Housing and Social Policy* (Routledge, 2005).

Peter Squires is Professor of Criminology and Public Policy at the University of Brighton, and has written extensively in the field of criminology, youth justice and anti-social behaviour. Peter is co-author (with Dawn Stephen) of *Rougher Justice: Anti-social Behaviour and Young People* (Willan, 2005) and he has recently edited the volume *ASBO Nation* (The Policy Press, 2008).

Helen Woolley is a chartered landscape architect and a senior lecturer in the Department of Landscape at the University of Sheffield. She is also a board member of the multi-disciplinary Centre for the Study of Children and Youth. Helen's research has included themes of open spaces and social inclusion, with a particular reference to children and young people. She is author of the book *Urban Open Spaces* (Spon Press, 1983) and lead author of *Inclusion of Disabled Children in Primary School Playgrounds* (Joseph Rowntree Foundation and National Children's Bureau, 2005). Her research and consultancy activities include working with a range of government departments and agencies; in particular, she is a CABE Space enabler.

Introduction

Andrew Millie

Following electoral success in 2005, Tony Blair announced that his third term 'big idea' was to create a society of 'respect'. According to Blair, 'there is a disrespect that people don't like. And whether it's in the classroom, or on the street, or on town centres on a Friday or Saturday night, I want to focus on this issue.' A government 'Respect Task Force' was established in September 2005 and a *Respect Action Plan* was launched in January 2006. This cross-departmental agenda built on earlier work targeting anti-social behaviour – a topic that had became something of an obsession during the Blair years, with its emphasis on the tough enforcement of standards of behaviour (Burney, 2005; Squires, 2008; Millie, 2009). But with the 'Respect Agenda' Blair was also going to be tough on disrespect (and maybe tough on the causes of disrespect?). Blair took some inspiration from the work of Richard Sennett (2003), if not necessarily Sennett's exact ideas (of which more later). In fact, in a speech to launch the *Respect Action Plan* (Respect Task Force, 2006), Blair stated that 'Richard Sennett has written persuasively about the way the basic courtesies diminish with increasing material inequalities.' How Blair intended to make people more courteous is another matter. Sennett was less favourable about Blair, and following the launch of the *Respect Action Plan* he commented:

> Is it any surprise to you that a politician who elicits less and less respect from his public thinks that the public has a problem with respect. Blair wasn't worried about this in 1998. This Whitehall project is just the wrong end of the telescope. The issue isn't how individuals can behave better but how institutions can behave better. (Sennett, 2006)

Like that of anti-social behaviour before it, the definition of 'respect' was left vague, maybe deliberately so. According to the *Respect Action Plan*,

> people are still concerned that the values the majority hold dear are not shared by a selfish minority. People do care when respect is disregarded – people find dropping litter and queue jumping irritating. But more serious

> anti-social behaviour like constant noise and harassment
> from neighbours ruins lives – particularly in the poorest
> communities. (Respect Task Force, 2006: 3)

Thus, disrespectful behaviour was equated with serious anti-social behaviour, but also with more minor annoyances such as queue jumping. Whether the government should be involved in promoting orderly queuing is another thing (but I suppose queuing is another British obsession!). What is telling is a concern for 'the values of the majority'. This book presents a collection of essays that consider the question of who decides behavioural acceptability in the UK, and what is respectable behaviour. If behavioural acceptability is decided by the majority of citizens, are they necessarily right? And if someone holds a minority view, does this make them disrespectful of the majority? With the government's emphasis on enforcing standards of behaviour, the consequences of such behavioural interpretation become very important. Further, according to the *Respect Action Plan*: 'Respect cannot be learned, purchased or acquired it can only be earned' (Respect Task Force, 2006: 30). This makes for a great sound bite, but is it true?

'Respect' is not solely a Blairite issue, with David Cameron of the Conservative Party also launching his 'Real Respect Agenda' in January 2006 (Conservative Party, 2006). Gordon Brown (2006) has similarly talked of 'respect' and the influence of his parents in the formation of his 'moral compass' – with their belief in 'duty, responsibility, and respect for others'. Politics is an unpredictable game, and in June 2007 Gordon Brown succeeded Blair as Labour Prime Minister. Perhaps in an attempt to distance himself from Blair, in the following January Brown called an end to the Respect Task Force, much to the delight of the Opposition. In *The Times* (Ford, 2008) Conservative spokesman James Brokenshire was reported as saying, 'Respect promised so much and has delivered so little. The Government hasn't even completed a proper assessment of where it thinks its various interventions are working.'

But the reported demise of 'respect' was a little premature. Yes, the Respect Task Force had not been given enough time to fully implement its planned programme – or to evaluate its effectiveness – but in October 2007 much of the government's work on anti-social behaviour and respect continued and was simply shifted to a new 'Youth Taskforce' established at the Department for Children, Schools and Families, under the guidance of Secretary of State Ed Balls. A *Youth Taskforce Action Plan* followed in March 2008. Within this document the new Prime Minister's position was made clear:

a strong society requires that where individuals – including young people – overstep the boundaries of acceptable behaviour they are made to face up [to] their responsibilities. Tackling the causes of bad behaviour helps to ensure lasting change. That is why we want to see young people who get into trouble made to take the help they need to mend their ways. (Gordon Brown, in Youth Taskforce, 2008: 34)

The government's position is one of *securing respect*, with a heavy emphasis on enforcing standards of behaviour; for instance, that young people will be 'made to take the help they need'. The extent to which the government can insist on a respectful citizenry is a common theme for this volume – but first, I want to focus on what 'respect' might actually mean. Like anti-social behaviour, it is an extremely slippery concept, but it has something to do with morality, mutuality, reciprocity and maintaining standards of behaviour in public places. These broad themes are considered in this introduction. In the final section an outline of the rest of the volume is provided.

Respect and morality

Just as Gordon Brown has emphasised his 'moral compass', Blair before him saw morality as central to the New Labour project and, according to Sennett (2005), 'throughout his career Tony Blair has worried about how government might enforce morality'. The idea that morality can be enforced is a strange one and begs the question, *whose* morality? In Chapter One Elizabeth Burney outlines the origins of New Labour's focus on anti-social behaviour and respect. Much of this is tied in with the party's communitarian leanings; however, it is also allied to Blair's *particular* brand of Christian Socialism. In a speech made in 2001 to the Christian Socialist Movement Blair set out his moral standpoint:

> Our values are clear. The equal worth of all citizens, and their right to be treated with equal respect and consideration despite their differences, are fundamental. So too is individual responsibility, a value which in the past the Left sometimes underplayed. But a large part of individual responsibility concerns the obligations we owe one to another. The self is best realised in community with others. Society is the way we realise our mutual obligations – a society in which we all belong, no one left out.... Equal worth, responsibility,

community – these values are fundamental to my political creed. (Blair, 2001)

The government's White Paper on anti-social behaviour published two years later had a similar emphasis on 'respect and responsibility' (Home Office, 2003). These ideas were also highlighted in the *Respect Action Plan*, where it was stated that '[respect] cannot be achieved by Government alone ... ultimately every citizen has a responsibility to behave in a respectful way and to support the community around them in doing the same' (Respect Task Force, 2006: 3). The key point of this 'Third Way' (Blair, 1998; Giddens, 1998; 2000) point of view is that every individual deserves equality of respect; but with this comes individual responsibility to community.

In Chapter Two Geoffrey Pearson provides compelling evidence that anti-social behaviour and disrespect are hardly new phenomena. In fact, the meaning of 'respect' has been a concern of moral philosophy for centuries. Moral philosophy can be a minefield for the uninitiated, and debates on respect are no different. Being a relative novice in this area I will be brief; but if the reader wants to look further I can recommend the work of Stephen Darwall (1977), Thomas Hill (2000), Joseph Raz (2001) and Carla Bagnoli (2007). Of most relevance is the work of Immanuel Kant (eg 1964 [1785]), on whom all these authors draw. Central to a Kantian conception of respect is the notion of human dignity, that 'respect for the moral law entails treating persons (oneself included) always as ends in themselves and never simply as means' (Darwall, 1977: 36). In effect, human dignity dictates that people should never be considered means to an end; in this sense, as Joseph Raz (2001: 125) has put it, 'Respect for people is, and is generally acknowledged to be, a central moral duty.' According to Thomas Hill (2000: 69), a Kantian perspective is that:

> human beings are to be regarded as worthy of respect as human beings, regardless of how their values differ and whether or not we disapprove of what they do.

This is a view in marked contrast to that put forward by the British government, and promoted in the *Respect Action Plan*. The government's position is based on a moral perspective where respect is associated with achievement, where respect 'can only be earned'. However, according to Hill, a Kantian view is of an equality of respect derived from human dignity: 'simply by virtue of their humanity, all people qualify for a status of dignity, which should be recognized respectfully by everyone'

(Hill, 2000: 70). With this in mind, the earlier quotation from Blair's 2001 speech becomes somewhat muddled. Blair's initial contention was that all citizens have 'equal worth' and have a 'right to be treated with equal respect'. This fits with a Kantian moral philosophy; yet the view that 'every citizen has a responsibility to behave in a respectful way' equates respect with merit and achievement. From this point of view those deemed to be respectful have greater moral worth. Correspondingly, individuals who have not earned the community's respect are seen logically as lower, as disrespectful or anti-social 'others'. This is a dilemma that has concerned moral philosophy; as Stephen Darwall (1977: 37) has put it:

> How could respect be something which is due to all persons? Do we not also think that persons can either deserve or fail to deserve our respect? Is the moralist who claims that all persons are entitled to respect advocating that we give up this idea?

Darwall attempted to resolve the dilemma by conceiving of two types of respect. First, he identified recognition respect, according to which persons are 'entitled to have other persons take seriously and weigh appropriately the fact that they are persons in deliberating about what they do' (1977: 38). This is closest to Kant's original idea of persons as ends and not means, and also Blair's (2001) contention that people have a 'right to be treated with equal respect'. According to Darwall there is also appraisal respect, whose 'exclusive objects are persons or features which are held to manifest their excellence as persons or as engaged in some specific pursuit' (1977: 38) – something more akin to esteem and respect being earned; or, as Darwall put it, 'when we speak of someone as meriting or deserving our respect, it is appraisal respect that we have in mind' (1977: 39). While dividing respect into two makes for neat philosophical argument, in reality, how we think and how we act respectfully includes elements of both recognition and appraisal respect working together (despite the inherent contradictions).

There is also the influence of and search for self-respect, whether this be the dignity that comes from others' recognition, the satisfaction of a job well done, or even intertwined with street gang, drug dealer or familial honour codes (eg Bourgois, 1996; and also examined by Peter Squires in Chapter Ten, this volume). Also of relevance to self-respect may be the Biblical instruction to 'Love your neighbour as yourself',[1] the implication of which is that love for yourself is equal to love for others, and that they are interdependent. Perhaps this is also true for respect? As Carla Bagnoli (2007: 114) has observed: 'It is when we reflect on our own status of rational agents that we encounter others: we encounter them as self-originating sources of legitimate claims.' But with the individualism that has accompanied contemporary – or late modern – consumer culture there is a danger that respect for the self will dominate respect for others, that everyone will shout 'respect me!' And, as noted elsewhere (Millie, 2006), the result will be calls that, 'it is my right to behave how I like, and for others to behave how I would expect them'. Such demands are clearly disrespectful of the other. Bagnoli (2007: 117) talks of community ties and autonomy, and says that both are important:

> Recognizing others as having equal standing commits us to enter dialogical practices of exchanging reasons, but it does not force us to share the content of these reasons. We can respectfully disagree. In fact, respect requires that we do not impose our views on others, but it also requires that we engage in a frank dialogue with them.... The conclusion of this dialogue may be informed disagreement ...

Alongside self-respect, recognition and appraisal respect for others, the notion of respect for authority or social position can be added to the mix. For instance, the type of respect sought within and across street gang culture will often be tied to authority and status (and relatedly, appraisal respect). Thomas Hill (2000: 89–90) uses the more familiar example of motherhood:

> Suppose someone says, 'She has not been a particularly good mother, but she is my mother, after all, and I must respect her as such.' Here the point is ... to acknowledge that merely holding a certain position, or standing in a certain relationship to another, is sometimes enough to warrant a (presumptive) claim of respect. This should not be surprising, because social roles, positions, and relationships are often defined in normative terms, by the rights, responsibilities, and privileges that are constitutive of them.

Someone can have respect for their parents because they are their parents (and not because they are necessarily good parents). Similarly, a judge may be respected as a judge, irrespective or whether he or she is any good at the job. This later example brings us to the related concept of deference. Over the past 50 years there has been a clear decline in

deference for traditional hierarchies – as illustrated in the classic 1960s
TV comedy sketch from The Frost Report featuring John Cleese (as
upper class), Ronnie Barker (middle class) and Ronnie Corbett (working
class). Corbett gets the best one-liner, telling the others 'I know my
place'. Few would want a return to such automatic subordination
(Harris, 2006; McCarthy and Walker, 2006); but, deference is not the
same as respect, in terms of either recognition or appraisal respect, or
even in terms of respect for authority (see also Sennett, 2003). It is a
point identified in the government's *Respect Action Plan* that:

> We should build a culture of respect for the modern age,
> based on values of mutuality and shared responsibility
> rather than deference and hierarchy. (Respect Task Force,
> 2006: 5)

What is missing from deference, but present in most people's ideas of
respect, is the notion of mutuality. It is to mutuality and the related
idea of reciprocity that I now turn.

Mutuality and reciprocity

When asked to comment on the *Respect Action Plan*, the Archbishop
of York John Sentamu replied that:

> If we expect young people to be respectful, we should show
> respect. If they are not treated lovingly and forgivingly, they
> will be unforgiving. If we do not trust them, they will not
> trust us. (2006)

Sentamu was expressing the idea of mutuality, something that Richard
Sennett (2003) has proposed as central to the creation of respectful
society. Sennett took the idea of respect away from a Kantian view
based on equality of humankind. Rather than simple egalitarianism,
where all are treated as equals, Sennett saw social life more as a
performance, where 'mutuality requires expressive work. It must
be enacted, performed' (2003: 59). Drawing on his own musical
background, Sennett compared society to a musical performance,
where all players have an implicit understanding of others' needs to
create a harmonious and musical experience. In translating this to the
social, Sennett conceded, 'an enormous gap exists between wanting
to act well toward others and doing so' (2003: 59). Sennett's emphasis
on talent has a lot in common with Darwall's idea of appraisal respect.

However, an important point is made, that respect is not a passive state, that it has to be performed. And for *true* mutuality, this action – or performance – needs to be reciprocated by others. This is slightly different to Archbishop Sentamu's view, based on Christian morality where respect (and love, forgiveness and trust) is enacted *not* with any expectation of reciprocity, but in the hope that others will learn from one's actions.[2] In this form, respect is also concerned with *empathy* and seeing things from the other's point of view – an idea linked to *tolerance* of the other, and explored in detail by Jon Bannister and Ade Kearns in Chapter Seven. In that 'respect' is something that is enacted, or performed (and for that matter, a verb), it could also relate to Auguste Comte's (1968 [1851–54]) notion of *altruism*.

The view that respect ought to be given without expectation of reciprocity may be the ideal, but Sennett's idea of mutuality is a useful guide for contemporary living. As already noted, it is Sennett's idea of mutual respect that inspired Tony Blair in the first place. Where Sennett differed from the New Labour Respect Agenda was in his emphasis on respect between the state and the citizenry, that this *has to be* in both directions. As will be explored in the chapters that follow, much of the Respect Agenda has been characterised by respect on the government's terms. And for those who overstep the government's definition of respectful behaviour, there will be serious consequences. But for those attempting to enforce and secure respect, Sennett gave the following warning:

> the vagaries of personal character lead people to their own separate interpretations. The command 'Respect others!' could not simply be obeyed by following a strict, single set of rules; subjective desire governs the willingness to obey, and the manner in which people might respond. (Sennett, 2003: 59)

The government cannot simply tell its citizens to be respectful. If Sennett and Sentamu are correct, this is made doubly difficult if the state does not show its citizens respect – or more precisely, if it does not show respect to *all* of its citizens.

Respect for the 'other'

In much of the policy literature and political rhetoric, the government has produced a dichotomised view of a respectful, law-abiding 'us' and an anti-social, disrespectful 'them'. In so doing, the state is being the opposite of respectful. A simple divide between us and them was reinforced by Gordon Brown (2007) in his first speech to the Labour Party Conference as Prime Minister:

> So yes we will strengthen the police. Yes we will strengthen our laws. But preventing crime for me also means all of us as a community setting boundaries between what is acceptable and unacceptable behaviour – with clear penalties for stepping over the line. Boundaries that reflect the words I was taught when I was young – words upon which we all know strong communities are founded: discipline, respect, responsibility.

If individuals remain within Brown's boundaries, then they will be respected; if they do not, then there are clear repercussions. It is a view that has also found favour among the Conservatives. According to David Cameron (2006): 'If the consequence of stepping over the line should be painful, then staying within the bounds of good behaviour should be pleasant. And I believe that inside those boundaries we have to show a lot more love.' Notions of 'outsiders' and 'insiders', or 'us' and 'them' have been common themes in sociological enquiry (eg Becker, 1963; Elias and Scotson, 1965; Young, 2007), and are explored further in John Flint and Ryan Powell's Chapter Nine on Scottish sectarianism (with particular reference to the work of Norbert Elias).

Seeing others as something inferior to one's self is clearly disrespectful, yet this is the message from government. It is a form of moral contempt for those who are not quite like us. As Hill has noted (2000: 59), 'people stigmatized as inferior may still feel, quite rightly, that they "get no respect"'. According to Sennett, when interviewed in *The Guardian* by Stuart Jeffries (2006), there is an additional danger that those stigmatised may respond in a wholly unintended fashion; for instance: 'With adolescent males there is a tipping point between good behaviour and antisocial behaviour in which if you say "I'm going to get you, I'm going to whip you into shape" that's a red rag to a bull.'

Respect in public spaces

Much of the policy on respect and anti-social behaviour is played out in public spaces, as this is where encounters with 'others' are most likely. The chapter by Jon Bannister and Ade Kearns (Chapter Seven) and my own chapter on cosmopolitanism (Chapter Eight) explore such issues further. But I want here to mention briefly the work of Erving

Goffman on people's behaviour in public (eg 1963; 1967). Goffman provided a fascinating mix of sociology, psychology and psychiatry in examining aspects of 'the "circles of the self" which persons present draw around themselves, and for which the individual is obliged to show various forms of respect' (1963: 242). These circles range from 'face engagement', 'social occasion', through to 'social gatherings' that occur within a social situation. According to Goffman, social situations are inherently moral in character, with those present expected to adhere to the specific moral requirements of each situation; if someone fails to meet these standards, 'some kind of public cognizance is taken of his failure' (1963: 240).

Of direct relevance to this volume, Goffman recognised that there are different behavioural expectations in different social situations, and that the same behaviour can be differently interpreted by different people. The variety of interpretations means that a simplistic assessment of acceptable and unacceptable behaviour is not helpful:

> a moral rule is not something that can be used as a means
> of dichotomizing the world into upholders and offenders.
> Indeed, the more comparative information we gather about
> a moral rule, the less easy it becomes to make statements
> about an individual who breaks it (Goffman, 1963: 241).

Such dichotomising is exactly what politicians in the UK have been guilty of in creating a moral discourse that separates a 'law-abiding majority' from an anti-social or disrespectful 'other'.

Respect and plurality

Linking back to a Kantian perspective (Hill, 2000), one way of viewing respect is that there are plural norms of behavioural acceptability, depending on the situation. In fact, these norms can shift in time and space, making simplistic assessments of respectful 'us' and disrespectful 'them' all the more hazardous. The notion of plurality is one that has been embraced by postmodernists (eg Milovanovic, 1997; Bouteillier, 2002), and equally those who talk in terms of late modernity (eg Bauman, 2000; Young, 2007). It was also a theme explored by Matza (1964; 1969), and famously by Berman (1982) in his book *All that Is Solid Melts into Air*. Such a perspective at first seems attractive, as it is inclusive of all opinion, culture and life-style. However, according to Downes and Rock (1982: 4), the problem with pluralism is that 'no coherent and definitive argument can ever completely capture it'. This may be true, but is such a situation always problematical? The government's view of anti-social behaviour is that 'you know it when you see it' (Millie, 2009). I would argue that a more nuanced understanding of 'anti-social behaviour' and 'disrespectfulness' is needed, one based on mutuality and understanding of alternative – or plural – perspectives. That said, there ought to be ultimate limits on what is acceptable behaviour, and thus, a moral standpoint that fully embraces plurality has its dangers. Thomas Hill (2000: 63) has expressed this view rather well in identifying a need for a middle ground between, 'dogmatic moralism that would impose all of our values upon everyone and an uncritical relativism that would accept everything, no matter how cruel, in the name of diversity'.

The Respect Agenda

It seems sensible at this point to introduce the main points of the government's Respect Agenda, as outlined in the *Respect Action Plan* (Respect Taskforce, 2006) and *Youth Taskforce Action Plan* (Youth Taskforce, 2008). Despite claims that work to tackle anti-social behaviour is not focused on youth, the main emphasis of both these plans was children, young people and their families. This is clearly shown in the Table I.1.

There are obvious overlaps between the two plans. The government's focus on children and young people has been strongly influenced by the actuarial literature on risk and protective factors for onset of anti-social or criminal behaviour (eg Farrington, 1995; Prior and Paris, 2005; France, 2008). The basic premise is that, by getting upstream of the problem, it can be dealt with before it escalates or even before it emerges. This approach has its critics and is examined in this volume by Alan France and Jo Meredith (Chapter Three), and by Judy Nixon and Caroline Hunter (Chapter Five). The perspective is summarised by Paul Roberts (2006: 37), although he is unsure why 'respect' has become its defining quality:

> it remains unclear, however, why lack of respect for others should be singled out as *the fundamental cause*. Might lack of respect not be a symptom of defective moral education in the home, in school, and in the wider community?

At first glance the Youth Taskforce approach reads as less enforcement heavy than the *Respect Action Plan*. This might have been expected, with a shift from the Home Office to the Department for Children,

Table 1.1: The government's Respect Agenda

Respect Action Plan (2006)	Youth Taskforce Action Plan (2008)
Activities for children and young people	Positive activities for young people
Improving behaviour and attendance in schools	Improved delivery for young people everywhere
Supporting families	Our vision for young people, building on success
Dealing with the 'most challenging families'	Helping every parent do the best for their child
Effective enforcement and community justice	A deeper response to anti-social behaviour by young people
Strengthening communities	Developing this plan and working with partners

Schools and Families. The Youth Taskforce is also more closely tied to other government agendas, such as *Every Child Matters* (Chief Secretary to the Treasury, 2003) and the *Children's Plan for England* (DCSF, 2007). And in the launch of the Taskforce in 2007, Secretary of State Ed Balls stated that: 'Every anti-social behaviour order marks a failure ... It's a failure every time a young person gets an ASBO. It's necessary – but it's not right ... I want to live in the kind of society that puts ASBOs behind us' (reported by Blackman in the *Daily Mirror*, 2007).

But despite this softer rhetoric, the new plan (and the post-Blair Labour government) still held on to the centrality of tough enforcement. The *Youth Taskforce Action Plan* (2008: 5) proposed a triple-track approach, but two of the three were enforcement objectives ('tough enforcement' on unacceptable behaviour, and 'non-negotiable support'):

- tough enforcement where behaviour is unacceptable or illegal;
- non-negotiable support to address the underlying causes of poor behaviour or serious difficulties;
- better prevention to tackle problems before they become serious and entrenched, and to prevent problems from arising in the first place.

Enforcing or securing respect was still central to the Youth Taskforce, with the action plan having the tagline '*give respect, get respect – youth matters*'. To return to the earlier discussion, the government's view remained one of *earning* respect, rather than respect being due to all persons.

Outline of the book

So far, there has been little attention in the academic and policy literature to the UK government's push for respect – notable exceptions being Jamieson (2005), Bannister et al (2006) and Harris (2006). Kevin Harris's book on respectful neighbourhoods is a particularly interesting and useful contribution, but the Respect Agenda has been far broader than this, with multiple emphases on young people and children, families and parenting, respectful city living, plus issues of diversity, values and identity. The aim of this volume is to consider these broader themes. Government policy agendas come and go, and this may be true also for the Respect Agenda. However, the politics of moral and behavioural improvement – as exemplified by calls for respectful citizenship and for tackling anti-social behaviour – are likely to remain for some time, irrespective of which party is in power. For instance, at the last general election all three of the main parties had policies targeting anti-social behaviour (Millie, 2008). What is unique about the current government's push for respect is its emphasis on enforcement; there is far more stick than carrot, so to speak. While the contributors to this volume may not agree on everything, I do not think I am overstating it in claiming that there is general consensus that policies designed to focus on behavioural acceptability and anti-social behaviour in the UK need to be more clearly thought through. This volume hopefully provides a useful starting point for such enquiry.

The collection of essays is interdisciplinary, with contributors having interests in criminology, sociolegal studies, social policy, urban geography, housing, social history, sociology and landscape. It provides a critical account of a particular phase of government policy, but will have longer-lasting and broader relevance to discussions of behavioural acceptability as well as the accompanying moral and behavioural politics. By exploring wider theoretical, philosophical and policy ideas and discourses, it also has direct relevance to debates on 'othering' and criminalisation. It should also be of interest to those exploring issues of youth, citizenship, responsibility, identity, urban living, community and housing. The collection builds on recent publications on anti-social behaviour (Millie et al, 2005; Flint, 2006; Squires, 2008; Millie, 2009) and crime, community and British urban policy (Atkinson and Helms, 2007).

The book is divided into five key and related strands, with each part consisting of two chapters by leading academics. Part One provides context for the contemporary focus on 'respect' and in Chapter One Elizabeth Burney explores the politics behind the Respect Agenda. She traces New Labour's fascination with 'respect' back to the early 1990s. Influences included aspects of Christian Socialism, communitarianism, Anthony Giddens' (1998; 2000) 'Third Way' politics and Richard Sennett's work on 'respect'. The key political players for New Labour were Tony Blair, Gordon Brown and Jack Straw, and to a certain extent Frank Field, as well as important and influential lobbying from the 'Social Landlords Crime and Nuisance Group'. Why 'respect' became such an important focus during this period is considered. In Chapter Two Geoffrey Pearson goes much further back in tracing the history behind the Respect Agenda – or as he states: 'The Respect Agenda implies a version of history'. This *version* of history centres on an assumed social decline and a corresponding decline in respect. In considering life on the streets of late nineteenth- and early twentieth-century Britain, Pearson puts such a claim into serious doubt. In 1983 Pearson published his highly influential work on *Hooligans: A History of Respectable Fears*. Using similar themes, in 1989 he wrote a paper for a collection in honour of John Barron Mays, edited by David Downes. With the permission of David Downes (and of the original publishers), an updated version of this paper is provided here, as the late Victorian and early Edwardian discourses on hooliganism have clear parallels with contemporary calls for respect from anti-social yobs.

At the heart of the government's work on anti-social behaviour and respect has been the assumed misbehaviour of young people and children. This is the focus of the second part. In Chapter Three Alan France and Jo Meredith consider the 'new' responsibilities of youth, the fact that they are increasingly perceived as potential 'citizens'. France and Meredith argue that this 'transition towards citizenship' is closely tied to New Labour's call for respect. And to gain respect young people need to behave in a respectful and morally upright way; as the authors note: 'By drawing upon the concept of respect in political and policy terms he [Blair] aimed to re-moralise the immoral minority.' Key to this re-moralisation was work with families (a theme also examined by Nixon and Hunter in Chapter Five) as well as early intervention work with the young. France and Meredith also consider the place of education and employment in nurturing respect. They conclude that a culture of respect is possible, but this needs to be mutual and inclusive of young people; that 'treating the young as having to "earn" respect is counterproductive'. This is a theme developed in Chapter Four by

Helen Woolley, but this time focusing on the place of children and young people in public open spaces. After defining what is meant by public open space, Woolley focuses on the visibility of the young in public. She uses two quite different – albeit related – examples, focusing on skateboarders' use of public open spaces and the provision of 'play' for children. For both examples Woolley concludes that spaces are heavily controlled by adults, be it by social, legal or physical means. It seems we want children and young people to play, but only on our terms. Woolley argues that being less controlling would demonstrate greater trust and respect for children and young people.

The third part considers the place of families and wider communities in the Respect Agenda. In Chapter Five Judy Nixon and Caroline Hunter make the important point that the control of anti-social behaviour has become a gendered issue. Drawing on their own empirical research into Family Intervention Projects, the authors provide strong evidence that parents are frequently held responsible for the misbehaviour of their children – and more particularly that this blame is most often put on mothers, 'where the failure of women to control the behaviour of members of their families is presented as a failure of parenting and citizenship'. The consequences can be severe, including loss of home. Alongside this focus on parental responsibility, Nixon and Hunter see such policy and legislation as reflecting a move from private to public patriarchy, a position clearly at odds with a true reading of respect. In Chapter Six Peter Somerville takes respect into a broader arena, providing a theoretical examination of the role of communities in nurturing respect. Somerville looks at the roles of civility, solidarity, sociability and trust in creating the conditions for mutuality. And drawing on the work of Erving Goffman, Barbara Misztal, Richard Sennett and others, he sees respect as a possible basis for cooperative interaction. According to Somerville, there needs to be room for self-governance – a notion related to informal social control – involving 'a balance between the formality of codes of behaviour' and 'the informality of everyday processes'. In trying to nurture respect, the government could allow room for *co*-governance, thereby demonstrating trust in its citizens.

Much of what is regarded as 'disrespectful' behaviour occurs in public (and semi-public) spaces within cities, and this is the focus for Part Four. In Chapter Seven Jon Bannister and Ade Kearns consider Britain's reputation for tolerance, and whether cities characterised by tolerance are possible. They take the view that key to the creation of 'dynamic' tolerance is engagement leading to mutual respect and empathy. Also linked to mutual respect are civility and, hopefully, fewer 'intolerable' behaviours. Yet, according to Bannister and Kearns, the alternative is a city defined by segregation and exclusion, leading to demands for others to respect *your* rights, and then to greater *in*tolerance (or at least static tolerance). Unfortunately the Respect Agenda has more in common with this alternative, characterised by the 'othering' of a 'disrespectful' minority. This idea is taken up in Chapter Eight (my contribution), looking at the role of urban cosmopolitanism in encouraging cities of respect. The place of plurality within the consumerist neoliberal city is discussed, with consumption regarded as the dominant force within the city. People with other uses for public spaces – such as groups of young people congregating, street people or other categories of 'them' – are invariably excluded and regarded as an anti-social or disrespectful 'other'. Borrowing from Tim Cresswell, such groups are seen as 'out of place', as they do not fit in with an urban aesthetic based on consumption. As framed as a 'willingness to engage with the Other' (cf Hannerz, 1990), cosmopolitanism is considered as a possible way forward for encouraging mutual respect in the city. Drawing on Jane Jacobs and Richard Sennett, 'respect' is seen as part of an urban performance that is inclusive of the 'other'.

In Part Five, the relationship between respect and individual and group identities and values is considered. In Chapter Nine John Flint and Ryan Powell focus on sectarianism in Scotland as expressed in education and football. For instance, the governance of sectarianism in Scottish football is regarded as 'an ambitious project aimed at changing cultural values and identities as well as the manifestation of these identities in public space'. According to Flint and Powell, this has much in common with anti-social behaviour and respect agendas. Drawing on the work of Norbert Elias, they see such agendas as part of a contemporary civilising offensive, 'through which new mechanisms of governance are utilised to inculcate perceived decivilising elements within society'. In Chapter Ten Peter Squires takes a different perspective, this time focusing on the discourses of respect and identity that accompany contemporary 'street' cultures, and how 'street respect' compares to the official discourses of the Respect Agenda. Drawing on a diverse range of sources – including, for instance, Jock Young, Sveinung Sandberg, former footballer Michel Platini, and the comedy 'street' character, Ali G – Squires provides a theoretical framework for considering what could be termed 'state' and 'street' respect. He highlights the importance of reputation and individual 'worth' for both types of respect and suggests that tolerance and better opportunities are needed.

As Peter Squires notes in Chapter Ten, 'There has truly been a proliferation of "respect" talk of late'. I hope with this book we have not just added to this talk. Instead, I hope the book challenges and provokes debate about moral and behavioural politics and, more specifically, the place of respect within late modern society. The concluding chapter brings the findings of these various chapters together and considers the possible future for 'securing' respect.

Notes

[1] Matthew 22: 39, New International Version translation; also Leviticus 19: 18.

[2] The Biblical view is that others will witness something of God in your actions, that you are being a true witness of the character and nature of God – however, simply being an example to others is probably a good start.

References

Atkinson, R. and Helms, G. (eds) (2007) *Securing an Urban Renaissance: Crime, Community and British Urban Policy*, Bristol: The Policy Press.

Bagnoli, C. (2007) 'Respect and membership in the moral community', *Ethical Theory and Moral Practice*, 10(2), 113–28.

Bannister, J., Fyfe, N. and Kearns, A. (2006) 'Respectable or respectful? (In)civility and the city', *Urban Studies*, 43(5/6), 919–37.

Bauman, Z. (2000) *Liquid Modernity*, Cambridge: Polity Press.

Becker, H. (1963) *Outsiders: Studies in the Sociology of Deviance*, New York, NY: The Free Press.

Berman, M. (1982) *All that Is Solid Melts into Air: The Experience of Modernity*, New York, NY: Penguin Books.

Blackman, O. (2007) 'Asbos are a failure', *Daily Mirror*, 27 July. Available at: www.mirror.co.uk/news/top-stories/2007/07/27/asbos-are-a-failure-115875-19528541.

Blair, T. (1998) *The Third Way: New Politics for the New Century*, London: Fabian Society.

Blair, T. (2001) 'PM's speech to the Christian Socialist Movement at Westminster Central Hall', 29 March. Available at: www.number-10.gov.uk/output/Page3243.asp.

Blair, T. (2006) 'PM's Respect Action Plan launch speech', 10 January. Available at: www.number-10.gov.uk/output/Page8898.asp.

Bourgois, P. (1996) *In Search of Respect: Selling Crack in El Barrio*, Cambridge: Cambridge University Press.

Boutellier, H. (2002) *Crime and Morality: The Significance of Criminal Justice in a Post-modern Culture*, Dordrecht: Kluwer Academic Publishers.

Brown, G. (2006) Speech to the Labour Party conference, 25 September.

Brown, G. (2007) 'Prime Minister's speech to the Labour Party conference', 24 September.

Burney, E. (2005) *Making People Behave: Anti-social Behaviour, Politics and Policy*, Cullompton: Willan Publishing.

Cameron, D. (2006) 'Making our country a safe and civilised place for everyone', Speech to the Centre for Social Justice, 10 July. Available at: www.conservatives.com.

Chief Secretary to the Treasury (2003) *Every Child Matters*, Cm 5860, London: HMSO.

Comte, A. (1968 [1851–54]) *System of Positive Polity*, New York, NY: Burt Franklin.

Conservative Party (2006) 'David Cameron unveils the real Respect Agenda', 10 January.

Darwall, S.L. (1977) 'Two kinds of respect', *Ethics*, 88(1), 36–49.

DCSF (Department of Children, Schools and Families) (2007) *The Children's Plan: Building Brighter Futures – Summary*, London: DCSF.

Downes, D. and Rock, P. (1982) *Understanding Deviance: A Guide to the Sociology of Crime and Rule Breaking*, Oxford: Oxford University Press.

Elias, N. and Scotson, J.L. (1965) *The Established and the Outsiders: A Sociological Enquiry into Community Problems*, London: Frank Cass & Co Ltd.

Farrington, D.P. (1995) 'The development of offending and anti-social behaviour from childhood: key findings from the Cambridge Study in Delinquent Development', *Journal of Child Psychology and Psychiatry*, 36, 929–64.

Flint, J. (2006) *Housing, Urban Governance and Anti-social Behaviour: Perspectives, Policy and Practice*, Bristol: The Policy Press.

Ford, R. (2008) 'Gordon Brown ditches respect agenda on youth crime', *The Times*, 11 January. Available at: www.timesonline.co.uk/tol/news/politics/article3168611.ece.

France, A. (2008) 'Risk factor analysis and the youth question', *Journal of Youth Studies*, 11(1), 1–15.

Giddens, A. (1998) *The Third Way: The Renewal of Social Democracy*, Cambridge: Polity Press.

Giddens, A. (2000) *The Third Way and its Critics*, Cambridge: Polity Press.

Goffman, E. (1963) *Behavior in Public Places: Notes on the Social Organization of Gatherings*, New York, NY: The Free Press.

Goffman, E. (1967) *Interaction Ritual: Essays in Face to Face Behaviour*, Chicago, IL: Aldine.

Hannerz, U. (1990) 'Cosmopolitans and locals in world culture', in M. Featherstone (ed) *Global Culture*, London: Sage, pp 237–52.

Harris, K. (2006) *Respect in the Neighbourhood: Why Neighbourliness Matters*, Lyme Regis: Russell House Publishing.

Hill, T.E. (2000) *Respect, Pluralism, and Justice: Kantian Perspectives*, Oxford: Oxford University Press.

Home Office (2003) *Respect and Responsibility: Taking a Stand Against Anti-social Behaviour*, Cm 5778, London: Home Office.

Jamieson, J. (2005) 'New Labour, youth justice and the question of "respect"', *Youth Justice*, 5(3), 180–93.

Jeffries, S. (2006) 'With respect: Stuart Jeffries meets Richard Sennett, Tony Blair's intellectual mentor', *The Guardian*, 14 January. Available at: www.guardian.co.uk/politics/2006/jan/14/ politicsphilosophyandsociety.books.

Kant, I. (1964 [1785]) *Groundwork on the Metaphysics of Morals*, trans. H.J. Paton, New York, NY: Harper & Row.

Matza, D. (1964) *Delinquency and Drift*, New York, NY: John Wiley & Sons.

Matza, D. (1969) *Becoming Deviant*, Englewood Cliffs, NJ: Prentice-Hall.

McCarthy, P. and Walker, J. (2006) 'R-E-S-P-E-C-T, find out what it means to me: The connection between respect and youth crime', *Crime Prevention and Community Safety*, 8(1), 17–29.

Millie, A. (2006) 'Anti-social behaviour: concerns of minority and marginalised Londoners', *Internet Journal of Criminology*. Available at: www.internetjournalofcriminology.com.

Millie, A. (2006) 'Crime as an issue during the 2005 UK general election', *Crime, Media and Culture*, 4(1), 101–11.

Millie, A. (2009) *Anti-social Behaviour*, Maidenhead: Open University Press.

Millie, A., Jacobson, J., McDonald, E. and Hough, M. (2005) *Anti-social Behaviour Strategies: Finding a Balance*, Bristol: The Policy Press.

Milovanovic, D. (1997) *Postmodern Criminology*, New York, NY: Garland.

Pearson, G. (1983) *Hooligan: A History of Respectable Fears*, Basingstoke: Macmillan.

Prior, D. and Paris, A. (2005) *Preventing Children's Involvement in Crime and Anti-social Behaviour: A Literature Review*, Research Report No 623, Nottingham: Department for Education and Skills.

Raz, J. (2001) *Value, Respect, and Attachment*, Cambridge, Cambridge University Press.

Respect Task Force (2006) *Respect Action Plan*, London: Home Office.

Roberts, P. (2006) 'Penal offence in question: Some reference points for interdisciplinary conversation', in A. von Hirsch and A.P. Simester (eds) *Incivilities: Regulating Offensive Behaviour*, Oxford: Hart Publishing, pp 1–56.

Sennett, R. (2003) *Respect: The Formation of Character in an Age of Inequality*, London: Penguin Books.

Sennett, R. (2005) 'What our grannies taught us: the government cannot enforce respect when it has failed to earn it', *The Guardian*, 19 May. Available at: www.guardian.co.uk/politics/2005/may/19/uk.comment.

Sennett, R. (2006) 'Views on respect: Richard Sennett', *BBC News Online*, 9 January. Available at: http://news.bbc.co.uk/1/hi/uk/4589616.stm.

Sentamu, J. (2006) 'View on Respect: Archbishop of York', BBC Online, 9 January. Available at: http:\\news.bbc.co.uk/1/hi/uk/4589636.stm.

Squires, P. (2008) *ASBO Nation: The Criminalisation of Nuisance*, Bristol: The Policy Press.

Young, J. (2007) *The Vertigo of Late Modernity*, London: Sage.

Youth Taskforce (2008) *Youth Taskforce Action Plan: Give Respect, Get Respect – Youth Matters*, London: Department for Children, Schools and Families.

Part One
Respect in context

ONE

Respect and the politics of behaviour

Elizabeth Burney

Who can be against 'respect'? And who can be in favour of 'anti-social behaviour'? These twin, Janus-faced mantras have guided many government initiatives and new laws since New Labour came to power in 1997. Their effects (or lack of them) are the subject of subsequent chapters in this book. This chapter seeks to set out the ideology behind the various initiatives described, and asks whether slogans with ill-defined targets are sufficient to change public behaviour.

> The importance of the notion of community is that it defines the relationship not only between ourselves as individuals but between people and the society in which they live, one that is based on responsibilities as well as rights, on obligations as well as entitlements. Self respect is in part derived from respect for others. (Tony Blair, speaking at Wellingborough, 19 February 1993)

This speech of Tony Blair's, made when he was shadow Home Secretary, and in the wake of the James Bulger murder, contains several themes which he had spoken of before, and was to do many times subsequently. The individual in relation to society and community; rights as well as responsibilities; and respect for others as well as for oneself – all were to become drivers of policy under the New Labour government.

Where did these ideas derive from? They were not particularly visible in post-war Labour thinking, based on equality and the beneficent effects of the welfare state, as well as 'liberal' attitudes to individual rights. As John Rentoul has written:

> Blair's great triumph as shadow Home Secretary was to move the debate from traditionally 'liberal' themes to a 'tough' message on crime and the family based on the concept of duty.... In return for society fulfilling its side of

the moral bargain by giving people a better life, people had responsibility to give something back to the community and obey its rules. And because mutual obligations originate in family responsibilities, the family must be strengthened. (Rentoul, 2001: 199–200)

This philosophy began with Tony Blair's personal Christian faith, acquired while a student at Oxford, and his simultaneous adoption of politics in the form of Christian socialism. As he said in 1995: 'My Christianity and my politics came together at the same time' (Rentoul, 2001: 35). There were echoes of the socialist past as, for example, launching the *Respect Action Plan* (Respect Task Force, 2006), he quoted R.H. Tawney's words: 'What we have been witnessing is the breakdown of society on the basis of rights divorced from obligations.' But for Blair a special inspiration came from the work of the philosopher John Macmurray, to which he was introduced as a student.

To cite Rentoul again:

What was distinctive about Macmurray was that he combined his Christian socialism with an attack on liberalism which resembled that of the conservative followers of Edmund Burke, who emphasise the family and tradition as the bonds that hold together organic communities, and who oppose individualism and rationalism. In this Macmurray anticipated the 'communitarian' philosophy of North American thinkers such as Charles Taylor and Michael Sandel. (p 42)

When Blair, together with Gordon Brown, visited the United States at the end of 1992, they were both struck with the success of Bill Clinton in adopting a 'tough on crime' stance, formerly the province of the Republicans. But Blair was also impressed with the way that communitarian thinking had been put into practice by Clinton as state governor, emphasising personal responsibility in return for opportunities.

The best-known exponent of communitarianism, Amitai Etzioni, explained a large agenda: 'We are a social movement aiming at shoring up the moral, social, and political environment. Part change of heart, part renewal of social bonds, part reform of public life' (Etzioni, 1993: 247). He also described that:

> A communitarian perspective recognises that the preservation
> of individual liberty depends on the active maintenance of
> the institutions of civil society where citizens learn respect
> for each other as well as self-respect ... (p 253)

Soon such sentiments began to penetrate mainstream Labour thinking. Anthony Giddens' *The Third Way* (1998) has several references to ideas of this kind: he states: 'One might suggest as a *prime motto for the new politics, no rights without responsibilities*' (p 63, original emphasis). But, unlike Etzioni, Giddens believed that 'government can, and must, play a major part in renewing civic culture' (p 79). Earlier in the book, he lists what government exists to do and includes:

> More controversially, have a civilising aim – government
> reflects widely held norms and values, but can also help shape
> them, in the education system and elsewhere. (p 48)

In a speech to the South African parliament in 1999, cited by Fairclough, Blair explained that

> the Third Way needs a concept of a modern civic society
> that is founded on opportunity and responsibility, rights and
> duties going together. Society has a duty to its citizens and
> its citizens have a duty to society. (2000: 38)

As Fairclough points out, "'community" has come to be understood in moral terms which emphasise that "responsibilities" are the other side of "rights"' (p 38).

An active government role in promoting good behaviour was therefore an accepted part of the New Labour philosophy. Combined with a pledge on 'toughness', it shaped policy and legislation from the very beginning of the new administration.

Confronting anti-social behaviour

When Tony Blair became leader of the Opposition following the death of John Smith in 1994, Jack Straw took his place as shadow Home Secretary. He immediately adopted a hands-on approach to what he saw as a plague of bad behaviour afflicting many communities – the very antithesis of the mutual respect aspired to in the thinking outlined above. In June 1995 the Labour Party published proposals in a hard-hitting document entitled *A Quiet Life: Tough Action on Criminal*

Neighbours. In complete contrast to the theoretical presentations of community harmony, the opening paragraph proclaimed: 'Across Britain there are thousands of people whose lives are made a misery by the people next door. Their behaviour may not just be unneighbourly, but intolerable and outrageous' (Labour Party, 1995: 1). There followed a number of examples (mainly taken from Straw's own constituency of Blackburn) and some very detailed legislative proposals for what was then called a 'Community Safety Order'. In due course, and with little significant change, these proposals made their way into policy under the newly elected Blair government, and thus into the 1998 Crime and Disorder Act, where the new legal power was known as the Anti-Social Behaviour Order (thus laying the emphasis not so much on the community itself, as on the censured actions of individuals).

Much has been written about the genesis and development of the Anti-Social Behaviour Order (ASBO) (see for instance Burney, 2005). For the purposes of this chapter it is important to emphasise that the pressure to act against 'intolerable and outrageous' behaviour came from local politics as much as from central government ideas. The areas most affected were the de-industrialised and marginalised communities located in Labour heartlands of the North and the Midlands. The 1995 paper refers specifically to its proposals having been developed with the help of policy advisers to Coventry City Council, which had pioneered the use of injunctions to target certain troublemakers. Mention has already been made of Jack Straw's evidence from Blackburn.

Other local councils, and MPs in their surgeries, were confronted with complainants who were suffering from harassment and nuisance but who were unable to gain respite through existing channels of the criminal justice system. In various speeches Tony Blair emphasised that it was Labour voters in poor areas who bore the brunt of crime and anti-social behaviour, which was why these issues were no longer seen as the preserve of the Tory Party but must be at the heart of his government's agenda.

Social landlords were at the sharp end of dealing with bad behaviour, and already had quite tough powers under the 1996 Housing Act passed by the Conservatives. But they felt something more comprehensive was needed, and an influential lobby group was developed, the Social Landlords Crime and Nuisance Group (SLNG), which gained the ear of Jack Straw.[1] This was an example of the growing tendency for single-issue pressure groups to do their utmost to influence government policy, and in this case they succeeded.

Presenting the proposed new legislation to the House of Commons, Jack Straw explicitly distanced himself from the libertarian opinion formers who had traditionally been close to the Labour Party. He told the House that 'the bill represents a triumph of community politics over detached metropolitan elites' (*Hansard*, House of Commons, 8 April 1998, col 370). He wrote in *The Times* newspaper (9 April 1998):

> For many years, the concerns of those who lived in areas undermined by crime and disorder were ignored or overlooked by people whose comfortable notions of human behaviour were matched only by their comfortable distance from its worst excesses.

He explained that 'in the period before last year's general election, my colleagues and I spent our time talking to those at the sharp end of the problems of crime and disorder – victims, the police, magistrates, local councils'. Straw claimed to have shaken off the influence of pressure groups concerned with things like human rights – although, as described above, he may simply have exchanged one type of pressure group for another, such as social landlords.

It was a significant shift in rhetoric and policy to lay the emphasis on meeting demands directly culled from encounters with local leaders and the general public, especially from the complaints brought to constituency surgeries. The development of behaviour-oriented policies, both popular and populist, continued throughout the entire Blair administration. The ASBO is the most obvious example of this. Where authorities hesitated to use this and similar powers, even though popular with the public, they were held up to blame by the Home Secretary, especially when David Blunkett took over the office (see below).

One politician outstanding for his condemnation of anti-social behaviour was Labour's Frank Field, whose book *Neighbours from Hell* (2003) was a stirring polemic which described the sufferings of his constituents in Birkenhead through the behaviour of certain families. He laid the blame squarely on the failure of parents to instil values of respectable behaviour, or 'common decencies' which had been built up over generations. The blame attributed to parents – and more particularly mothers – is explored in Chapter Five by Judy Nixon and Caroline Hunter. According to Field:

> These virtues, which became almost universally practiced, ensured that the family's behaviour promoted a thoughtfulness for its other members as well as its neighbours. But the

attitudes, behaviour and customs thus established are under threat.

A growing number of families no longer understand the importance of these virtues to their neighbour's immediate well-being, or to their own family's interests. In a significant respect, the drive to respectability has not only been thwarted but has gone into reverse. (p 2)

Field looks back nostalgically at the working-class culture of mutual support and organisation, which he believes was stifled when the welfare state substituted state-controlled centralised systems of welfare for local responsibilities. In this he echoes the views of Norman Dennis (Dennis and Erdos, 1993), at the right-wing Institute of Economic Affairs, who contrasted the undisciplined society of absent fathers and single mothers with the stable working-class communities he had known in North-East England. He would agree with Field, who argues that, when Thatcherism in turn demolished welfarism and collectivism, what was left was unchecked individualism. With this, 'those social virtues, centring around a respect for others, plays increasingly less of a role, or no role at all' (Field, 2003: 5–6). Field argues:

> The three social virtues which I believe to be premier are politeness, considerateness and thoughtfulness … the practice of each underpins a sense of common, or shared, decency … A cornerstone of civilised living has been the development of an innate courtesy which, as the nineteenth century Bishop Paget remarked, consists of the respect of the self-respect of others. (2003: 31)

Field's book contains some stark stories about the foul behaviour of children towards neighbours, and the powerlessness felt by the victims. His eyes were first opened when a group of elderly pensioners came to see him ('respectably' dressed as befitted a visit to their MP) and described how their lives had become intolerable.

> Young lads who ran across their bungalow roofs, peed through their letterboxes, jumped out of the shadows when they returned home at night, and, when they were watching television, tried to break their sitting room windows, presumably with the hope of showering the pensioners with shattered glass. (Field, 2003: 10–11)

He then started collecting similar stories from his constituency and elsewhere, amounting to a frightening picture of yobbish anarchy. Certain families stood out as generating the worst behaviour, although he also charts the general decline in respect for authority and public property.

Frank Field's solutions to restoring order and a sense of responsibility range from a contractual ceremony when a birth is registered, to the removal of benefits from persistently anti-social families (an idea which is gradually becoming a more mainstream Labour argument). He sees the police as potential 'surrogate parents', dishing out penalty points, which turn into an ASBO the third time – again, the use of the police as on-the-spot arbiters of behaviour is an idea which has increasingly turned to reality in recent legislation. Teaching of parenting skills is another Field priority which is now well embedded in government policy, in the form of the Parenting Order introduced in the 1998 Crime and Disorder Act.

The 'Together' campaign and the 2003 Anti-Social Behaviour Act

The arrival of David Blunkett as Home Secretary in 2002 heralded a tougher era of behavioural politics. Dismayed at the low level of use of ASBOs, he introduced last-minute changes in the 2002 Police Reform Act which made it possible to attach ASBOs to criminal convictions in the magistrates' and Crown courts. This measure has since been responsible for the majority of ASBOs.

Blunkett's own background and his long experience on Sheffield City Council gave him an authoritative voice in the quest for civic renewal. In a book (Blunkett, 2001) he set out a detailed programme for mutual responsibility between individuals and communities and for making public institutions responsive to the communities they serve. The authoritarian tone adopted in ministerial policy documents was not evident.

However, the tone changed when the policy of enforcing respect and civic responsibility was truly launched with the publication, in March 2003, of the White Paper *Respect and Responsibility – Taking a Stand Against Anti-Social Behaviour* (Home Office, 2003a). In his introduction, Blunkett stated 'Our aim is a "something for something" society where we treat one another with respect and where we all share responsibility for taking a stand against what is unacceptable.'

'Taking a stand' indicated the idea, which was to grow in importance, that communities should themselves exercise control over their black sheep. Though no doubt not intended as an encouragement to vigilantism, it could have been interpreted as such. The practice of 'naming and shaming' ASBO recipients can impart an air of vengefulness, but has been defended by the government as necessary for enforcement, and given qualified endorsement by the House of Commons Home Affairs Select Committee (HoC, 2005).

The White Paper foreshadowed the contents of the 2003 Anti-Social Behaviour Act, particularly in new measures to enforce parental responsibility through the extension of Parenting Contracts and Orders and Fixed Penalty Notices. Schools were reluctant to become involved, especially in applying for ASBOs for children excluded for bad behaviour – this provision has so far remained a dead letter, completely unused (Burney and Gelsthorpe, 2008). Youth Offending Teams (YOTs) were to get powers to apply for ASBOs for children who had not appeared in court, but who were deemed to be acting in a criminal or anti-social manner. If there had been any doubt, it was now clear that the enforcement of respect was to focus on errant families and their children. Support to dysfunctional families was also mentioned, but enforcement was the main message.

Many of the proposed new measures dealt with disorder and incivilities in public spaces. Blunkett still bought into the 'broken windows' thesis of Wilson and Kelling (1982), that minor versions could lead directly to an increase in crime, although the causation had already been largely disproved (Sampson and Raudenbush, 2001; Taylor, 2001). Thus graffiti, kerb crawling, begging and anti-social behaviour around licensed premises were among the targeted behaviours, as well as the obviously criminal crack houses. Blunkett claims in his autobiography (2006: 463) that, but for him, measures clamping down further on social tenants and on environmental incivilities would not have been included in this rag-bag legislation. Along with the introduction of Penalty Notices for Disorder – dispensed on the spot by police – the enforcement of civil behaviour spread to city centres, and especially the night-time economy. The 'remoralisation' of city centres was further enhanced by strong powers to deal with drunken behaviour in the 2006 Violent Crime Reduction Act.

'Together' was the message in the White Paper's title (Home Office, 2003a) – solidarity among respectable citizens must be the bedrock of the drive against anti-social behaviour. This word became the title of the campaign launched amid fanfare in October 2003, before 700 delegates from across the country and attended by both Tony Blair and David Blunkett. It was orchestrated by the recently appointed Louise Casey, director of the Anti-Social Behaviour Unit based in the Home

Office whose action plan was being launched. Casey, an outspoken and fervent campaigner who had previously moved from the voluntary sector to become the government's 'Homelessness Czar', was to set the tone for a five-year programme, preaching and supplying advice to local agencies. She led a team made up of departmental agencies and practitioners from different backgrounds who could speak with authority to their counterparts in local areas, be it on enforcing housing, environmental or policing sanctions.

An evangelistic tone was adopted from the start. Tough speeches from Blair and Blunkett at the launch of the campaign paid little heed to possible social causes of bad behaviour. Some truly dreadful examples were presented from victims who had 'taken a stand'. Social workers were not to be trusted: Blunkett said there would be enforcement without 'garbage from the 60s and 70s about being non-judgemental', underlining once more that New Labour had moved away from the soft-centred attitudes of yore. Among further populist rhetoric, he said that people paid to do the job of keeping order must be held to account locally – officials and policemen who did not use the new powers against anti-social behaviour should be sacked.

Tony Blair poured scorn on the ability or willingness of the criminal justice system to deal with anti-social behaviour – he too urged local people to use the powers provided. Respect, self-respect and local leadership formed his mantra. He wished to 'sharpen community justice' and 'interfere with people's freedom if they are interfering with other people's freedom'. He laid a lot of emphasis on the use of Fixed Penalty Notices (FPNs) to enable the police to deal out instant justice. He explained:

> Respect is a simple idea. We know instinctively what it means. Respect for others – their opinions, values and way of life. Respect for neighbours. Respect for the community that means caring about others. Respect for property that means not tolerating mindless vandalism, theft and graffiti. And self-respect, which means giving as well as taking.
>
> Respect is at the heart of a belief in society. It is what makes us a community, not merely an isolated group of individuals (Tony Blair, Speech at launch of 'Together' campaign, 14 October 2003)

The action plan, entitled *Together: Tackling Anti-Social Behaviour* (Home Office, 2003b), spelled out the steps to be taken to (in David Blunkett's words in the introduction) 'create a decent, civil society in which people can shape their own lives and participate fully in their local community' (p 1). The communitarian basis of the campaign was clear.

The methods depended upon spreading the message of enforcement to local communities and the officials who had to use the various powers. 'Trailblazers' were chosen among local authorities to demonstrate good practice and proselytisers from the Anti-Social Behaviour Unit toured the country, whipping up enthusiasm for the crusade against anti-social behaviour. Local politics sometimes intruded – there were different degrees of enthusiasm for the new powers under different councils.

The 2003 Anti-Social Behaviour Act simultaneously provided even more weapons in this war, as outlined in the earlier White Paper (Home Office, 2003a) with the most controversial provision giving the police powers to create local Dispersal Order areas within which any group (two or more people) thought to be acting anti-socially could be sent away and forbidden to return within 48 hours. A curfew for under-16s could also be attached – a provision soon legally challenged.

Introducing the second reading of the Anti-Social Behaviour Bill to the House of Commons, David Blunkett spoke of it as:

> a symbol of the need for cultural change. It is about putting alongside prevention and remedial action the key enforcement measures that send a signal to those involved in anti-social behaviour. (*Hansard*, House of Commons, 8 April 2003, col 136)

Clearly, the civilising mission of government, in his view, depended upon scaring people into the right kind of behaviour, and punishing them if necessary.

Blunkett left the Home Office in 2004. His successor, Charles Clarke, was less inclined to issue threats against anti-social behaviour. But Tony Blair still kept a firm hand on the issue. A landmark policy paper, the *Respect Action Plan*, published in January 2006, was produced by a team in the Cabinet Office, under Blair's eye. But it was issued on behalf of the Respect Task Force, the new name for Louise Casey's Anti-Social Behaviour Unit (illustrating precisely how 'respect' had become absorbed into enforcement). The tone was in some ways milder than previous statements on the subject of enforcing good behaviour, since there was more emphasis on support, especially to parents and young people, for instance by funding local youth activities and parenting classes. But the new ideas on organisation and funding to promote pro-social behaviour in families, schools and communities alternated with stress on enforcement on non-compliant persons – such as 'challenging' families who could be made to undergo training in special units. Clearly, no respect was to be accorded to people whose behaviour deserved censure. They were still to be regarded as outsiders, not part of the communities to which they belonged.

Hazel Blears was appointed Minister for Respect. 'Respect' became a banner attached to anything relating to the menu of policies passing through the hands of the Task Force. When a Youth Offending Team wrote in to ask for information on the Respect Agenda to pass on to magistrates, it was puzzled to receive a large cardboard box in reply. Inside were a large number of grey baseball caps neatly inscribed in pink lettering 'Give Respect, Get Respect' – the slogan adopted to spread the message. (Surely the JPs were not expected to wear this headgear in court!)

The shrill tone subsided with the appointment of Gordon Brown as Prime Minister in 2007, the transfer of Louise Casey to a less high-profile job, and the disbanding of the Respect Task Force (not to mention the fact that the Tories had adopted their own version of 'respect'). As noted in the Introduction, the 'agenda' was moved to the new Department for Children, Schools and Families and absorbed into a Youth Taskforce, promoting positive outcomes – but nevertheless tacitly acknowledging that youths had always been the main focus of anti-social policies. The new tone was shown by Ed Balls, the minister responsible, quoted as saying that he would be glad if there were no more ASBOs, though he recognised that they were sometimes needed. 'Respect' in its new guise had shaken off the enforcement focus. The head of the Youth Task Force, Anne Weinstock, is a civil servant who was formerly the director of the Supporting Children and Young People Group within the Department of Children, Schools and Families. In a press notice from the department (5 October 2007) she was quoted as saying:

> I want this new unit to be at the forefront of work to ensure that we expand opportunities for all young people outside of school and are able to intervene early to prevent problems from escalating. With support from Government, community and parents, young people will have an opportunity to give, and get respect from our communities. (Respect website, 2007)

Focus on parenting

As the scapegoating of young people was gradually downplayed politically, from 2003 onwards political momentum gathered around the question of parental responsibility for children's behaviour – an issue which had always been present but which became ever more central to policy and practice. The enhanced powers for use of the Parenting Order enacted in the 2003 Anti-Social Behaviour Act proclaimed a message that pointed the finger at parents. Alongside government funding aimed at increasing parental training opportunities, especially in areas with significant reports of anti-social behaviour, the most 'challenging' families were to be subject to special powers which could force them into intensive training units where they would be taught how to behave and control their children (see Nixon and Hunter, Chapter Five). Fifty Action Areas were designated for carrying out this treatment on an estimated 1,000 families. As Hazel Blears put it in a 2005 speech:

> we are investing £1.25 million to ensure that those parents who persist in letting their kids run wild, or behave like yobs themselves, will face intensive rehabilitation ... backed by the threat of enforcement.

Politicians were encouraged to focus on parenting styles as a key to developmental delinquency by academic findings showing the bad effects of harsh, inconsistent or negligent parenting (reviewed in Farrington, 2007; see also Farrington, 1978; 1991; McCord, 1979; Wilson, 1980; Riley and Shaw, 1985; Loeber et al, 2008). But they also knew that they were on a popular cause. A poll commissioned by the Respect Task Force in 2006 found that four out of five people supported the idea that parents should be held responsible for their children's bad behaviour. Other findings included:

- 53% thought that parents not bringing up their children appropriately caused anti-social behaviour;
- 55% thought that better parenting would do most to reduce crime;
- 80% agreed that parents should be held responsible for the bad behaviour of their children and that they should be made to take help if need be.

Increasingly, again following academic findings and evidence of successful programmes (Barlow, 1997; Farrington and Welsh, 1999; Utting, 2003; Moran et al, 2004), government attention turned to early-years parent training and, inspired by the work of David Olds (Olds et al, 1998), even ante-natal supervision of mothers seen as at risk of producing anti-social children. Tony Blair and Gordon Brown both appeared to endorse this policy, in spite of sharp criticism of seemingly labelling children in the womb.

The Conservatives were not to be outdone in this field. David Cameron has focused on families and parents as the key to what he calls 'the broken society'. Increasingly, reports of violent crimes by teenagers turned to blaming parents. Inspired by the murder of Gary Newlove by a group of yobbish youths, the Conservative Party chairperson, Caroline Spelman, called for parents to do community service alongside their children (Wintour, 2008) – a policy practised in some jurisdictions in the US.

Rescuing civil society

Given the importance of the family in communitarian philosophy as the foundation stone of a society based on respect, it is no surprise that policies were formed on that basis. Such policies reflected public opinion, academic research, and ordinary experience. But the choice of punitive rhetoric and legislative powers was not inevitable. Although Etzioni (1993) calls upon communities to rally against the miscreants in their midst, moral authoritarianism expressed in exclusionary rhetoric and practice is not an inevitable characteristic of communitarian approaches.

As Gordon Hughes (1996) has pointed out, other perspectives can be adopted. Instead of excluding 'morally deficient' members of the underclass, an egalitarian approach would focus on the uneven distribution of power and wealth and the righting of past social injustices. A more participatory democracy at local level would replace unresponsive bureaucratic systems. There could also be a place for restorative justice, using Braithwaite's (1993) 'reintegrative shaming', particularly community conferencing (although Hughes is aware that this might be used to repress the more vulnerable members of society).

The Respect Agenda was linked to a broader government project to revive civil society, as Blunkett argued in his Scarman lecture (Blunkett, 2003). The aim of the government's civil renewal programme was to build trust, cooperation and initiative among individual members of society and create more responsive local agencies. Social capital – the fund of common purpose within communities – needs to be built on 'bridging' across interest and cultural groups as well as 'bonding' within them (Putnam, 2000). To achieve these things it is, in Blunkett's words (2003: 1–2), 'critical to reconnect with the issue of respect, to ensure that people treat each other differently, that youngsters learn not to bad mouth and abuse those around them, but to be able to put a point of view or engage in a non-threatening or aggressive manner'.

Trust and respect are two sides of the same coin, but truly respectful societies accord that respect to everybody, young and old, regardless of life-style, ethnicity, etc. Instead, youths, the target of many of the repressive instruments of social control, tend to be viewed with suspicion rather than trust, and do not feel respected (Stephen and Squires, 2005; Prior et al, 2007). Rather, especially in deprived areas, they may become alienated, which bodes ill for the future of civil renewal.

Conclusion

It was a political choice to go down the exclusionary and punitive route, linking community renewal to the crusade against anti-social behaviour. As Prior et al (2007) point out, it would be possible to take any number of other issues linked to deprivation as the focus of community building. But the pressure to introduce tough measures (especially the ASBO) against very real problems of crime and disorder in certain areas was felt strongly at the beginning of the Blair government. Legislation is often seen as the answer to social problems, where real solutions, less eye-catching, lie in long-term efforts to improve social and economic conditions. This has been attempted, and much money expended, in neighbourhood regeneration schemes, training programmes, policing initiatives and so on. Sometimes, confidence and trust does build up where people can see that something is being done about crime and incivilities (Bottoms, 2006; Bottoms and Wilson, 2007). But the urge to 'give respect, get respect' rings hollow when people feel that in their ordinary lives the powers that be do not demonstrate respect to them by recognising their basic needs and aspirations and providing effective help and services.

Richard Sennett (2003) shows that respect has many roots and meanings. He ponders the difficulties of respect bridging inequalities of socio-economic status and ability. He has 'charted a necessarily complicated relationship between society and character which might, just, lead people to treat each other with mutual respect' (pp 245–6). Earning and giving respect belongs to the individuals involved. He concludes: 'Treating people with respect cannot simply occur by commanding it should happen. Mutual recognition has to be negotiated; this negotiation engages the complexities of personal character as much as social structure' (p 260).

Neither 'respect' nor 'anti-social behaviour' was ever defined in concrete terms – they are slogans, reduced to little more than encouraging people to be nicer to one another and targeting individuals whose behaviour upsets the public. Government-led propaganda can change behaviour if the target is clear and is backed by precise legislation (for example, seat belts, drinking and driving, smoking). But a general reform of manners requires a spontaneous, long-term, social sea change, emanating from the public (or at least powerful sections of it) rather than from government intervention. The occasional opinion poll or public meeting is no substitute. There is a lesson in the shift to Victorian manners and behaviour from the perceived excessive disorder of the late eighteenth century – a shift driven by the rise of a prosperous middle class and the campaigns of leading moral entrepreneurs (Wilson, 2007; see also Chapter Two, this volume, by Pearson).

Respect is not therefore going to be spread successfully through slogans and political speeches. Governments and politicians need to demonstrate respect for the population at every level themselves, by listening, understanding, and adapting policies to needs, rather than by diktat and punitive laws and practices. A drive for civil renewal that seems to rely primarily on enforcement against young people creates neither trust nor the 'mutual recognition' so subtly explored by Richard Sennett. The ideas behind the policies, as described by Tony Blair and David Blunkett, acknowledge the need for a responsive government and a holistic approach to communities: but in implementation the demand for tough powers and the populist use of exclusionary language *drowned* out other messages. Hopefully, the change of direction indicated in the creation of the Youth Taskforce will supply some of the missing ethos and action.

Notes
[1] The SLNG still exists, providing extensive information and advice to social landlords of all types, and publishes a newsletter entitled *Nuisance News*.

References

Barlow, J. (1997) *Systemic Review of the Effectiveness of Parent-Training Programmes in Improving the Behaviour of Children aged 3–10 years*, Oxford: Oxford University Press.

Blunkett, D. (2001) *Politics and Progress: Renewing Democracy and Civil Society*, London: Politico's.

Blunkett, D. (2006) *The Blunkett Tapes: My Life in the Bear Pit*, London: Bloomsbury.

Bottoms, A. (2006) 'Incivilities, offence and social order in residential communities', in A. von Hirsch and A. Simester (eds) *Incivilities: Regulating Offensive Behaviour*, Oxford: Hart Publishing, pp 239–80.

Bottoms, A. and Wilson, A. (2007) 'Civil renewal, control signals and neighbourhood safety', in T. Brannan, P. John and G. Stoker (eds) *Re-energizing Citizenship*, Basingstoke: Palgrave Macmillan, pp 63–90.

Braithwaite, J. (1993) 'Shame and Modernity', *British Journal of Criminology*, 33(1), 1–18.

Burney, E. (2005) *Making People Behave: Anti-Social Behaviour, Policy and Politics*, Cullompton: Willan Publishing.

Burney, E. and Gelsthorpe, L. (2008) 'Do we need a "naughty step"? Rethinking the parenting order ten years on', *Howard Journal of Criminal Justice*, 47(5), 470–85.

Dennis, N. and Erdos, G. (1993) *Families without Fatherhood*, 2nd edition, London: Institute of Economic Affairs.

Etzioni, A. (1993) *The Spirit of Community. The Reinvention of American Society*, New York, NY: Touchstone.

Fairclough, N. (2000) *New Labour, New Language*, London: Routledge.

Farrington, D. (1978) 'The family backgrounds of aggressive youths', in L. Hersov, M. Berger, and D. Shaffer (eds) *Aggression and Anti-social Behaviour in Childhood and Adolescence*, Oxford: Pergamon, pp 73–93.

Farrington, D. (1991) 'Childhood aggression and adult violence: early precursors and later life outcomes', in D. Pepler and K. Rubin (eds) *The Development and Treatment of Childhood Aggression*, Hillsdale, N.J.: Erlbaum.

Farrington, D. (2007) 'Childhood risk factors and risk focused prevention', in M. Maguire, R. Morgan and R. Reiner (eds) *The Oxford Handbook of Criminology*, 4th edition, Oxford: Oxford University Press.

Farrington, D. and Welsh, B. (1999) 'Delinquency prevention using family-based interventions', *Children and Society*, 13(4), 287–303.

Field, F. (2003) *Neighbours from Hell: The Politics of Behaviour*, London: Politico's.

Giddens, A. (1998) *The Third Way: The Renewal of Social Democracy*, Cambridge: Polity Press.

Home Office (2003a) *Respect and Responsibility – Taking a Stand against Anti-Social Behaviour*, Cm 5778, London: Home Office,

Home Office (2003b) *Together: Tackling Anti-Social Behaviour. Action Plan*, London: Home Office.

HoC (House of Commons Home Affairs Select Committee) (2005) *Anti-Social Behaviour*, London: Stationery Office.

Hughes, G. (1996) 'Communitarianism and law and order', *Critical Social Policy*, 16(49), 17–41.

Labour Party (1995) *A Quiet Life: Tough Action on Criminal Neighbours*, London: Labour Party.

Loeber, R., Farrington, D.P., Stouthamer-Loeber, M. and White, H.R. (2008) *Violence and Serious Theft: Development and Prediction from Childhood to Adulthood*, New York, NY: Routledge.

McCord, J. (1979) 'Some child-rearing antecedents of criminal behaviour in adult men', *Journal of Personality and Social Psychology*, 37(9), 1477–86.

Moran, P., Ghate, D. and van der Merwe, A. (2004) *What Works in Parenting Support? A Review of the International Evidence*, Research Report 574, London: Department for Education and Skills.

Olds, D., Pettitt, L.M., Robinson, J., Henderson, C., Eckenrode, J., Kitzman, H., Cole, B. and Powers, J. (1998) 'Reducing risks for antisocial behavior with a program of prenatal and early childhood home visitation', *Journal of Community Psychology*, 26(1), 65–83.

Prior, D., Farrow, K., Spalek, B. and Barnes, M. (2007) 'Anti-social behaviour and civil renewal', in T. Brannan, P. John and G. Stoker (eds) *Re-energizing Citizenship*, Basingstoke: Palgrave Macmillan, pp 91–111.

Putnam, R. (2000) *Bowling Alone: The Collapse and Revival of American Community*, New York, NY: Simon and Schuster.

Rentoul, J. (2001) *Tony Blair: Prime Minister*, London: Little, Brown.

Respect Task Force (2006) *Respect Action Plan*, London: Home Office.

Respect website (2007) 'Government spotlight on young people with creation of new Youth Taskforce', News, 5 October. Available at: www. respect.gov.uk/news/article.aspx?id=11900.

Riley, D. and Shaw, M. (1985) *Parental Supervision and Juvenile Delinquency*, Home Office Research Study 83, London: Home Office.

Sampson, R. and Raudenbush, S. (2001) *Disorder in Urban Neighbourhoods: Does it Lead to Crime?* Washington, DC: National Institute of Justice.

Sennett, R. (2003) *Respect: The Formation of Character in a World of Inequality*, London: Allen Lane.

Stephen, D. and Squires, P. (2005) *Community Safety, Enforcement, and Acceptable Behaviour Contracts*, Brighton: Health and Social Policy Research Centre, University of Brighton.

Taylor, R. (2001) *Breaking Away from Broken Windows*, Boulder, CO: Westview Press.

Utting, D. (2003) 'Prevention through family and parenting programmes', in D. Farrington and J. Coid (eds) *Early Prevention of Adult Antisocial Behaviour*, Cambridge: Cambridge University Press.

Wilson, B. (2007) *Decency and Disorder, 1789–1837*, London: Faber and Faber.

Wilson, H. (1980) 'Parental supervision: a neglected aspect of delinquency', *British Journal of Criminology*, 20(3), 203–35.

Wilson, J. and Kelling, G. (1982) 'The police and neighbourhood safety: broken windows', *The Atlantic Monthly*, March, 29–38.

Wintour, P. (2008) 'Tory backing for punishment of parents alongside child offenders', *The Guardian*, 11 April. Available at: www.guardian.co.uk/politics/2008/apr/11/conservatives.children.

TWO

'A Jekyll in the classroom, a Hyde in the street': Queen Victoria's hooligans

Geoffrey Pearson

The Respect Agenda implies a version of history. As the Respect Task Force has put it, 'when respect for self, others and community breaks down, anti-social behaviour takes hold'.[1] It is therefore a history of *breakdown* and erosion: young people *no longer* respect the law, *no longer* respect their parents and neighbours, they *no longer* show any obedience to authority in all its forms, there is *now* a carnival of disorder in the streets of the 'broken' society. This in itself implies a time-scale, pointing to a time when communities were harmonious, whole and unbroken; when parents were dutiful; and children obedient and loyal to their elders and betters, uncorrupted by demoralising popular entertainments.

Within the remembered traditions of the 'British way of life' it is the Victorian era, particularly the golden years of late Victorian and Edwardian society – the times of our grandparents, our great-grandparents and their parents – that occupy a privileged position as a time of unrivalled tranquillity. The cosy fug of the music hall, the rattle of clogs on cobbled streets, the unhurried pace of a horse-drawn civilisation – before the motor car, before the cinema, before the sweeping changes of the twentieth century and their attendant disorientations – here, we are repeatedly encouraged to believe, is the original home of 'Old England' and a life ordered by tradition and familiarity. It may be helpful, then, to reflect on what the Victorians themselves thought about 'Victorian values', the morals of their own young people in the 'good old days', and their own version of the Respect Agenda.

My strange title is taken from a collection of essays, *Studies of Boy Life in Our Cities*, brought together by E.J. Urwick in 1904, three years after Queen Victoria's death. It did not paint a very reassuring picture of the youth of the nation, reflecting the anxious mood of late Victorian and Edwardian Britain (as it actually existed) about declining standards and the erosion of the old traditions. There was mention of 'Hooligan' gangs in London, for example, who went in for street-fighting battles, as well as assaults on innocent passers-by, and who do not appear to have had a great deal of respect for the police (Pearson, 1983). The family was widely believed to be in meltdown, and 'the break-up or weakening of family life' was on the editorial agenda of *The Times* no less than 'the break-up or impairment of the old ideas of discipline or order' in the cities, where there was 'something like organised terrorism in the streets'.[2] The excessive leniency of the law was indicted frequently enough. The baleful influence of the music hall entertainments and 'penny dreadful' comics were said to be encouraging immorality and imitative 'copycat' crime among the young. The failure of the elementary system of Board Schools (otherwise known jokingly as the 'Bored Schools') to exercise effective controls upon the rising generation was also subject to widespread condemnation. And so it was, with children and youths allegedly running riot outside school hours, that Urwick had summed up the faltering disciplines of his era. 'It is a common experience', he observed, 'to find a boy a Jekyll in the classroom, and a Hyde in the street' (1904: 295).

The streets were made to play in

> Balls of every size whistle mysteriously past his ears; swift moving shapes, reared aloft on a single roller-skate rattle by; artists are sketching portraits on any available surface ... all are taking place in a kind of rhythmic chant, unceasing, discordant, cheerful ... Such is the wanderer's first introduction to the London boy. As the hours draw on, and twilight gives place to dusk, and dusk turns to darkness, the numbers remain undiminished ... The street and not the house ought to be regarded as the home ... There they remain until it is dark, and often in summer till dawn begins to break. (Bray, 1904: 3, 23, 25)

Street life at the beginning of the twentieth century, here described for us by Reginald Bray, who worked in the boys' club movement in Camberwell, was a swarm of activity. 'The children in my particular part', said another commentator at the time, 'are playing until twelve o'clock at night from about the age of four years ... the place is alive with them at night' (HMSO, 1904). The world of children, as the historian Jerry White (1980: 144) has described it, 'etched itself in sound ... the only modern parallel would be a school playground at break-time. But this was a break-time which lasted the best part of a day and lingered on through the night'. Indeed, it was a common joke among those involved in the boys' and girls' clubs, and in the elementary schools, that if children were asked to explain the purpose of streets, they would reply that 'The streets were made to play in' (Paterson, 1911: 108). And play in them they did, as indicated by Reginald Bray in another lively portrait of the dizzy whirl of street life:

> In the streets crowds of children, hustled together into a noisy throng, render impossible all chance of unimpeded pleasure; a football descends, like a bombshell, on a group of girls intent on the thrilling amusement of hop-scotch, and tiresome pedestrians ruthlessly break into the most exciting skipping exhibition; a swarm of maidens quarrel for the possession of a rope that has fallen from a cart; and a hundred boys assiduously angle for some solitary fish as it swims uneasily in the oleaginous waters of the canal. (1907: 44–5)

Norman Douglas's *London Street Games*, which first appeared in 1916, listed hundreds upon hundreds of children's games, with strange rules and even stranger names – 'Woggles', 'Wriggly-worm', 'Zig-zag', 'Bedlam', 'Tree-hee', 'Nixie', 'Paper truncheons', 'Hitting the sun', 'Kick-can policeman', 'Knock him down donkey', 'Hammers on', 'Green man rise-o', 'Bangings', 'Alley gobs', 'Bogie man', 'Chinese orders', 'Dead soldiers', 'Inch it up', 'String-he', 'Hitting the mummy', and so on (1931). Most of these games are now entirely forgotten, although some of them can be recognised as variants of 'Tig', 'Relieve-Oh', 'O'Reilly Says', 'Bobbers and Kib', whip-and-top, marbles, swings improvised from lamp-posts, and ball games – with innumerable local improvisations in the rules, and where the spelling of the names of the games was always uncertain because this was (and is) an essentially non-literate oral tradition of childhood that is passed on, from generation to generation, by word of mouth, rhymes and songs (Opie and Opie, 1969; 1977; 1985).

But this was not an age of innocence. Some of these street games could be extremely rough affairs, spilling over into 'larking', rowdyism and vandalism, or involving the use of foul play and foul language. Douglas described one game called 'Release' which he said was played by some of the bigger boys, a kind of 'tig' that required you to clobber your opponent about the head. 'Old people bar the game', he said, 'because you always get your clothes torn.' But that was only the half of it, because it was also a game that frequently ended in tears, rough banter and fighting:

> "D'ye want a claht over the jor?" says one, "Cos yer never did touch me 'ead, so there."
>
> "Ole Ikey seed me doos it."
>
> "Liar. 'Cos 'e wos t'ovver side o' the street."
>
> "E never. Yer wos on the grahnd when I crahned yer napper."
>
> "Liar. Yer sez I wos a-layin dahn when all the time I wos on me stumps. Yer finks I'm up the pole to 'ear yer tork. Knock 'arf yer fice orff."
>
> "Not 'arf. Yer know I touched yer nut 'cos don't yer remember me a-standin on yer arms?"
>
> "Ef yer wants on eye bunged up or a punch on the snaht – "
>
> "Well ef I'm a liar y'ore the biggest. So yer lumps it. I'm going to be blowed ef I play wiv a lahsy blisterin blitherin blinkin blightin bloomin bleedin blasted barstard wot's got a mover wot's got a bloke wot's – "
>
> "Garn! Piss up yer leg, an play wiv the steam." (Douglas, 1931: 19–20).

Nor, if we should be tempted into romantic judgements on the healthy vigour of these old street traditions, should we forget that the battle for territorial space had already been engaged between the young and the older generations. The increased police vigilance, which led to many young men and boys being brought before the courts for playing street football or gambling with pennies at pitch-and-toss, has often been commented upon (Gillis, 1975; Humphries, 1981). Even so, it was not always that straightforward. It was not only children who were implicated in these conflicts over playing games in the street, but also grown men. And although plainclothes police officers were sometimes deployed in order to counter these kinds of street nuisances, some London magistrates appear to have been reluctant to prosecute on police evidence alone, unless local people came forward to offer proof of annoyance by street games. The police view, on the other hand, was that neighbours were often afraid to give evidence because of possible reprisals. In internal memoranda on these controversies, the police thought that 'it is common sense to assume that rough men cannot play football or cricket in a street without causing annoyance' and that if they waited for things to reach such a pitch that neighbours would actually come forward to offer evidence, then 'thickly populated busy districts such as this would become impassable'. Senior officers suggested as a solution that, rather than prosecute under the section of the Police Acts concerning annoyance, they should employ the section concerned with 'discharging missiles'. The delicate legal issue then arose as to 'whether a cricket ball or a football comes within the meaning of the word "missile"'.[3]

Hedged about with difficulties such as these, it would appear that the police often stood back from these kinds of problems and simply allowed this turbulent street life to take its course.[4] Some indication of the hidden dimensions of the problem can be gleaned from a small-scale police experiment in some areas of London in 1903 and 1904 when, for a few months, a handful of plainclothes men were stationed on special duties in order to combat street rowdyism. The result was that 3,499 arrests and summonses were made, mostly in seven police districts, with a heavy concentration in 'L' district, where four men made 1,067 arrests within 12 months.[5] And this, given the scale of the operation, can only have been scratching the surface.

The struggle over street games and rowdyism was only part of a more general picture. Quite apart from physical assaults on the police, to which we will turn in a moment, there was any number of other troubles and conflicts, sometimes reaching quite serious proportions. In one area of Southwark in the late 1890s, for example, persistent attempts had been made to prevent children from using the drying areas on the roof of a tenement block as a playground. Doors and bolts had been fixed, but it was said that in a three-month period 'fourteen dozen locks' had been broken, the children had burned down the doors, and even iron gates that were fitted had not stopped them from gaining access to the roof, from where they had repeatedly showered people below with volleys of stones.[6] We also hear of schools being vandalised by children, of obstructions placed on railway lines, and the police had once more found it necessary to station plainclothes men on London's bridges in order to stop children and youths from throwing stones (and spitting and urinating) on the boats that passed below, causing annoyance and danger to their passengers.[7] In 1896 while sculling at Putney, an oarsman had been sunk by a stone-throwing youth, and the following year there was a complaint that a yacht's skylight had been broken at Lambeth Bridge and then 'a shower of horse dung greeted us at Chelsea'. It should also be said that names given by some of the boys arrested for these offences – David Stones and Arthur Gobbing, for example – suggest the possibility of a hoax.

There were also complaints of damage and fires started by children throwing rockets and fireworks, sometimes aimed at passing cyclists or to frighten horses. Attacks on cyclists by gangs of stone-throwing youths and children, a kind of 'highway robbery' according to the *Bicycling Times*, were said to be too frequent; and in one case a South London cowboy was brought before Lambeth court for lassoing cyclists – 'a kind of horseplay that must be stamped out at once' said the magistrate, with good reason. School 'treats' and outings were another focus for these concerns, and in Streatham and Brixton it was said that 'van loads' of children frequently passed through the neighbourhood 'discharging fireworks and throwing them indiscriminately at passers-by'.[8] Another favourite 'street game' was to jump onto the back of a cart in order to steal a ride, and also to bundle its contents off into the thieving arms of one's friends following behind (Samuel, 1981). Soon the new-fangled motor car would be putting in an appearance, with a flurry of complaints to the police that children in some neighbourhoods had taken to lying down in the street in the path of oncoming motor vehicles in order to halt their progress, so as to take a closer look at this wonder of the modern age, to steal a ride on the back, or even to assault the motorist. Indeed, in the face of such a threat, serious consideration was given to whether it should be a compulsory requirement to fit motor cars with netting or spikes at their rear in order to prevent such practices.[9] And amid all this, there were graffiti, too. Here is one example from this era, said to depict 'the little disagreements which are natural to healthy children': 'This [pointing to a drawing of a girl] is Fanny Ives and she is going to have a smack in the jaw for hitting Nellie Western.'[10]

These aspects of the bustling, horse-drawn street life of late Victorian and Edwardian cities were a matter of great concern to many commentators at the turn of the century. Not only in terms of their nuisance value and potential danger, but also for what they indicated about the moral consequences of urban life for the rising generation. 'The daily doings of a small boy out of school', wrote Alexander Paterson in what was an otherwise sympathetic portrait of working-class life before the Great War, 'form a rapid succession of inconsequent episodes, calculated to produce smart, resourceful, but unreliable men at the age of fourteen.' 'The games they play in the street or court', he continued, 'are wildly lawless … friendships grow old in a day, fights are forgotten in an hour. Life is a giddy kaleidoscope of danger, catastrophe, and unexpected windfalls' (Paterson, 1911: 108).

For Sir Robert Baden-Powell, founder of the Boy Scout movement and always something of a maverick in these matters, it was no bad thing that a boy schooled in the customs of the street was 'as sharp as a needle'; nor that the kinds of incidents that excited his interest were 'an arrest, or a passing fire engine, or a good fight between two of his neighbours – especially if one is a woman' (Baden-Powell, 1919: 27). But more commonly it was feared that the excitements of town life produced a merely superficial intelligence, as when Reginald Bray, in his powerful Christian pastoral thesis *The Town Child*, remarked upon the disorienting effect which street life must inevitably have on the character of the young:

> The effect on character is easily traced. Children who have acquired the habit of sharing the life of a crowd find the routine existence of the individual insipid and distasteful; they become more noisy and uncontrolled in their ways, less tolerant of any restraint ... Life lacks the elements of permanence, of significance, of idealistic imaginings. The aimless wandering of a child down the street is symbolic of his whole existence. He is dodging now this vehicle and now that; he is halting now to gather the dusty treasures from a coster's barrow providentially upset, now to watch a herd of bullocks swept into the slaughterhouse; here he is pressing urgently into the heart of a drunken quarrel, there he is flying from some shopkeeper whose wrath his pleasing amenities have aroused; at one moment he is clambering up a lamp-post, at another he is pouring the vials of his contempt on a stranger ... here walking, here running, here idling, now laughing, now crying, now shouting, he drifts ... no particular destination to be reached, no special street to be crossed, no definite task to be worked through, and no final goal of all desire to be attained. (Bray, 1907: 48, 51)

For Bray, as for so many of his contemporaries, the result of all this was a perceived alteration in the temperament of the English people. 'A deliberate slowness in action was once the characteristic of the Englishman,' Bray thought. 'He would look around a situation before he leapt into it.' Whereas now, there was 'a wild spirit of unrest ... nerves are ever on the strain ... the crowd of the town in a moment flashed into a delirious mob' (Bray, 1907: 145–6).

The judgement was echoed elsewhere, often combining allegations of the physical deterioration of the working class with this equally worrying temperamental shift. For Jack London, for example, the effect of urban living was not only that 'the children grow up into rotten adults, without virility or stamina, a weak-kneed, narrow-chested, listless breed'. There was also the same marked change in the national character. 'The traditional silent and reserved Englishman has passed away', he wrote in 1902. 'A new race has sprung up, a street people … The pavement folk are noisy, voluble, high-strung and excitable' (London, 1963: 39, 137).

Were the streets also made to fight in?

These troubled discourses about the children of late Victorian society and their part in its restless street life, together with the new streak of excitability and violence among the people, came into sharp focus around the desperate energies of London's 'Hooligan' gangs. The word 'Hooligan' emerged some time in the 1890s, and although its origins remain obscure it probably came out of the popular culture of the Victorian music hall. It was not, however, until the late summer of 1898 that it entered into common English usage, when, in the aftermath of an excessively rowdy August Bank Holiday celebration in London, it grabbed the headlines (Pearson, 1983).

At first it was not entirely clear what the words 'Hooligan' and 'Hooliganism' meant, although they were used freely enough in the press and elsewhere to describe assaults, street robberies and attacks on policemen, together with what was known as the 'free fight', which must have been a major public institution, sometimes consuming the energy of several hundred people at a time. But when the word 'Hooligan' had settled down – and at first it was invariably graced with a capital 'H' – it transpired that the original 'Hooligans' were what we would now call a youth culture. Young men in slum neighbourhoods had adopted a uniform dress style of bell-bottom trousers cut tight at the knee, heavily ornamented leather belts, neck-scarves, a distinctive style of peaked cap (peak to the front rather than to the back as so often nowadays), and short-cropped hair with a donkey fringe. In some areas of London there were trend-setters in the Hooligan fashion: the 'Velvet Cap Gang' from Battersea, for example, the 'Plaid Cap Brigade' from Poplar, and the 'Crooked Stick' division from South London. And one young man caused some amusement when he appeared before a London Police Court with such a daringly exaggerated 'donkey fringe' that it sounded remarkably like a 'Mohican' hairstyle, which was to come into fashion many years later with some of the more outlandish Teddy Boys, and then the Punks: 'His hair had been clipped as closely as possible to the scalp, with the exception of a small patch on the crown of his head, which was pulled down over the forehead to form a fringe.'[11]

In other cities similar gangs were known by different names. In Birmingham they were called 'Peaky Blinders' or 'Sloggers', while in Manchester and Salford they were known and feared as 'Scuttlers' and later as 'Ikes' or 'Ikey Lads'.[12] There were also similar youth factions in late nineteenth-century Australian cities, where they were known as 'Larrikins', and for some years 'Larrikin' continued to be used in Britain as a synonym for 'Hooligan' (McLachlan, no date; Pearson, 1983). The 'Peaky Blinders' and 'Scuttlers' can be traced back for some years before the word 'Hooligan' appeared, although they wore the same clothing styles as the London gangs. From Salford in 1890 a Police Court Missioner (forerunners of the modern probation officers) described how the Scuttlers wore a uniform of 'narrow-go-wide' trousers, a 'puncher's cap' and narrow-toed, brass-tipped clogs; and he was particularly struck by the ornamental patterns on their belts, which they made with metal pins and studs:

> These designs include figures of serpents, a heart pierced with an arrow (this appears to be a favourite design), Prince of Wales' feathers, clogs, animals, stars, etc., and often either the name of the wearer of the belt or that of some woman.

He also listed weapons that had been confiscated from Scuttlers when their street fights had been broken up:

> Old cutlasses, pokers, pieces of strap having iron bolts affixed to the end, the tops of stone 'pop' bottles fastened at the end of a piece of string and used for whirling round the head, specially made pieces of iron … knives and loaded sticks. But the favourite weapons are stones and belts … the most dangerous part of the belt is the buckle. (Devine, 1890: 2)

These street fights, or 'Scuttles' as they were known in Manchester and Salford, were often quite formalised affairs, with a time and place for the encounter set in advance. Street would fight against street, neighbourhood against neighbourhood, or pub against pub, and they must have been a formidable spectacle: one 'Scuttle' reported from Newton Heath, a neighbourhood not far from 'inner city' Ancoats, in 1890 involved between 500 and 600 youths in a pitched battle in Holland Street.[13] In London the pattern was much the same, with

'Fulham Boys' against 'Chelsea Boys', 'Chelsea Boys' against 'Battersea Boys', or 'Chapel Street' against 'Margaret Street'. In Hammersmith it was alleged in *The Sun*[14] that the gangs were 'NOT "HOOLIGANS" BUT WORSE', while in South London it was said that they wore 'boots toe-plated with iron, and calculated to kill more easily'. Whereas from the East End, Walter Besant (1901: 167) provided a more detailed inventory of the Hooligans' street-fighting equipment:

> They arm themselves with clubs, with iron bars, with leather belts to which buckles belong, with knotted handkerchiefs containing stones – a lethal weapon – with sling and stones, with knives even, with revolvers of the 'toy' kind, and they go forth and fight the lads of Brook Street. It is a real fight.

A few months before the 'Hooligan' was officially christened by the news media, the London *Echo* had already remarked that 'No one can have read the London, Liverpool, Birmingham, Manchester and Leeds papers and not know that the young street ruffian and prowler, with his heavy belt, treacherous knife and dangerous pistol, is among us.'[15] Discussing 'Those Pistol Cases', The *Daily Graphic* had agreed that they 'are getting much too frequent' and that 'the latest pistol cases have almost all been of boys, hardly in their teens, deliberately using pistols as weapons of aggression ... those "gangs" of young ruffians ... seem to think little more of discharging them than they would of throwing stones'.[16] Gun licensing was undoubtedly extremely lax, and there can be no doubt that firearms were used in the tussles of adult mobsters and that youths were sometimes caught in possession of pistols and revolvers.[17] Even so, whether Hooligans were engaged in regular shoot-outs in the street is another matter altogether, and it seems likely that the gentlemen of the press who advanced such stories occasionally got carried away with themselves. Indeed, there were complaints from a number of well-informed sources that the whole business of the 'Hooligan' was the result of 'silly season' sensationalism and that it was merely 'press-manufactured Hooliganism'. Even so, one of those sources, Charles Booth's survey of poverty in London (1903), went on to state that in spite of exaggeration in the press 'there is real ground for complaint' and further asserted that 'Criminals are heroes to the young'.[18]

However real their weaponry, the 'Hooligan' gangs were real enough, and they were to become notorious in the years leading up to the Great War. Apart from their internecine warfare, the press gave a good deal of coverage to incidents in which gangs of youths had pushed people off the pavement, or knocked them down without provocation. 'A gang of roughs', for example, 'who were parading the roadway, shouting obscene language, playing mouth organs, and pushing respectable people down. The young ruffians were all armed with thick leather belts, on which there were heavy brass buckles.'[19] The frequent reports of this nature probably derived from the practice known as 'holding the street', a violent ritual of territorial supremacy in some working-class neighbourhoods which sounds not unlike the more recent practice at football grounds of 'holding the End' (see Flint and Powell's Chapter Nine and Squires' Chapter Ten for contemporary issues of respect, disorder and sectarianism at football grounds). As Walter Besant described it in 1901:

> The boys gather together and hold the street; if anyone ventures to pass through it they rush upon him, knock him down, and kick him savagely about the head; they rob him as well ... the boys regard holding the street with pride.[20]

One final dimension of this unfriendly street life, in which the Hooligans were again implicated, was the fierce traditions of hostility to the police in many working-class neighbourhoods. Policemen attempting to make arrests would commonly be set upon by large crowds of bystanders, sometimes numbered in hundreds, to the battle-cry of 'Rescue! Rescue!' and 'Boot 'im!'. While trying to separate a man and woman who were quarrelling in the street, for example, London policemen were 'set upon by a crowd of 200 persons, who called out "Boot them", and they were assaulted and kicked'. Elsewhere, at Alexander Park Race Day, when police arrested a pickpocket 'the constables were surrounded by a crowd, who kicked them and brutally ill-treated them, and released the prisoner'.[21] As one final example, at the height of the Bank Holiday outrages in 1898 various newspapers picked up on what one described as a 'Midnight Riot' in the vicinity of Euston Road, when policemen attempted to deal with a disorderly woman who 'began to shriek, and ... screamed that she was being choked'. Surrounded by a hostile crowd that began to hiss and hoot, one officer swept a semi-circle with his truncheon to make space while another blew his whistle for assistance. 'Unfortunately for the constable', we are told, 'this only had the effect of bringing reinforcements to the mob.' A roar went up of 'Rescue! Rescue!' and among those alerted to the commotion were the notorious Somers Town Boys.[22]

Such was the hostility to the police that they frequently found it necessary to turn a blind eye to legal infringements, or risk serious disorder and injury. Here, in an internal memorandum of 1900, a police superintendent explains the difficulties of enforcing what were called 'petty offences' under the Police Acts, in this case two men fighting in the street while surrounded by a crowd:

> It is often quite impossible for one constable to apprehend persons who are fighting and are surrounded by a rough crowd and to attempt to do so would in many cases lead to a much more serious breach of the peace.[23]

There were any number of reports of this kind in the press, and nor was it only 'Hooligans' who were involved. Attacks on the police and resistance to arrest touched upon complex structures of loyalty and popular tradition in working-class neighbourhoods, and these traditions carried through into the 1920s and 1930s, when policing the rougher areas of the major cities was still an extremely hazardous business (Bean, 1981; Cohen, 1979; White, 1979; 1983). Even so, before the Great War the police were treated very badly indeed. To give some idea of the scale of the problem, in the early 1900s approximately one in four of London's entire uniformed police strength was assaulted each year in the course of duty, and one in ten of these would be on the sick list for a fortnight or more.[24] So, however much the popular press may have magnified some aspects of the 'Hooligan' affair, there can be no doubting the truthfulness of the *Pall Mall Gazette*'s assessment of the policeman's lot in 1901, only one month after Queen Victoria's death:

> The constable in certain districts is apparently looked upon as the common enemy whom it is right to kick and beat … A policeman's lot is not a happy one when he attempts to arrest disorderly persons who have the active sympathy of a crowd of roughs.[25]

The rough justice meted out to London's policemen can be usefully compared to the even rougher justice sometimes doled out in the Police Courts. A case comes to hand of a band of holidaymakers returning home to the Elephant and Castle from a railway excursion to Herne Bay late one summer's evening, when a bottle fight broke out among the merrymakers, as a result of which a man was killed. It was an unremarkable story, which did not excite too much interest in the South London press, where there were frequent headlines such as 'Kick a Man Like a Football' and reports of throwing glasses and bottles at pub landlords; but what does seem remarkable is that the only charges brought were against three men who were hauled before the magistrates, charged with assault, fined 20 shillings each, and required to pay the doctor's bill on the dead man.[26] Life was evidently cheap in the streets of Old England.

Organised sport to the rescue: football, fact and fantasy

> Col. Fox: 'When you spoke just now about Hooligans, or what are commonly called Larrakins … is it the lowest stratum, or simply the lads who have greater energy – what is commonly called "devil" … owing in the majority of cases to boys having superfluous energy?'
>
> Mr. Eyre: 'I do, distinctly. I feel that if adequate provision were made for their recreation, almost the whole of this Larrakin business would vanish.'
>
> Col. Fox: 'That is to say, if you provided them with footballs and made them kick footballs, they would not be so inclined to kick policemen in the street?'
>
> Mr. Eyre: 'That is so. They simply want recreative facilities.'
> (HMSO, 1904, qus 3663–5).

The 'Hooligan' (who when mentioned here in evidence before the Physical Deterioration Committee of 1904 was still confused with his Australian cousin the 'Larrakin') was to embark on a spectacular official career in the early years of the twentieth century. He would appear, if not in person then at least in name, before numerous committees of inquiry into the troubled state of the nation. He loomed large in the inspirations for Baden-Powell's Boy Scouts. Gymnasia would be thrown up and playing fields laid down in his honour. He would be feared by some as the herald of a dark hour in the nation's affairs, while others would see him as a likely recruit for the nation's armed forces. And eventually, his name not only would travel the globe as a standard term in any number of languages, but in 1922 would also be included in that select list of insults which Members of Parliament were forbidden to use when describing each other (*Hansard*, 1922; Neuberger, 1993; Weissman, 1978).

It must be said at once, however, that the inconsistencies revealed by those who spoke on the Hooligan's behalf were no less remarkable than 'Hooliganism' itself. In Colonel Fox's terms, as part of the evidence gathered by the Physical Deterioration Committee of 1904, the 'Hooligan' was understood as a hulking lad full of the 'devil'. And while this was not an uncommon view, elsewhere he was seen as the end-point of the process of urban degeneration, as when *The Spectator* first remarked on the 'London Larrikins' by identifying them as a 'reverted type ... one of the very central ideas of evolutionary doctrine' that was produced by 'every kind of artificial civilisation'.[27] Widely understood as the result of ignorance, 'the violence of the hobbledehoy Hooligan' nevertheless appeared before the Scottish Royal Commission on Physical Training in 1903 as 'a product of the Education Act' (HMSO, 1903), a view echoed in the pages of the *Catholic Pulpit*, where these 'pagan bandits of the metropolis' were said to have come about 'because these children are so well educated' and hence 'so capable of resisting the authorities'.[28] So often described as the product of poverty and poor housing, the 'Hooligan' was held up before the 1909 Poor Law Commission (of all places) as an exemplification of 'the youth, who even now has too much pocket-money' (Webb and Webb, 1909: 273). Indeed, the chameleon figure of the 'Hooligan' was capable of providing a crystallising focus for many of the overlapping, and sometimes contradictory, social apprehensions of his age.

When the Hooligan had first made his social entrance, flogging was the remedy most often advocated. On the use of pistols by young people, the *Daily Graphic* took the view that 'if birching and short sentences will not stop it, then more birching and longer sentences will have to be tried'.[29] The refusal of Parliament to extend the powers of whipping (which were largely restricted to the birching of boys under 14 years of age) was regarded as a sign of morbid sentimentality. But with a growing feeling that 'Hooliganism' represented a more general dislocation among the nation's youth (and not just a criminal 'hard-core'), this narrow punitive response gave way to initiatives that stressed the need to firm up the existing system of elementary education. And this is where organised sport and games assumed a new importance in national affairs, although again for contradictory reasons.

Undoubtedly, the central contradiction was whether or not Hooliganism was symptomatic of the process of 'urban degeneration' which had been feared since the 1880s, although it was brought into sharp focus by the public scandal concerning allegations about the appalling physical condition of recruits for the Boer War. The danger, as Charles Masterman saw it in *The Heart of the Empire*, was that urban over-crowding and squalor threatened 'a perpetual lowering in the vitality of the Imperial Race in the great cities of the Kingdom':

> Turbulent rioting over military successes, Hooliganism, and a certain temper of fickle excitability has revealed to observers during the past few months that a new race, hitherto unreckoned and of incalculable action, is entering the sphere of practical importance – the 'City type' of the coming years; the 'street-bred' people of the twentieth century; the 'new generation knocking at our doors'... The result is the production of a characteristic *physical* type of town dweller: stunted, narrow-chested, easily wearied; yet voluble, excitable, with little ballast, stamina or endurance. (Masterman, 1902: 7–8)

We have seen this response before, although Masterman's was one of the earliest and most authoritative judgements on the question. Even so, the contradiction is in full flower: a narrow-chested, listless people who are at the same time excitable and dangerous. On the one hand, then, the inspiration for organised sports was to beef up the physique of the 'Imperial Race', which is how Baden-Powell boomed off in *Scouting for Boys*:

> Recent reports on the deterioration of our race ought to be taken as a warning to be taken in time before it is too late. One cause which contributed to the downfall of the Roman Empire was the fact that the soldiers fell away from the standards of their forebears in bodily strength. (Baden-Powell, 1908: 208)

On the other hand, there were those such as Urwick who could not reconcile complaints about 'the decline of physical energy' with 'a class of boys bursting with animal energy' (Urwick, 1904: 265). So that on this different reckoning, as Lord Meath put it in 1903, 'a great deal of this hooliganism and riot and rowdyism is simply because our lads have no means of working off their energies'. 'If you want to get hold of the roughest and worst class of hooligan', he explained to the Scottish Royal Commission on Physical Training, 'there is nothing better than starting boxing classes' (HMSO, 1903: qu 8403). From her experience of the London boys' club movement, Mrs Josceline Bagot agreed: 'What these boys really like is fighting. So we get them into the club and have them trained in boxing … and they learn to do it properly' (HMSO, 1904: qu 4528).

Any number of competing claims were made upon the Hooligan's leisure time, in fact: boxing clubs and Bible classes, fresh-air funds and camping holidays, gymnasia and physical jerks, football pitches and swimming clubs, Continuation Schools, training ships and military drill. There was 'nothing more attractive to a lad than drill', according to Lord Meath, 'especially if it is a real drill; and more particularly, if it is connected with shooting' (HMSO, 1903: qu 8434). Here Mrs Bagot was inclined to disagree, however, because 'the old-fashioned sergeant with peninsular ideas does not go down with the boys' (HMSO, 1904: qu 4705). Baden-Powell would have found himself much in agreement with such a view, in that he disapproved of drill because it stunted individual initiative, whereas, as he explained to the National Defence Association, 'Scouting attracts the Hooligans':

> We say to a boy, 'Come and be good.' Well, the best class of boy – that is, the Hooligan – says, 'I'm blowed if I'm going to be good!' We say, 'Come and be like a red Indian, and dress like a Scout', and he will come along like anything. (Baden-Powell, 1910: 446)

There was, no doubt, a certain amount of humbug and wishful thinking in this kind of response, because on all the available evidence it seems more likely that the Boy Scout movement found its recruiting base among youth from lower middle-class and respectable working-class backgrounds (Springhall, 1972). In any case, what did the Hooligan want with a uniform? He already had his own.

But it was typical of the Edwardian frame of mind that it should entertain sometimes quite extravagant hopes for the rising generation, and no less typical that the Hooligan should so often find himself in the company of military men. 'As for Hooliganism', Lord May explained, 'high spirits that would be of use on board a man-of-war or on the march find vent in "bashing" the casual pedestrian or demolishing coffee stalls.'[30] 'We want sailors', said Commander Deverell of the Clyde Training Ship, and 'even although they were hooligans, I think that a lot of good might be brought out of them' (HMSO, 1903: qu 627). Indeed, it sometimes seemed within these worried discourses as if the rough-fighting Hooligans were just the kind of warrior class needed to stiffen the backbone of the imperial armies.

Physical training and exercise, then, could be understood both as a means to improve the physique of a wasted urban population and as a crude instrument to burn off the excess energy of rowdy youths: as in Colonel Fox's recommendation to have Hooligans trained to kick footballs instead of policemen. Charles Russell adopted a similar outlook in his *Manchester Boys* (1905: 68): 'Those boys who do play football are far less likely to display their energies in unpleasant ways, in the streets of the city on a Saturday night, after a two miles' walk to their ground and a hard ninety minutes' play.' And with an eye to cost-benefit analysis and the public purse, he thought 'it may then be well to consider ... if the almost complete dearth of public playing fields can in any way be met, without heavy cost to the rates'.

An equally important consideration, however, was that organised sports might open up an avenue towards moral instruction. 'In fact, it is the thin end of the wedge', Colonel Fox thought while interrogating another witness to the Physical Deterioration Committee, 'it gives them a more manly spirit and habits of cleanliness; and if so, might you not look upon it as a step towards religion?' (HMSO, 1904: qus 4697–8) 'Take football seriously,' urged the *Boys' Brigade Gazette*, 'it may prove to be one of the roads leading to the Kingdom of Heaven ... only it must be *football*, and not merely playing at playing at football.'[31] There was invariably a moral objective to hand, even though it was perhaps more usually smuggled in as a hidden agenda behind the physical jerks and fresh-air fun, as in the following advice from Bradford in 1905:

> The slum children have to be taught how to play ... Much of the hooliganism of our slums is due to the pure weariness of lads who have never acquired the art of recreation – whose games are shoving one another into the mud and 'chi-hiking' every decent-looking person they meet ... The end, while it should be moral improvement, of course, in every case, should be carefully concealed as to the ethical purpose; and the children should be allowed to assemble without a suspicion that they are going to be made good. Our aim at first should be to make them innocently happy. I have no doubt that, in the case of the lowest, there would be need of more vigorous control. But what I insist on is that the whole moral purpose of the undertaking should be implicit rather than open or defined. (Whiteing, 1905: 18)[32]

The public school ethos of 'playing the game' was an organising concept in the mental landscape of so much of this philanthropic endeavour. We all know the motto that the battle of Waterloo was won on the playing-fields of Eton, and late Victorian and Edwardian England knew it too: even though it was a historical howler of the most elementary kind. The early public schools had been not only the sites of gross public disorder, when it was occasionally found necessary to bring in the troops to suppress schoolboy rebellions, but also deeply hostile to both the spirit and the reality of organised games. Games had been regarded as a waste of time and effort, and it was only through a most uneven pattern of struggle and change in the second half of the nineteenth century that the public schools were converted to the belief in their moral and physical advantages (Mangan, 1981). But certainly, by the end of the century the dominant ethos was that the best character training for the growing youth was to be found in the discipline of 'all pulling together' in a common cause, playing in your place and 'playing the game'. And it was that generation of respectable England that had passed through the reformed public schools who not only produced a number of the founding members of the Football League teams, but who more generally set about spreading the gospel of sportsmanship to the un-sporting working classes. In the late 1890s, for example, Ernest Ensor's observations on 'The Football Madness' had introduced him to people in the manufacturing towns of the north of England 'whose warped sporting instincts are so difficult to understand, even when they are so familiar', that he feared that 'soon the only football played, as used to be the case, for the love of the game, will be seen among University men' (Ensor, 1898: 754, 757). And so it was that respectable England set about the business of teaching the young that there was more to football than just kicking a ball about, and that it was to be regarded as a training for life.

It was 'through sport that you can best get hold of a boy', said Baden-Powell (1919: 27). But here was the rub: organised sport, and football in particular, had already got hold of the boy to such an extent that it was thought that the game 'occupies too high a place in the minds of the working classes', especially when this led to mass absenteeism from work in order to watch Wednesday afternoon matches (HMSO: 1904, qus 3209, 4473). So that if the public image of the Hooligan suffered from a mass of contradictions and inconsistencies, this was no less true of his sporting saviour. 'Football', Baden-Powell had announced in *Scouting for Boys* (1908), 'is a grand game for developing a lad physically and morally', but it was also 'a vicious game when it draws crowds of lads away from playing themselves to be mere spectators to be mere onlookers at a few paid performers':

> Thousands of boys and young men, pale, narrow-chested, hunched up, miserable specimens, smoking endless cigarettes, numbers of them betting, all of them learning to be hysterical as they groan or cheer in panic unison with their neighbours – the worst sound of all being the hysterical scream of laughter that greets any little trip or fall of a player. One wonders whether this can be the same nation which had gained for itself the reputation of a stolid, pipe-sucking manhood, unmoved by panic or excitement, and reliable in the tightest of places. (Baden-Powell, 1908: 338)

We have met this mode of response to an imagined alteration in the English national character before, and here Baden-Powell characteristically saw the shadow of the Fall of Rome hanging over the football stadiums: 'They paid men to play their games for them, so that they could look on without the fag of playing, just as we are doing in football now ... Well, we have got to see that the same fate does not fall upon our Empire' (Baden-Powell, 1908: 314). The same brooding concern was to be found elsewhere. 'Race suicide is possible', exclaimed one commentator writing under the cloak of anonymity on 'Sport and Decadence', who thought that 'the mad craze for "athletics by other people"' was 'amongst the most disheartening symptoms of the hour'. Going to football matches was 'but an excuse for loafing or worse', while also reflecting the tendency 'towards effeminacy and self-indulgence'. The lure of professionalism, moreover, and what was taken for the dumb admiration of 'crack' sportsmen, was said to have discouraged active participation in sport because young men were 'frightened by the grotesque criterion of excellence set up for them'. Or, when they did still play, it was according to a distorted system of values:

> Young men have lost the brilliant dash ... the all-for-the-side-and-the-world-well-lost spirit ... Today we see 'old heads on young shoulders' with a vengeance; boys play like old stagers, with an eye to the list of averages, and a scientific caution which in the young is almost repulsive.[33]

This was obviously an ex-public-school man writing, and the same snobbish emphasis could be detected elsewhere, as when Ensor mocked the 'bewildering maze of figures' that appeared in the sporting press, analysing the number of goal kicks, corner kicks and so on in each game:

A passion for statistics seems to have spread all over England
... Compulsory education has established far and wide
an abstract love of decimals ... The ex-Board-School
boy cannot do without his favourite study. (Ensor, 1898:
759–60)

But while Ernest Ensor may have lost his way in the maze of sporting
statistics, in Alexander Paterson's working-class South London the boys
who gathered on the street corner (and who called themselves 'The
Heads') were masters of the art:

For the greater part of the year football holds the stage ...
A most amazing knowledge is betrayed of the personal
appearance, character, and moral weakness of each individual
player. Their native village, the year of their birth ... are all
matters of common-knowledge to the cigarette-smoking
enthusiasts. None of the Heads are without a cricket or
football guide in their inside pocket ... and thither they
will refer in argument for the day of Tunnicliffe's birth,
or the average weight of Aston Villa's forwards. (Paterson,
1911: 144–5)

The 'Heads' also applied this 'genius for hero-worship', it was said,
to 'boxers or wrestlers, runners and cyclists, weight-putters, and dog
fanciers', who were 'assumed to be national celebrities, their times,
weights and records stored away in minds that seem capable of
containing little else'. It was a matter of some puzzlement to respectable
England that working-class youths latched on to heroes such as these.
From the Midlands, for example, Arnold Freeman (1914) seemed quite
perplexed that the Birmingham boys whom he studied knew the names
of football stars and music hall acts, but did not recognise the name
of the chancellor of Birmingham University! As Charles Russell saw
it from Manchester, hero-worship was no bad thing in itself. The sad
fact of the matter, however, was that the heroes too often set a bad
example, the 'professional foul' being recognised as but one aspect of
the spirit of commercialism which handed out lessons in sharp practice
and deception:

Time after time, in his own way, he has noticed stale and bad
goods from the wholesale market, sold as fresh in the streets.
At football, in match after match, he has seen the unfair trick
applauded, as if it were something of distinct virtue. The

want of truthfulness is, perhaps, more noticeable than any other evil in the rising generation. (Russell, 1905: 49)

Ensor also condemned the spirit of professionalism in football, where winning was everything and 'rough play, so long as it escapes punishment from the referee, is one means to an end, and delights the crowd'. 'The worst feature of professional football is its sordid nature,' he said. It reminded him of slavery with its 'transfer money', which smacked of 'bribery and corruption' (Ensor, 1898: 755).

Russell, however, whose ear was a bit closer to the ground than many of his contemporaries', could not wholly condemn his beloved Manchester boys, because 'if all the juvenile spectators whom they judge so harshly wished to play, there would be absolutely no grounds whatever upon which they might do so'. In any case, football was already the rage among the youth – giving the lie to so many of these accusations against passive spectatorship. Indeed, we can judge the importance of these street traditions in the game's popular origins by the use of the term 'wall pass' in football even today, which certainly did not emerge from playing football on open fields. 'In courts and alleys', Charles Russell observed, 'on vacant plots of land, on brickfields, indeed where any open space at all may be found, attempts are made to play the game, even although the football may be but a bundle of tightly rolled up string-bound papers.' 'Every little croft [which in Manchester means a patch of cinder waste] and every available field is seized upon by some team or another,' he continued, and 'in back streets and quiet corners desperate games are played with "tanner pills" or tightly rolled balls of paper' (Russell, 1905: 67–8; 1913: 100).

In Birmingham, too, football was said to be 'the greatest single interest in the life of the ordinary working boy'. 'Some do not care for it,' Arnold Freeman reported, 'a few play themselves, but most of them spend Saturday afternoon in watching "Birmingham" or "the Villa". No subject arouses their enthusiasm like football. Nothing is so hotly contested or so accurately known' (Freeman, 1914: 151–2). Freeman offered vivid glimpses into the lives and preoccupations of Birmingham youth by means of interviews and personal diaries which he encouraged them to keep of their daily pursuits at home and work. The diaries commonly showed every spare minute being used for a kick-around. Here, for example, is a real fanatic who worked in a factory making wire handles for lard pans. On Saturday morning it was work as usual, starting at eight o'clock. Then:

> I knocked off at 12.30. I drew my money and then went home [and] had dinner ... At about 1.30 went with some friends and played Football for about two hours and then went to the match Birmingham v. Preston North End ... At First it was an exciting game first the ball would be up one end of the field and then up the other end.

> Bir. got a runaway through A.R. Smith who centred to Hall who missed. Play went into mid field for about 15 minutes where Preston's inside right secured the ball and run down the field passed to the centre who dribbled through the goal. Birm. then began to Press but did no good and in the second Half missed several open goals. Preston won by 1.0.

In the evening he had wandered about Jamaica Row and the Rag Market with his friends 'watching things being sold'. On Sunday it was breakfast in bed for the young working man, followed by football and more football:

> SUNDAY: – Had bread and bacon and two cups of tea for breakfast. Got up at 9.50 got ready and went out. I went for my friends and we went on some waste ground and played football until about 2 o'clock went home.
>
> In the afternoon we gathered together and saw some lads who live the other end of our street and asked them if they would play us at football this was agreed and we went on the ground and kicked off we were the winners of that match by a list of 8 goals to 5. After that we went to the coffee house and stayed there for a while and then went home to tea at 6.15. (Freeman, 1914: 115)

Charles Russell filled in other details of the popular organisation of sport, some of which he thought were encouraging while others were not. He found it somewhat amusing that 'nowadays, football teams of quite small boys frequently consider it necessary to "train" as they call it, if they are to win their matches'. 'A certain amount of weight-lifting' was practised, together with 'the use of chest-expanders, and of running exercises', although he regretted that this was not accompanied by 'any decrease in the number of cigarettes smoked, [or] any curtailment of the weekly excitement of the music hall'. Both Russell and Paterson (1911: 160–1) noted the increasing popularity of long-distance running among city youths. Russell described 'this hare and hounds by gaslight' amid

Manchester's notorious rain and fog as a strange performance, 'mainly through the busy streets ... passers-by regard them as suffering from some mild form of lunacy, for disporting themselves in such a fashion'. But he was happy that these turn-of-the-century joggers were 'nearly always those who smoked little, or not at all'. By contrast:

> In a football game of rough lads, sixteen to eighteen years of age, I have seen perhaps a dozen of them light a cigarette at half-time, or a full-back even puffing his smoke during the progress of the game. (Russell, 1905: 56, 58–60)

And there were other aspects of the popular game that he and his generation did not like:

> The language and conduct of players leave a very great deal to be desired. Tempers are easily roused, and a boy often neglects an opportunity of really playing the game well in order that he may, as he terms it, 'get his own back' for an injury inflicted on himself ... There is also a lamentable lack of any fine sense of sportsmanship ... It is not thought dishonourable to win a game by an entirely false claim for a goal ... In the case of competitions in which there is an age limit, lads who are older than the limit will unblushingly sign statements to the effect that they are one or two years younger, and consider that they have done something rather to be complimented upon. (Russell, 1905: 64)

Even worse, although Russell admired the 'business-like methods' employed by boys as young as ten or twelve years of age when they formed themselves into a league team, sometimes they were a little too businesslike. The boys would organise a subscription in their neighbourhood to provide themselves with football shirts, a ball, ground rent and possibly even goalposts. And while there was nothing wrong with this, the goalposts, 'Sad to state, are frequently obtained in the dark hours of the August and September nights, from grounds where they have been carefully erected for older and more substantial teams'. Russell had also heard of pavilions and changing rooms spirited away by 'midnight marauders' (Russell, 1905: 61–2; Russell and Russell, 1932: 92).

Amid this tangled web of factual evidence as to what football and other games amounted to in the lives of young working-class men and boys, some quite spectacular fantasies were also entertained as to how organised sport might help to regulate this wayward energy. Not only in terms of physical fitness and the often vaguely defined sense of a moral training, but also more specifically in order to combat class antagonisms. Because, however fanciful it might seem to us now, football was sometimes seen as a means of defeating the spread of socialist ideas and the 'selfishness' of radical trade unionism.

Arthur Hope's essay on 'The Breaking Down of Caste' in Whitehouse's *Problems of Boy Life* had offered one indication of this sentiment, recommending joint activities such as camping and sport between boys of different social backgrounds:

> Class distinctions are difficult to maintain amid the healthy rivalries of the open air, and 'footer shorts' and naked bodies make for equality ... It is not likely that boys who have regularly met in such an atmosphere will retain many shreds of class antipathy, whatever their sphere of after-life may be. (Hope, 1912: 302)

For Baden-Powell, however, who in his writings developed this political theme more deliberately than anyone else, the promise of football was not this kind of scaled-down miniature of class war. It was not meeting your opponents on the field of play that counted for him, but learning through organised games and 'fair play' a discipline of rules by which the larger contest should be conducted. In *Scouting for Boys* he had sketched the broad outlines of his approach, suggesting that football was 'a grand game for developing lads physically and morally, for he learns to play with good temper and unselfishness, to play in his place and "play the game", and these are the best training for any game of life' (Baden-Powell, 1908: 338). Later, summing up a few years of experience in *Aids to Scoutmastership* (1919: 27), he elaborated his political understanding of the functions of organised games and 'fair play':

> It is through sport that you can best get hold of a boy. Many of our working class lads have never known what it was to play any regular games with strict rules ... discipline, sense of fair play, or keenness for winning simply for the honour of the thing without thought of prizes or rewards. All these come very quickly, with a little organised play.

This might easily be mistaken for no more than a general character training, although as he scattered broadsides against 'false doctrine, heresy and schism', which were 'definitely preached to workers by means of leaflets and addresses', and 'wrong ideas and fallacies' that were 'actually and deliberately taught to children in Socialist schools', and which led to 'industrial ignorance' and 'the ruinous unrest now prevalent', Baden-Powell appreciably firmed up the political agenda of organised games:

> An ulterior point is that they can breed morale, *esprit de corps*, and fair play. It should be 'the thing' for the boys never to bear envy or to mention unfairness of judging or the opponents' tactics when their team is defeated, and whatever disappointment they may feel they should show only cordial praise for the other side. This means true self-discipline and unselfishness, and it promotes that good feeling all round which is so much needed for breaking down class prejudice in our people. (Baden-Powell, 1919: 27, 86–7)

The problem as he saw it was that unemployment and dead-end jobs were producing 'numbers of poor and disheartened men – the easy prey for political demagogues, without any sense of fair play or even of their own best interests'. He thought that the discipline of 'fair play' should also be applied in the industrial sphere, where he urged employers to harness a boy's sense of fairness early in his working life by insisting on '*strict adherence to instructions*, with the feeling that such obedience is "playing the game" for the good of the business'. The scoutmaster's aims, and the satisfaction from his work, were thus: 'Having worked to prevent the recurrence of those evils which, if allowed to run, would soon be rotting the nation … [the aim] is to teach the boys to "play the game", each in his place … Each has his allotted sphere of work' (Baden-Powell, 1919: 23, 38–40, 82).[34]

Within these deliberations of the sporting enthusiasms of young people there are repeated hints of disorder of one kind or another among this unruly urban population which had come all-too-terribly alive in the person of the 'Hooligan'. For some faint hearts, such as the Reverend Peter Green in his description of boys' club work in *How to Deal with Lads* (1911), football itself was such a disorderly influence that it was more trouble than it was worth. Others wished that the boys would give themselves up to the more genteel influence of cricket, although of course this was something they would never do, any more than they would give up their allegiance to the local football team – Villa, Arsenal, City. Indeed, contrary to those who bewailed the loafing spectatorship of the working class, football had already gained such a popular momentum that it was clearly going to prove difficult to domesticate the game. Nevertheless, more robust characters, such as Baden-Powell, saw that youthful enthusiasm for sport provided a missed opportunity for placing some badly needed regulating force upon the rising generation. And crucially, in a bitterly divided society, football had one important advantage over cricket, in that it was incontestably a team game. So, in the first edition of *Scouting for Boys*:

> A house divided against itself cannot stand … For this you must begin, as boys, not to think of other classes of boys to be your enemies … You have to stand shoulder to shoulder … You must sink your differences … We are like bricks in a wall, we each have our place … Self-sacrifice pays all round. (Baden-Powell, 1908: 319–20)

From our own historical vantage point it is not clear what on earth all this had to do with 'Hooliganism'. But the 'Hooligan', of course, was both real and imagined. And according to the fevered imagination of late Victorian and Edwardian England, it seemed clear enough at the time. 'Victorian values', as we have seen, reflected a very different way of life – but not a way of life that in any way resembles the dreamy nostalgia that now attaches to Victorian society and 'Victorian values'. Rather, it was a society that often felt as if it were about to burst apart at the seams.

Conclusion? 'Everything changes, nothing moves'[35]

Times change. And along with them, the relations between police and public, which have certainly been much worse at other times, and might possibly never have been better; the endlessly mutating contours and structure of the typical household, in which the only constant is that the family always seems to be in decline; and the shifting nature of education, work and leisure. One indisputable and decisive break with the past is the twilight of the street, which as Le Corbusier foresaw, is now the unrivalled realm of the motor car: 'A city made for speed is made for success' (1929: 179). No more carefree street games, then, and with the demise of street life the street is experienced as having fallen into the possession of an army of hoodies, aggressive beggars, muggers, chavs and binge drinkers. The Respect Agenda, with its assorted baggage of ASBOs, parenting orders and neighbours from hell, is simply a new chapter of this gloomy, ceaseless narrative of decline. And within this narrative the younger generation, their morals perceived to be perpetually spiralling downward and always younger in the onset of their depravity, figures both as a lament for things lost and a harbinger of worse to come. The question poses itself: when will we break from the shackles of the past and learn to face the future? Although the problem is that this cultural pessimism cannot be resolved by political action, because it is political action itself that brought it into being.

Notes

[1] Respect Task Force, www.respect.gov.uk.

[2] *The Times*, 6 February 1899, 16 August 1899 and 17 August 1898.

[3] Metropolitan Police Commissioner Papers, 'Local Supervision: Playing Games in the Street – Magisterial Comments, 1906–1911', MEPO 2/992 (The National Archives).

[4] Metropolitan Police Commissioner Papers, 'Prisoners – disorderly conduct: Act under which a charge may be made, 1900–1907', MEPO 2/1010 (The National Archives).

[5] Metropolitan Police Commissioner Papers, 'Strength: Suppression of Rowdyism, 1904', MEPO 2/727 (The National Archives).

[6] *Illustrated Police News*, 16 July 1898.

[7] 'Railway Outrages: Who is the Wrecker?', *News of the World*, 11 September 1898; *Manchester Evening News*, 10 and 13 September 1898; *South London Chronicle*, 13 August 1898; Metropolitan Police Commissioner Papers, 'Local Supervision: Stone Throwing from Bridges, 1895–1900', MEPO 2/362 and 'Local Supervision: Walthamstow, 1898–1906', MEPO 2/467 (The National Archives).

[8] Metropolitan Police Commissioner Papers, 'Lighted Coloured Matches etc. thrown from Vehicles onto Roads: Requests by Public to Stop this Practice, 1896–1898', MEPO 2/7161 (The National Archives); *Bicycling News*, 10 August 1898; *News of the World*, 9 October 1898.

[9] Metropolitan Police Commissioner Papers, 'Traffic: Dangerous Practices. Children running behind, riding on, and being drawn by vehicles, 1898–1914', MEPO 2/1257 (The National Archives).

[10] *Westminster Budget*, 12 August 1898.

[11] *Daily Graphic*, 6 August 1898.

[12] For detailed accounts of different aspects of the 'Scuttler' phenomenon, see Davies (1998; 1999; 2008).

[13] Home Office Papers, 'Scuttling', HO45/9723/A51956 (The National Archives).

[14] *The Sun*, 6 August 1898 and 7 August 1898.

[15] *The Echo*, 7 February 1898.

[16] *Daily Graphic*, 15 February 1898.

[17] Metropolitan Police Commissioner Papers, 'Pistols Act, 1903: definition of a "weapon", 1907–1909', MEPO 2/1044 and 'Firearms: issue of gun licences to persons under age, 1907–1909', MEPO 2/1162 (The National Archives); Pearson, 1983: 101–6.

[18] See also 'The Police Court and its Problems: An Interview with Mr. Thomas Holmes', *The Young Man*, vol 15, 1901: 327; *South London Chronicle*, 6 August 1898.

[19] *Daily Graphic*, 25 August 1898.

[20] Besant, 1901, p 177.

[21] *Reynolds's Newspaper*, 2 October 1898; *Illustrated Police News*, 1 October 1898; Pearson, 1983: 85–9.

[22] *Daily Mail*, 15 August 1898; *News of the World*, 14 August 1898; *Evening News*, 13 August 1898; *The Sun*, 13 August 1898.

[23] Metropolitan Police Commissioner Papers, 'Prisoners – disorderly conduct: Act under which a charge may be made, 1900–1907', MEPO 2/1010 (The National Archives).

[24] *Report of the Commissioner of the Police of the Metropolis 1899*, Cd 399 (HMSO, 1900); *Royal Commission on the Duties of the Metropolitan Police*, vol 2, Minutes of Evidence, Cd 4260 (HMSO, 1908), qu 79; Metropolitan Police Commissioner Papers, 'Prisoners: assaults on police, 1900–1905', MEPO 2/531 and 'Traffic: coffee stalls in streets, 1901–1909', MEPO 2/570 (The National Archives).

[25] *Pall Mall Gazette*, 19 February 1901.

[26] *South London Chronicle*, 27 August 1898.

[27] *The Spectator*, 27 August 1898.

[28] *Catholic Pulpit*, vol 5, no 55, July 1898.

[29] *Daily Graphic*, 15 February 1898.

[30] *Pall Mall Gazette*, 12 February 1901.

[31] *Boys' Brigade Gazette*, quoted in Baden-Powell, 1919: 27.

[32] I am grateful to Rowena Allcock for bringing my attention to this source.

[33] Anon, 'Sport and Decadence', *The Quarterly Review*, vol 212, no 421, October 1909, pp 487, 495, 501–2 and passim.

[34] Compare the unfriendly exchange of letters in *Baden-Powell Exposed!* (Young Communist League, 1927).

[35] Horkheimer, 1947: 159.

References

Baden-Powell, R.S.S. (1908) *Scouting for Boys*, London: Horace Cox.

Baden-Powell, R.S.S. (1910) 'Boy Scouts', *National Defence*, 4 (August), 434–47.

Baden-Powell, R.S.S. (1919) *Aids to Scoutmastership*, London: Herbert Jenkins.

Bean, J.P. (1981) *The Sheffield Gang Wars*, Sheffield: D. & D. publications.

Besant, W. (1901) *East London*, London: Chatto & Windus.

Booth, C. (1903) *Life and Labour of the People of London: Notes on Social Influences*, London: Macmillan.

Bray, R.A. (1904) 'The Boy and the Family', in E.J. Urwick (ed) *Studies of Boy Life in Our Cities*, London: J.M. Dent, pp 1–101.

Bray, R.A. (1907) *The Town Child*, London: Fisher Unwin.

Cohen, P. (1979) 'Policing the working class city', in B. Fine et al (eds) *Capitalism and the Rule of Law*, London: Hutchinson, pp 118–36.

Davies, A. (1998) 'Youth gangs, masculinity and violence in late Victorian Manchester and Salford', *Journal of Social History*, 32(2), 349–69.

Davies, A. (1999) '"These viragoes are no less cruel than the lads": young women, gangs and violence in late Victorian Manchester and Salford', *British Journal of Criminology*, 39(1), 72–89.

Davies, A. (2008) *The Gangs of Manchester: The Story of the Scuttlers, Britain's First Youth Cult*, Preston: Milo Books.

Devine, A. (1890) *Scuttlers and Scuttling*, Guardian Printing Works.

Douglas, N. (1931) *London Street Games*, 2nd edition, Dolphin Books.

Ensor, E. (1898) 'The football madness', *Contemporary Review*, 74 (November), pp 750–60.

Freeman, A. (1914) *Boy Life and Labour: The Manufacture of Inefficiency*, London: King.

Gillis, J.R. (1975) 'The evolution of juvenile delinquency in England, 1890–1914', *Past and Present*, 67, 96–126.

Green, P. (1911) *How to Deal with Lads: A Handbook of Church Work*, London: Edward Arnold.

Hansard (1922) House of Commons, 5th Series, 153, cl 1500.

HMSO (1903) *Report of the Royal Commission on Physical Training (Scotland)*, Vol 2, Minutes of Evidence, Cd 1508, qu 6059.

HMSO (1904) *Report of the Inter-Departmental Committee on Physical Deterioration*, Vol 2, Minutes of Evidence, Cd 2210, qus 4546, 4551.

Hope, A. (1912) 'The breaking down of caste', in J.H. Whitehouse (ed) *Problems of Boy Life*, London: King, pp 287–306.

Horkheimer, M. (1947) *Eclipse of Reason*, Oxford: Oxford University Press.

Humphries, S. (1981) *Hooligans or Rebels? An Oral History of Working Class Childhood and Youth, 1889–1939*, Oxford: Blackwell.

Le Corbusier, M. (1929) *The City of Tomorrow and its Planning*, London: The Architectural Press.

London, J. (1963) *The People of the Abyss*, London: Arco (1963 edition).

McLachlan, N.D. (no date) 'Larrikinism', unpublished MA thesis, Melbourne: Melbourne University.

Mangan, J.A. (1981) *Athleticism in the Victorian and Edwardian Public School*, Cambridge: Cambridge University Press.

Masterman, C.F.G. (1902) *The Heart of the Empire*, London: Fisher Unwin.

Neuberger, J. (1993) *Hooliganism: Crime, Culture and Power in St Petersburg, 1900–1914*, Berkeley, CA: University of California Press.

Opie, I. and Opie, P. (1969) *Children's Games in Street and Playground*, Oxford: Oxford University Press.

Opie I. and Opie, P. (1977) *The Lore and Language of Schoolchildren*, St Albans: Paladin.

Opie, I. and Opie, P. (1985) *The Singing Game*, Oxford: Oxford University Press.

Paterson, A. (1911) *Across the Bridges*, London: Edward Arnold.

Pearson, G. (1983) *Hooligan: A History of Respectable Fears*, Basingstoke: Macmillan.

Russell, C.E.B. (1905) *Manchester Boys*, Manchester: Manchester University Press.

Russell, C.E.B. (1913) *Social Problems of the North*, London: Mowbray.

Russell, C.E.B. and Russell, L.M. (1932) *Lads' Clubs: Their History, Organisation and Management*, London: Black (1932 edition).

Samuel, R. (1981) *East End Underworld*, London: Routledge & Kegan Paul.

Springhall, J.O. (1972) 'The Boy Scouts, class and militarism in relation to British youth movements 1908–1930', *International Review of Social History*, 16(2), 125–58.

Urwick, E.J. (ed) (1904) *Studies of Boy Life in Our Cities*, London: J.M. Dent.

Webb, B. and Webb, S. (1909) *Minority Report of the Poor Law Commission*, Kelley (1973 edition).

Weissman, N.B. (1978) 'Rural crime in Tsarist Russia: the question of hooliganism, 1905–1914', *Slavic Review*, 37(2), 228–40.

White, J. (1979) 'Campbell bunk: a lumpen community in London between the wars', *History Workshop*, 8, 1–49.

White, J. (1980) *Rothschild Buildings: Life in an East End Tenement Block, 1887–1920*, London: Routledge & Kegan Paul.

White, J. (1983) 'Police and people in London in the 1930s', *Oral History*, 11(2), 34–41.

Whiteing, R. (1905) 'Clubs for kiddies: teaching slum children how to play', *The Bradford and District Congregational Magazine*, January, p 18.

Part Two
Respectful young people and children

Giving respect: the 'new' responsibilities of youth in the transition towards citizenship

Alan France and Jo Meredith

Introduction

There is growing political anxiety that 'respect' among the young is a major social problem of our time (Respect Task Force, 2006a). Youthful immorality and poor behaviour have been seen as major components of the 'youth question' for a very long time (as evidenced by Geoffrey Pearson in Chapter Two), yet there is a perception that it has increased in recent years (France, 2007). For example, in a recent consultation by the Joseph Rowntree Foundation young people's negative behaviour was defined by many adults as a 'social evil' in the twenty-first century (Watts, 2008).[1] Similarly, there has been growing anxiety about a 'crisis' in childhood. Concerns are being expressed about how young people's morality and respect for the world they live in is being undermined by the type and pace of social change (Children's Society, 2007). Such a perspective is not unique to public attitudes or politicians, with the media industry and political commentators regularly proposing that the immorality and lack of respect among the young is a worrying signifier of the decline of modern civilised society. Such concerns lead to continual calls for government to intervene and find ways to reinstate core values of the past (Critcher, 2003).

As previously explored, in 2006 the then Prime Minister, Tony Blair, set about increasing and reaffirming 'respect', especially among the young, as a core British value (Respect Task Force, 2006a). In the discussion that follows we explore how this approach has infiltrated government thinking and shaped policy towards the young. We argue that such an approach is narrow and unproductive in helping to create a 'culture of respect' among young people. If respect is to be a useful way of mobilising the young, then it has to have a broader definition and give recognition to notions of 'mutual' respect and 'self-respect'. These, as we shall show, have been missing from recent youth policy debates. If these are not addressed, the concept of respect as a workable solution to the 'youth problem' will not bring about any substantial changes and will only continue to create cynicism and a 'lack of respect' from the young towards those who claim to be helping them become future responsible citizens.

The politics of respect

As a way of tackling anxieties about the 'lack of respect', Tony Blair and New Labour launched the *Respect Action Plan* in January 2006. The action plan built on a number of previous initiatives which New Labour had introduced to tackle anti-social behaviour.[2] However, it differed in that it aimed to address the deeper, underlying issues which are often seen as the cause of anti-social behaviour (Respect Task Force, 2006b). Blair suggested that the major cause of anti-social behaviour was the decline of respect in modern society and therefore he wanted to create a momentum towards a moral restructuring. By drawing upon the concept of respect in political and policy terms he aimed to remoralise the immoral minority. He argued that a 'small number' of families and young people (usually disadvantaged) were the cause of the majority of society's ills, usually identifiable through their 'bad behaviour' and their lack of respect for others and the society they live in (Respect Task Force, 2006a). Based on these assertions, government set about constructing and encouraging a new framework of core values that aimed to provide clear guidance to professionals, parents and young people about what 'respect' should mean (Respect Task Force, 2006a). As part of this, the Respect Task Force was established and Louise Casey was appointed as Respect Commissioner with direct responsibility for delivery of the action plan. While it was denied that the *Respect Action Plan* was aimed specifically at the young, or that it related only to anti-social behaviour, in reality the main thrust was specifically the targeting of policies to prevent young people from engaging in behaviour such as 'loud music, graffiti, offensive and threatening remarks, dumping rubbish, harassment and intimidation' (Respect Task Force, 2006a: 5). Such behaviours are very similar to those defined by the Home Office as 'anti-social' (Harradine et al, 2004). This connection to anti-social behaviour was further emphasised by the Respect Task Force being initially located in the Home Office, and the appointment of a previous director of the Anti-Social Behaviour Unit as the Respect Commissioner. What is striking about the notion of 'respect' in the

Respect Action Plan is a strong focus on the prevention and cessation of anti-social behaviour, particularly aimed at young people and their families. Less attention is paid to the notion of fostering a 'culture of respect' at all levels of the community.

When Gordon Brown took over the role of prime minister in 2007, the issue of respect in policy changed and seemed to have less significance. The task of delivering the *Respect Action Plan* was relocated into the Department of Children, Schools and Families and became the responsibility of the Youth Taskforce.[3] 'Respect' was integrated into a new *Youth Taskforce Action Plan* (Youth Taskforce, 2008), which was seen as a more holistic approach. The most striking change was that, despite the new action plan having the subtitle of *Give Respect, Get Respect – Youth Matters*, there was very little mention of respect within it. There remained discussion about the work done by the Respect Task Force, but no firm commitment to taking the notion of 'respect' forward in policy. While the focus on respect became reworked and filtered, with a stronger emphasis on more positive activities, the issue of tackling the difficult and anti-social behaviour of some of the most 'problematic' families did remain as core, especially within the range of new family policies. For example, 20 Intensive Intervention Projects, and 52 Challenge and Support Projects, aimed at stopping poor behaviour from escalating, were established (Youth Taskforce, 2008: 12). There also remained a strong focus on intervening early in the lives of families with children 'at risk' of anti-social behaviour (Jamieson, 2005; Social Exclusion Taskforce, 2007). However, as Brown's premiership has continued, the focus has shifted to youth crime reduction, as evidenced by the publication of the *Youth Crime Action Plan* in July 2008 (HM Government, 2008). Other strategies published in 2008, such as the *Tackling Violence Action Plan*, the *Youth Alcohol Action Plan* and the 10-year drug strategy *Drugs: Protecting Families and Communities*, all point towards a change in the priorities of the Brown government (Home Office, 2008a; DCSF, 2008; Home Office, 2008b). Yet these new policy initiatives still target the anti-social behaviour of 'problem' families and have been clearly influenced by the aims of the *Respect Action Plan*.

Within the *Respect Action Plan* the definition of 'respect' was given little attention, as there was an assumption that everyone understands what respect means. Thus, respect was defined as 'an expression of something that people intuitively understand … a common set of values, expressed through behaviour that is considerate of others' (Respect Task Force, 2006a: 5). There is an assumption that across society these values are clearly recognised. It is suggested they should include 'respect for others, their property and their privacy, civility, good manners and a recognition that everyone has responsibilities as well as rights' (Respect Task Force, 2006a: 5). Thus, when the government speaks of respect, it is usually a synonym for 'good behaviour', 'good manners' and 'responsibility'. In this context respect is seen as a core value of citizenship. Yet this definition of respect is narrow and simplistic, making calls to 'common sense' understandings of values. Respect is, in reality, a very complex concept, and can be:

> a mode of action, a form of treatment, a motive, an attitude, a feeling, a mode of valuing, a way of attending to things, a moral principle, a duty, an entitlement, a moral virtue or an epistemic virtue. (Dillon, 2003: 3)

Not only is its meaning complex, but it can also vary according to social context. As Dillon argues, it can be subjective, depending on the sociocultural conditions:

> What it is ... to have a status worthy of respect, what treatment and conduct are appropriate to a person or one with such status, what forms of life and character have merit – all of these are given different content in different sociocultural contexts. (Dillon, 2003: 31)

This suggests that respect is open to interpretation and can be defined in a number of ways. It is not unusual for respect to be understood as simply the notion of treating someone as you wish to be treated yourself. For example, '[it] implies appreciating their intrinsic value or significance and feeling that one ought to treat them as one would expect to be treated by them' (McCarthy and Walker, 2006: 26). However, this can also be dependent on what an individual (or group) perceives as respectful behaviour. For example, although the *Respect Action Plan* defines playing loud music as an example of disrespectful behaviour, if this were classical music at a garden party in the suburbs would it be seen as 'disrespectful'? Therefore respect remains a value judgement where the power to define what is 'respectful' and 'disrespectful' has an influence. The most pertinent example of how respect can take different and alternative meanings is how members of youth gangs show or gain respect through violent or threatening behaviour (Monti, 1995; Gaskell, 2008; see also Squires, Chapter Ten in this volume). Such a definition of respect is peculiar to a certain culture and the context is key. For example, for some disadvantaged young people, respect has to be earned by alternative means:

to be someone in the world, you have to have money ... a nice car, a nice yard. If you're from an estate where you feel you're never going to make that from a job then you do what you can to make yourself top dog. (Dwyer Hogg, 2008)

The importance of mutual and self-respect

In political philosophy it is recognised that respect is central to the very nature of being human. As explored in the introduction to this volume, Immanuel Kant argued we are all owed respect because we are free rational beings and that this status and worth has to be recognised (Dillon, 2003). It is a part of our human dignity and a necessity for living together as a collective. John Rawls saw respect as a 'primary' and 'social' good, suggesting that it is critical to a just and fair society (Rawls, 1971). Yet there is little recognition of such ideas in youth policy. Respect, in government policy, is seen as a static concept, whereas it can be a negotiated, two-way process where a relationship exists between being respected and showing respect (Dillon, 2003). Yet when such ideas are discussed in political debates about the young they tend to be somewhat circular, in that for someone to be shown respect by others, they must first earn it; but if they are shown no respect until they earn it, it is difficult to understand how they will learn to have respect for others. Of course the argument over mutual respect as 'earned' also creates dangers in that, by concentrating on 'what comes first', we fail to address young people's own concerns over how they may feel disrespected.

As part of the process of understanding respect, it is also important to recognise the related issue of having 'self-respect'. Self-respect can be defined as 'an attitude towards ourselves which is made public in the way in which we present ourselves' (Middleton, 2006: 75). 'The self-respecting person acknowledges their own value, their own worth and their own humanity' (Middleton, 2006: 67). In this context self-respect is gained through living our lives according to standards which we set for ourselves. We can have respect for ourselves through our achievements, no matter how unexceptional they may appear to others (Middleton, 2006). While we can gain self-respect in this way, we also look to others to affirm it, and 'repeated instances of lack of affirmation as a person of worth can undermine our sense of self' (Middleton, 2006: 69). Self-respect therefore can be gained through a sense of pride in our own achievements, but also through others recognising our contribution. It is also about status, which is related to our sense of autonomy; our ability to act for ourselves and make our own choices. Status self-respect also comes from a feeling of belonging, particularly to a certain group or community (Middleton, 2006). Being a member of a group by merit can instil a sense of self-respect. It is the community or group itself which is afforded respect by others, not necessarily the individual. In this context it is important that young people as a group are able to gain self-respect, as 'it seems evident that a person who lacks respect for themselves is likely to lack the ability to respect others' (Middleton, 2006: 63).

Rawls argues that the maintenance and expansion of self-respect should be a fundamental aspect of government policy (Rawls, 1971). A person's sense of worth needs to underpin the basis of citizenship and therefore social institutions should be built around the promotion of self-respect through access to civil liberties, political rights and resources that individuals require to be active citizens. Others have suggested that a decent society is one where individuals' self-respect is not damaged by social institutions (Margalit, 1996). For example, institutions should not humiliate or ignore people and should give recognition to those who are vulnerable. Issues of injustice and experiences of oppression by social institutions are seen as fundamental problems in trying to promote and support individual self-respect. If we therefore want to build a 'culture of respect' among the young that helps produce a better society for us all, then young people from all walks of life have to feel valued and respected in this process, with their experiences needing to live up to political rhetoric (Gaskell, 2008). As identified, this cannot be a one-way process; respect has to be given as well as received and it has to be enshrined in a policy framework that promotes self- and mutual respect. This is clearly not how the majority of young people experience policy today.

Building respect through status and recognition

Getting status and recognition for achievements is something young people should experience in the education system, yet even when pupils receive high grades and are seen to achieve, their success is not always recognised by the society around them. Despite the pass rate of A levels improving, there is a yearly debate within the media over whether standards have declined (McGaw et al, 2004). Various media outlets suggest that exams have been 'dumbed down' (Frean, 2007) or that these qualifications are 'irrelevant' for success in later life (Paton, 2007). There is also discussion over the merits of different subjects, with social sciences and media studies often derided as 'soft' subject choices behind traditional subjects such as maths and sciences (QCA, 2008: 10). Research suggesting that standards have dropped in some subjects has added weight to such debates (Kounine et al, 2008). These discussions show little respect or recognition for young people's achievements. Many young people and teachers find such deliberations in the media unhelpful and upsetting (Ipsos MORI, 2007). In this context, even successful young people can feel that the society around them does not respect their achievements.

However, it is in the area of paid work where young people can gain most self- and mutual respect, yet over the last 20 years the opportunities for certain groups to achieve this have become more limited. In government discussions over respect, the role of paid work has been marginalised. For example, while achieving full employment is central to government policy, the *Respect Action Plan* had nothing to say about the relationship between paid work and respect. This is a major gap in the respect policy agenda, as young people having good-quality paid work is important to how they earn respect and gain self-respect (MacDonald and Marsh, 2005). Sennett (2003) argues that in society it is seen as 'shameful' for an adult to be dependent on others, such as family or the welfare state: 'The hard human edge which eschews neediness and emphasizes self-sufficiency brings respect in the eyes of others and breeds self-respect' (Sennett, 2003: 101).

To avoid this feeling of 'shame' in the modern capitalist society, paid work remains an essential ingredient (Sennett, 2003). Making the transition to adult citizenship requires young people to move from 'dependency' to 'independency' and historically this has relied upon paid work as a major source of status and income (Jones and Wallace, 1992). Paid work is a central part not only of a young person's identity but also of how others see them, and having meaningful and paid employment remains essential to how a young person becomes defined and respected as an adult (France, 2007). As such, it is an important part of gaining both respect from others and self-respect. Historically, school-to-work transitions were seen as unproblematic (Carter, 1966), yet it is now well recognised that these transitions have radically changed (Furlong and Cartmel, 2007), with education and training being the main source of the post-school experience. Mizen suggests that since the 1980s these changes have seen the growth of what he calls the 'training state' (Mizen, 1995) and, as a result, the pathways into work have become more fragmented and complex.

Because of these changes, New Labour has prioritised tackling youth unemployment. This has been targeted at 'making work pay' and ensuring the benefit regime for those who are out of work does not create a disincentive to seek and remain in work (McKnight, 2005). The New Deal for Young People (NDYP), introduced in 1998, has been at the heart of this policy, with the express aim of reducing the number of 18- to 24-year-olds experiencing long-term unemployment (Mason, 1998). NDYP is mandatory for 18- to 24-year-olds who have been claiming Jobseeker's Allowance continuously for six months. The young unemployed have, at this stage, no choice but to become involved in New Deal. If they do not find employment after the four-month 'gateway stage', they automatically enter the 'option stage', where they must take up one of four options available to them. Choice is then limited to what might be available. A core aim of NDYP is to make sure that there is 'no fifth option of staying at home on benefit' (Field and White, 2007: 7). If an individual refuses to cooperate with New Deal, they face the prospect of losing their benefits (Finn, 2003).

Mizen (2004) suggests that New Labour, through New Deal, is creating a form of 'progressive competitiveness'. This focuses on vocationalism and skills development, over knowledge learning and purpose (Mizen, 2004). As a result, many of the jobs produced on the New Deal programme are low skilled, low paid and not career jobs with prospects (Mizen, 2004). Evidence suggests that many young people on NDYP do not feel they are treated well and can feel pressured into taking short-term agency work or 'crap jobs' rather than being able to wait for a 'reasonable job' (Finn, 2003: 174). Some young people also experience New Deal as a form of 'warehousing', where they encounter the programme as a form of 'churning', moving from the programme to unemployment and back again (Kemp, 2006). Issues also exist over how effective it can be in local areas (Turok, 1999) where local labour markets have collapsed, meaning that young people experience programmes such as New Deal as nothing but a way of getting them into poor or 'shit jobs' (MacDonald and Marsh, 2005).

This is not just an issue for the New Deal programme; with the collapse of the youth labour market many young people, especially in deprived communities, have a negative experience of finding work. For example, in MacDonald and Marsh's (2005) study of growing up in poor neighbourhoods, good-quality and well-paid work was very difficult to find. Young people could be very active but were under constant pressure from the state to become employed. When they were not successful they were often branded as failures or members of the 'undeserving' underclass and labelled as 'dole wallah' 'lazy scroungers' and 'bone idle'. Little recognition was given to the structural constraints they were living under or their positive attempts to 'get on' (MacDonald and Marsh, 2005). For many disadvantaged young people the only option available to them is to take work in the service or retail sectors, and this can hold little status. Service sector jobs are often perceived negatively, with unrealistic wages, long and unsociable hours, poor conditions and little opportunity for career development (Lindsay and McQuaid, 2004). Thus, young people working in these sectors tend not to feel respected or valued because of their poor conditions of employment. Such work does not promote self-respect or feelings of self-worth.

However, there is also a deeper issue of young people's paid work not being valued by society. Not only do young people often end up working in low-paid jobs, but the National Minimum Wage is lower for those aged 16 to 21 than for those aged 22 and over (Low Pay Commission, 2008). Such a position gives the impression that the government and employers do not value young people's work in the same way as they do adults'. This has an impact on young people's experience of poverty and inequality (France, 2008a). The British Youth Council argues that young people can feel exploited, powerless and, most importantly, discriminated against by the fact that they are paid a lower wage than those over 22 (British Youth Council, 2006). This not only makes them feel disrespected by the state, but can also impede their chances of making the transition from dependence to independence (British Youth Council, 2006). If we expect young people to feel valued and to have respect for themselves and others, then awarding them 'equal pay for equal work' (British Youth Council, 2006) would be a step in the right direction.

Respect, justice and feelings of fairness

For many young people their experiences of how policy makers, the media and society in general treat and respect them is negative (Children's Rights Alliance for England, 2008). Government has constructed a range of policies that undermine the rights of young people (UK Children's Commissioners, 2008). For example, Dispersal Orders and Anti-Social Behaviour Orders are seen as potential infringements of the UN Convention on the Rights of the Child (UNCRC) (UK Children's Commissioners, 2008) and also impact on how young people feel they are treated by the state (Children's Rights Alliance for England, 2008), potentially stigmatising them and increasing their chances of being future criminals (Margo, 2008). Thus, policy and its practice can, in many areas of young people's lives, be experienced as a form of harassment and discrimination.

Many young people, and especially some of the most deprived and disadvantaged, encounter policies of harassment in their everyday use of public space. For example, it is the young who are more likely to experience police 'stop and search' as a normal part of their everyday lives. Black (Bowling and Philips, 2002) and, more recently, Asian youths (Alexander, 2004) are more vulnerable to being stopped for little or no reason.

Similar concerns are raised over the introduction of the 'mosquito device'. This is targeted at the young and produces a high-pitched sound which only those aged under 25 can hear, with the aim of dispersing youth groups 'hanging around' public spaces and shops. While this is not supported by government, it has not been banned or outlawed, even though it indiscriminately harasses young people in their own communities (UK Children's Commissioners, 2008). Young people are also experiencing increased forms of surveillance (McCahill, 2002), such as the expansion of CCTV, with young people more likely to be followed and monitored than any other group, regardless of their behaviour (Norris and Armstrong, 1999).

But these policies can also have far-reaching impacts in that they create a climate in which some of the most vulnerable young people do not feel protected and safe in their own communities (France et al, 2007). For example, recent research has shown that young people aged between 10 and 25 are most likely to be victims of crime (Wilson et al, 2006). Young people are also six times more likely to be subject to some forms of victimisation (Jubb, 2003). Victimisation is not just about young people picking on other young people, although this can be important (Deakin, 2006). There is a growing body of evidence that shows adults victimise and intimidate young people through a wide range of practices (Brown, 2005). Those living in the most deprived communities are likely to experience higher rates of victimisation (Armstrong et al, 2005) and, while school is the place where most young people are victimised, public places such as 'the streets' and parks are sites where many experience being victimised on a day-to-day basis (Wilson et al, 2006; see also Chapter Four by Helen Woolley).

Developments in the Youth Justice System have also created a negative experience for many young people. New Labour has constructed a more punitive system that has marginalised welfare (Muncie, 2004). While New Labour prioritised the reduction of youth crime, there is a growing concern that its policies are stigmatising many young people and increasing their contact with the Youth Justice System (Solomon and Garside, 2008; Morgan, 2008). For example, one strategy used by the government to reduce persistent offending among a minority of young people was to introduce Intensive Supervision and Surveillance Programmes (ISSPs). Evidence of the effectiveness of these programmes has shown that a major impact has been increased net widening and use of custody (Solomon and Garside, 2008). Similar patterns are arising over the use of early intervention and prevention programmes. More young people are coming to the attention of the Youth Justice System earlier and for more minor offences (France, 2008b; Margo, 2008; Solomon and Garside, 2008).

The UK also detains more children and young people than any other European country, and they serve longer prison sentences (UK Children's Commissioners, 2008). Experiences in prisons are also a concern, with 30 young people having died in custody since 1990 and evidence of an overuse of physical restraint, strip searching and segregation (HM Chief Inspector of Prisons, 2008). This is especially relevant in Secure Training Centres, where physical restraint techniques were used over 7,000 times between January 2004 and September 2005 (HM Chief Inspector of Prisons, 2008). Government also increased the powers of prisons to use pain sanctions as a part of restraint mechanisms, such as use of nose, rib and thumb 'distraction' techniques. Violence and force are becoming a normal part of how discipline is managed in such institutions (Carlile, 2006).

It is also the case that not all young people are treated equally. Discrimination is a core experience of the young in British society. Age discrimination is one particular area of concern for young people, in that it infiltrates all aspects of their lives (Garnelas, 2007). Young people express anger and frustration at being treated differently in shops, on transport and in public services. Experiences such as being stopped from going into a shop because of their age, being ignored while adults are served first, being followed in shops or searched for no reason, undermine young people's respect for the adult world. Other, more structural, issues are also a concern; for example, not being allowed to open a bank account when under 16, or not receiving adult health services despite being old enough to get married or have children (Garnelas, 2007). Many young people feel these responses by adults are driven by stereotypes and misconceptions of young people (Youth Net and British Youth Council, 2006). In a recent survey 9 out of 10 young people felt that the media and politicians had little respect for the young, portraying them as a group to be feared and also the major perpetrators of anti-social behaviour. This misrepresentation was seen as shaping public policy and adult attitudes (Youth Net and British Youth Council, 2006).

Other forms of discrimination exist which shape young people's experiences of British society. For example, Black Caribbean and mixed White/Black Caribbean young people are one and a half times more likely to be identified as having behavioural problems at school. Similarly, they are five times more likely to be excluded from school for a fixed term (DfES, 2005). Concerns also exist over their experience in the Youth Justice System, with Black Caribbean young people being over-represented in a wide range of areas (House of Commons Education and Skills Select Committee, 2006). There are also issues around the treatment of some of the most excluded groups of young people; for example, those leaving care are still more likely to end up in prison, be homeless and to have future social problems (UK Children's Commissioners, 2008); and Gypsy and Traveller young people are more likely to be permanently excluded from school than others (UK Children's Commissioners, 2008).

While the government is keen to promote equal opportunities for all, this does not always extend to young people. For example, the 2006 Equality (Age) Regulations exclude young people under 18 years old from being treated the same over wages and benefits (France, 2008a). New legislation also aims to exclude them from protection in 'goods, facilities and services and the single public sector equality duty' (UK Children's Commissioners, 2008).

Respecting young people's voices and increasing participation

For the young, feelings of being respected can and do revolve around being 'listened to' and being involved in the decision-making processes in their lives (Children's Rights Alliance for England, 2008). The UK government has prioritised listening to young people, with their participation as a core policy objective, although how this is understood and acted upon is unclear (Tisdall et al, 2006; France et al, 2007). In line with Article 12 of the UNCRC, the government set out plans for young people to have a voice in the development of services and policies which impact upon their lives (UN Convention on the Rights of the Child: UK Second State Report, 1999). The government committed itself to valuing young people's contribution, to giving them an opportunity to be involved and to providing resources to help achieve this (CYPU, 2001). This has resulted in a wide range of initiatives being constructed that have aimed to increase young people's participation. These include Agenda 21 programmes, Single Regeneration Budgets, New Deal for Communities, the Children's Fund and the Local

Government Act (Kirby et al, 2003). Government has also recognised that young people's political contribution is at an all-time low (Youth Voting Network, 2003) and that it needs to take action to increase youth participation in democracy. One major development has been the UK Youth Parliament (DfES, 2004), which was formed in 1998 and has been supported by DfES with an annual grant. It currently has over 300 elected members representing different areas of the country, and its central objectives are to give young people a voice in the political process, to increase young people's participation in democracy and to empower young people to become more involved in positive activities in their communities (UK Youth Parliament, 2008).

Challenges and tensions remain around the types of participation being proposed, and ideas of building 'a culture of participation' tend to be constructed around young people making a contribution to public discussions and public services (Tisdall et al, 2006). What this approach struggles to engage with is helping young people to make decisions about their everyday lives. The types of decisions that are most important to the young revolve around their life in school, their families and their peers (Crimmens and West, 2004), yet many of the programmes that encourage listening and participation have failed to make this central. This lack of attention to personal decision-making continues to marginalise young people and helps to maintain the status quo rather than challenging it (Crimmens and West, 2004). Even in public decision-making processes young people's voices still seem to be marginalised. For example, there is much research on young people's perspectives of their communities and what needs to be changed, yet little seems to happen to suggest these types of activities might bring about change. In fact, the failure to do so can create greater cynicism and disaffection among the young (Kirby et al, 2003). This approach tends to promote a consumer-testing approach and an illusion of 'voice' rather than a reality (Cockburn, 2005; Middleton, 2006). The issues of power between adults and young people, or policy, professional practice and young people, are rarely considered in discussions over 'voice' and participation. These relationships tend to go almost uncontested and left alone (Crimmens and West, 2004). Similar problems exist with the UK Youth Parliament, and its success to date remains questionable (DfES, 2004). Challenges remain in constructing participation processes that replicate existing adult structures, which may not be the most effective ways of encouraging greater participation for all. For example, the Youth Parliament bears a strong resemblance to the adult system and evidence already suggests that the representation of excluded groups still remains a fundamental problem (DfES, 2004). Also, the Youth

Parliament remains relatively unknown across the youth population as a system of representing their issues (DfES, 2004).

At the heart of the participation debate is the question of citizenship. Young people are being 'trained' or educated for their future role as citizens (Garnelas, 2007). There have been moves towards developing young people as citizens through the introduction of citizenship education in the national curriculum. This is aimed at preparing young people to be citizens by teaching them their social and moral responsibility, about what community involvement means, and about political literacy (Advisory Group on Citizenship, 1998). However, what is absent in this debate is a recognition that citizenship is a 'lived' state, in which being a citizen is a social process where individuals are active in constructing themselves as citizens through norms, practices and meanings in everyday life (Isin and Turner, 2002; Smith et al, 2005). Citizenship in this context is a more dynamic and negotiated process that can involve power struggles over who is to be included or excluded. It is therefore important to recognise that citizenship is not simply a legal status but also a social–political practice of being recognised (Lister et al, 2007). Policy fails to actively acknowledge this in terms of the young, with the focus being on the making of future citizens (France et al, 2007). Policy sees young people as 'between' childhood and adulthood and 'in transition' towards adulthood, therefore the lived daily experiences of the young are given little attention. Citizenship education is concentrated on 'responsibilising' young people, making sure they understand what their core responsibilities are in being citizens (France, 2007). For example, within these discussions the emphasis is on participation as volunteering, where individuals are encouraged to 'give back' to others (France et al, 2007). Government's approach to both participation and citizenship is, then, very narrowly focused and does not acknowledge young people's lived experiences of citizenship.

Towards a 'culture of respect'?

Young people have expressed their frustration at the lack of respect they get from the adult world (Youth Net and British Youth Council, 2006; Children's Rights Alliance for England, 2008; UK Children's Commissioner's Report, 2008) and, as our discussion has shown, evidence exists as to why this is. For example, not only does policy fail to understand the importance of mutual or self-respect, it also discriminates and fails, in a number of areas, to protect the young and to listen to their concerns. The lack of respect for the young is also evident at the more local, neighbourhood level, where adults and professionals, such as the police, use power and the law in ways that show little respect to young people who are, in the majority of situations, going about their normal, everyday business (Jamieson, 2005). Such feelings of being 'disrespected' are, for many young people, reinforced by the media portrayal of the young as 'hooligans', 'problems', 'scroungers' and lacking any real respect for adults (Youth Net and British Youth Council, 2006). The continual call for the young to 'show some respect' as a core function and responsibility of citizenship denies the responsibilities that we, as adults, have to future generations. These factors combine to leave many young people feeling cynical about the actions of adults and, in many cases, marginalised or excluded from present and future citizenship. These feelings, while not justifications for young people being 'disrespectful', do raise issues about why the young, and especially those more on the margins, should respect an adult world that has little respect or recognition for them.

But it does not have to be like this. We need to consider how we might create a 'culture of respect' that is inclusive and effective for young people. First, there has to be a recognition in policy, in the media and within the interactions of the everyday activities of adults, that respect is a 'two-way process' and that treating the young as having to 'earn' respect is counterproductive. We as a nation have to start producing more positive messages to young people, showing that we recognise their achievements and that we are listening to what they have to say. Without such a 'culture' being developed, respect will not flourish. Second, we need to recognise that respect is learned through actions, not words alone. In this context citizenship is a lived experience (Smith et al, 2005) and we have to change the experience young people have. Education for citizenship has potential, but only if we create real experiences of citizenship in action.

There are examples of other ways to 'learn' about respect and its relationship to citizenship. One such approach is to instil a culture of democracy and respect as a vital aspect of the school ethos. An example of this is democratic schools, which encourage all members of the school, including pupils, to be involved in the decision-making process, with a representative school council as its centrepiece (Inman, 2002). Not only does this support citizenship education by giving young people the experience of participating in a democratic forum, it also promotes respect by showing young people that their views are respected and valued by all adults in the school (Inman, 2002). Similarly the UNICEF 'Rights Respecting Schools' initiative, where the ethos of the school is based on the UNCRC, is an example where respect can flourish. Young people encounter an environment where their rights and responsibilities to one another are embedded in the ethos and actions of the school. The impact of this kind of school philosophy is that pupils become more aware of and empathetic towards one another and the quality of classroom discussions improves (Covell and Howe, 2005). 'Rights Respecting Schools' has also shown improvement in pupil behaviour, with pupils more motivated to attend school and more empowered to take control of their own learning, which helps to improve achievement (Covell and Howe, 2005). These kinds of initiatives show that if young people are shown respect and their opinions are valued within school it creates a climate of mutual respect which improves young people's 'lived experience' of school. Improving the day-to-day experiences of pupils in this way also helps to improve behaviour, attendance and achievement (Massey, 2003) – the government's focus within education policy. Such a strategy is about creating a culture of respect that is embedded in the everyday lived experiences of being a citizen.

Notes

[1] The issue of victimisation was also acknowledged as the other side of this story.

[2] For example, Anti-Social Behaviour Orders (ASBOs), Parenting Orders, Fixed Penalty Notices, Penalty Notices for Disorder, Dispersal Orders, etc.

[3] The position of Respect Commissioner was dropped as a part of these plans.

References

Advisory Group on Citizenship (1998) *Education for Citizenship and Teaching of Democracy in Schools*, London: QCA.

Alexander, C. (2004) 'Imagining the Asian gang: ethnicity, masculinity and youth after "the riots"', *Critical Social Policy*, 24(4), 526–49.

Armstrong, D., Hine, J., Hacking, S., Armaois, R., Jones, R., Klessinger, N. and France, A. (2005) *Children, Risk and Crime: The On Track Youth Life-styles Surveys*, Home Office Research Study 278, London: Home Office.

Bowling, B. and Phillips, C. (2002) *Racism, Crime and Injustice*, London: Longman.

British Youth Council (2006) *The Submission to the Low Pay Commission on the Impact of the Minimum Wage for Young People*, London: British Council.

Brown, S. (2005) *Youth Crime*, Maidenhead: Open University Press.

Carlile, Lord (2006) *The Carlile Inquiry*, London: Howard League for Penal Reform.

Carter, M. (1966) *Into Work*, London: Pelican.

Children's Rights Alliance for England (2008) *Get Ready for Geneva: Submission to the UN Committee on the Rights of the Child*, London: CRAE.

Children's Society (2007) *The Good Childhood Inquiry*, London: The Children's Society.

Cockburn, T. (2005) 'Children as participative citizens: A radically pluralist case for "child friendly" public communication', Special Volume of *Journal of Social Sciences*, 9, 19–29.

Covell, K. and Howe, B. (2005) *Rights Respect and Responsibility in Hampshire Schools: Summary of the Report of the RRR Initiative.* www3. hants.gov.uk/education/hias/childrensrights/rrr-general.htm.

Crimmens, D. and West, A. (2004) *Having Their Say: Young People and Participation – European Experiences*, London: Russell House Publishing.

Critcher, C. (2003) *Moral Panics and the Media*, Buckingham: Open University Press.

CYPU (Children and Young People's Unit) (2001) *Building a Strategy for Children and Young People*, London: DfES.

DCSF (Department for Children, Schools and Families) (2008) *Youth Alcohol Action Plan*, London: DCSF.

Deakin, J. (2006) 'Dangerous people, dangerous places: the nature and location of young people's victimisation and fear', *Children and Society*, 20(5), 376–90.

DfES (Department for Education and Skills) (2004) *Review of the UK Youth Parliament*, London: DfES.

DfES (2005) *Ethnicity and Education, the Evidence of Minority Ethnic Pupils*, London: DfES.

Dillon, R.S. (2003) 'Respect' (*Stanford Encyclopaedia of Philosophy*), Available at: http://plato.stanford.edu/entries/respect/ [Accessed 25 April 2008].

Dwyer Hogg, C. (2008) 'Why do children carry knives? The view from the streets – This Britain, UK', *The Independent*, 28 June.

Field, F. and White, P. (2007) *Welfare isn't Working: The New Deal for Young People*, London: Reform.

Finn, D. (2003) 'The "employment-first" welfare state: lessons from the New Deal for Young People', *Social Policy and Administration*, 37(7), 709–24.

France, A. (2007) *Understanding Youth in Late Modernity*, Maidenhead: Open University Press.

France, A. (2008a) 'From being to becoming: the importance of tackling youth poverty in transitions to adulthood', *Social Policy and Society*, 7(4), 495–506.

France, A. (2008b) 'Risk factor analysis and the youth question', *Journal of Youth Studies*, 11(1), 1–15.

France, A., Sandu, A. and Meredith, J. (2007) 'Youth culture and citizenship in multicultural Britain', *Journal of Contemporary European Studies*, 15(3), 303–16.

Frean, A. (2007) '"Dumbed-down" English GCSE fails to challenge pupils, says watchdog', *The Times*, 16 March.

Furlong, A. and Cartmel, F. (2007) *Young People and Social Change: New Perspectives*, 2nd edition, Maidenhead: Open University Press.

Garnelas, C. (2007) *'We are all equal and that's the truth!' Children and young people talk about age discrimination and equality*, London: Children's Rights Alliance for England.

Gaskell, C. (2008) '"But they just don't respect us": young people's experiences of (dis)respected citizenship and the New Labour Respect Agenda', *Children's Geographies*, 6(3), 223–38.

Harradine, S., Kodz, J., Lernetti, F. and Jones, B. (2004) *Defining and Measuring Anti-Social Behaviour*, Home Office Development and Practice Report 26, London: Home Office.

HM Chief Inspector of Prisons for England and Wales (2008) *Annual Report 2006/2007*, London: Her Majesty's Inspectorate of Prisons.

HM Government (2008) *Youth Crime Action Plan*, London: HM Government.

Home Office (2008a) *Saving Lives, Reducing Harm, Protecting the Public: An Action Plan for Tackling Violence 2008–2011*, London: Home Office.

Home Office (2008b) *Drugs: Protecting Families and Communities: The 2008 Drug Strategy First Edition*, London: Home Office.

House of Commons Education and Skills Select Committee (2006) *Special Education Needs, Third Report, Session 2006–2006, Vol 1*.

Inman, S. (2002) *School Councils: An Apprenticeship in Democracy?* London: Association of Teachers and Lecturers.

Ipsos MORI (2007) *GCSEs and A Level: The Experiences of Teachers, Students, Parents and the General Public*, London: Qualifications and Curriculum Authority.

Isin, E.F. and Turner, B.S. (eds) (2002) *Handbook of Citizenship Studies*, London: Sage.

Jamieson, J. (2005) 'New Labour, youth justice and the question of "respect"', *Youth Justice*, 5(3), 180–93.

Jones, G. and Wallace, C. (1992) *Youth, Family and Citizenship*, Buckingham: Open University Press.

Jubb, R. (2003) *Youth Victimisation: A Literature Review*, Community Safety Practice Briefing, London: NACRO.

Kemp, P. (2006) 'Young people and unemployment: from welfare to workfare', in M. Barry (ed) *Youth Policy and Social Exclusion*, London: Routledge, pp 139–56.

Kirby, P., Lanyon, C., Cronin, K. and Sinclair, R. (2003) *Building a Culture of Participation: Involving Children and Young People in Policy, Service Planning, Delivery and Evaluation*, Nottingham: DfES Publications.

Kounine, L., Marks, J. and Truss, E. (2008) *The Value of Mathematics*, London: Reform.

Lindsay, C. and McQuaid, R. (2004) 'Avoiding the "McJobs": unemployed job seekers and attitudes to service work', *Work, Employment and Society*, 18(2), 297–319.

Lister, R., Williams, F., Anttonen, A., Bussemaker, J., Gerhard, U., Heinen, J., Johnasson, S., Leira, A., Siim, B. and Tobio, C. (2007) *Gendering Citizenship in Western Europe: New Challenges for Citizenship Research in a Cross-National Context*, Bristol: The Policy Press.

Low Pay Commission (2008) *National Minimum Wage 2008*, London: HMSO.

McCahill, M. (2002) *The Surveillance Web*, Cullompton: Willan Publishing.

McCarthy, P. and Walker, J. (2006) 'R-E-S-P-E-C-T, find out what it means to me: the connection between respect and youth crime', *Crime Prevention and Community Safety*, 8(1), 17–29.

MacDonald, R. and Marsh, J. (2005) *Disconnected Youth? Growing Up in Britain's Poor Neighbourhoods*, Basingstoke: Palgrave Macmillan.

McGaw, B., Gipps, C. and Godber, R. (2004) *Examination Standards: Report of the Independent Committee to the QCA*, London: Qualifications and Curriculum Authority.

McKnight, A. (2005) 'Employment: tackling poverty through "work for those who can"', in J. Hills and K. Stewart (eds) *A More Equal Society? New Labour, Poverty, Inequality and Exclusion*, Bristol: The Policy Press, pp 23–46.

Margalit, A. (1996) *The Decent Society*, Cambridge, MA: Harvard University Press.

Margo, J. (2008) *Make Me a Criminal*, London: IPPR.

Mason, C. (1998) 'New deal with marked cards', *Local Economy*, August, 176–86.

Massey, I. (2003) *The case for RRR – A paper.* Available at: www3.hants. gov.uk/caseforrrr.pdf [Accessed April 2008].

Middleton, D. (2006) 'Three types of self-respect', *Res Publica*, 12(1), 59–76.

Mizen, P. (1995) *The State, Young People and Youth Training: In and Against the Training State*, London: Mansell.

Mizen, P. (2004) *The Changing State of Youth*, Basingstoke: Palgrave Macmillan.

Monti, D. (1995) *Wannabe: Gangs and Suburbs and Schools*, Oxford: Blackwell Publishing.

Morgan, R. (2008) *Summary Justice: Fast – but Fair?* London: Centre for Crime and Justice Studies.

Muncie, J. (2004) *Youth and Crime*, 2nd edition, London: Sage.

Norris, C. and Armstrong, G. (1999) *The Maximum Surveillance Society*, Oxford: Berg.

Paton, G. (2007) 'Examiner admits that GCSEs are being dumbed down', *Daily Telegraph*, 31 August.

QCA (Qualifications and Curriculum Authority) (2008) *Inter-Subject Comparability Studies*, London: QCA.

Rawls, J. (1971) *A Theory of Justice*, Cambridge, MA: Harvard University Press.

Respect Task Force (2006a) *Respect Action Plan*, London: Home Office.

Respect Task Force (2006b) *Tackling Anti-social Behaviour: The Story So Far and the Move to Respect*, London: Home Office.

Sennett, R. (2003) *Respect in a World of Inequality*, New York: W.W. Norton & Co.

Smith, N., Lister, R., Middleton, S. and Cox, L. (2005) 'Young people as real citizens: towards an inclusionary understanding of citizenship', *Journal of Youth Studies*, 8(4), 425–43.

Social Exclusion Task Force (2007) *Reaching Out: Think Family*, London: Social Exclusion Task Force.

Solomon, E. and Garside, R. (2008) *Ten Years of Labour's Youth Justices Reforms: An Independent Audit*, London: Centre for Crime and Justice Studies.

Tisdall, E.K.M., Davis, J.F., Prout, A. and Hill, M. (eds) (2006) *Children, Young People and Social Inclusion: Participation for What?* Bristol: The Policy Press.

Turok, L. (1999) 'Urban labour markets: The causes and consequences of change', *Urban Studies*, 36(5/6) 893–915.

UK Children's Commissioners (2008) *UK Children's Commissioners' Report to the UN Committee on the Rights of the Child*, London: UK Children's Commissioners.

UK Youth Parliament (2008) UK Youth Parliament: Making Our Mark. Available at: www.ukyouthparliament.org.uk/ [Accessed 4 July 2008].

UN Convention on the Rights of the Child: UK Second State Report (1999). Available at: www.everychildmatters.gov.uk.

Watts, B. (2008) *What are Today's Social Evils? The Results of a Web Consultation*, York: Joseph Rowntree Foundation.

Wilson, D., Sharpe, C. and Patterson, A. (2006) *Young People and Crime: Findings from the 2005 Offending, Crime and Justice Survey*, Home Office Statistical Bulletin 17/06, London: Home Office.

Youth Net and British Youth Council (2006) *Respect? The Voice behind the Hood: Young People's Views on Anti-Social Behaviour, the Media and Older People*, London: Youth Net; The British Youth Council.

Youth Taskforce (2008) *Youth Taskforce Action Plan*, London: Department for Children, Schools and Families.

Youth Voting Network (2003) *A Young Person's Agenda for Democracy – One Year On*, London: Electoral Commission.

FOUR

Every child matters in public open spaces

Helen Woolley

Introduction

In 2003 the British government declared that *Every Child Matters* (Chief Secretary to the Treasury, 2003). The expression of this assertion was that children should be healthy, stay safe, enjoy and achieve, make a positive contribution and achieve economic well-being. One of the aims of this policy was to provide a more joined-up approach to children and young people's services in local government. A more recent development of this policy was the launch of the *Children's Plan for England*, in December 2007 (DCSF, 2007). This is intended as a 10-year programme with the aim 'to make England the best place in the world for children and young people to grow up' (DCSF, 2007: 3).

But how do these policies relate to children and young people and their relationship to open spaces? Are children and young people *respected* in public open spaces, especially in our increasingly physically dense and multicultural urban areas? This chapter explores the place of children and young people in public open spaces and considers whether they are accepted and respected (or otherwise). The chapter uses the examples of young people skateboarding and the provision of outdoor play spaces for children. It concludes that public open spaces are essentially controlled by adults. The implications for respect and citizenship are discussed. But first, it is worth considering what is meant by 'public open space'.

Defining public open space

There have always been debates about spaces and whether they are public or private, by both ownership and use. In recent years approaches to open space have included a range of definitions and constructs which have been based upon both physical and social understandings. Thus, one assertion is that open space is the land, the water on the land and, in addition, the space and light above the land (Tankel, 1963), a concept which can perhaps be easily identified with in light of the fact that people often like to go outside for the 'fresh air'. Another definition of open space is that it is the land and water in an urban area that is not covered by cars or buildings, or is any of the undeveloped land (Gold, 1980). Some might agree with this definition while others would not, because streets and roads and car parks are sometimes 'covered with cars', but at other times are not and are even played in by children and young people who see an affordance (Gibson, 1986) for a different activity. Another definition, based on the physical nature of spaces, states that open spaces are wide-open areas that can be fluid and that the city can flow into the park and the park can flow into the city (Cranz, 1982). However, this definition seems to limit itself to an understanding of parks as open spaces.

Public space

Some express their understanding of open spaces from a social rather than a physical approach, and these definitions relate not necessarily to open space, but move towards a concept of public space. Thus, public spaces have been defined as responsive, democratic and meaningful places that protect the rights of user groups (Carr et al, 1992). Others have discussed that 'public places are expected to be accessible to everyone, and are where strangers and citizens alike can enter with fewer restrictions' (Madanipour, 1999: 880). For some the public spaces of parks are considered to be the most democratic of spaces (Worpole and Greenhalgh, 1995). Thus, these definitions give an insight into an understanding that public spaces are, or at least should be, for use by anyone or everyone.

Other definitions of public space based on a social premise are perhaps less inclusive. For instance, the assertion that public space 'contains every single aspect of urban life that exists beyond home and beyond work' (Shonfield, 1998: 2) implies that open spaces which people might use during their working day – for instance at lunchtime – would not be considered as public space. One definition of public spaces which has a richness to it is that by Walzer (1986: 470), who states that:

> Public space is space where we share with strangers, people who aren't our relatives, friends or work associates. It is space for politics, religion, commerce, sport; space for peaceful coexistence and impersonal encounter. Its character

expresses and also conditions our public life, civic culture, everyday discourse.

However, the complexity of this definition, with layers of activities, carries an underlying assumption that public spaces are not for meeting or sharing experiences with relatives, friends or work colleagues. For instance, this understanding is alien with respect to the public space of parks, for it is clear that one of the main social uses of parks is for adults to accompany children, who are often relatives (Dunnett et al, 2002). A discourse which explores both physical *and* social attributes of public spaces, together with a discussion about public and private spaces, can be found in Madanipour (2003). This provides an understanding across time and cultures as to some of the complexities of public spaces.

Open space

For some, the definition of public space does not assume that the space which is an open space is outside. According to Worpole and Greenhalgh (1996), in work for the think-tank Demos, libraries, railway stations, churches, parks and squares are examples of public space. To these have been added, in more recent years, car boot sales and supermarket cafes (Mean and Tims, 2005).

A variety of academic, policy and practice definitions for *open space* have been identified during the last 30 years. Thus, Lynch (1981) suggested a typology of regional parks, squares, plazas, linear parks, adventure playgrounds, wastelands, playgrounds and playing fields. The London Planning Advisory Committee (Llewelyn-Davies Planning, 1992) defined a hierarchy of open spaces to include a small local park, local park, district park, metropolitan park, regional park and linear open space. One professional body suggests a typology that is based upon land use, whch includes urban and rural spaces but which adds on cultural and visual value (ILAM, 1996). It has also been argued that definitions which are hierarchical can overlook the smaller open spaces one might choose to use close to home (Morgan, 1991). For some it is the functional or multifunctional nature of open spaces which is important. Thus, Eckbo (1969) understands that open spaces provide for relaxation and recreation, conservation of wildlife, natural and agricultural resources, scenery and the shaping and control of urbanisation. The multifunctional social, health, environmental and economic benefits are also affirmed (Woolley, 2003a), while Barber (2005) discusses the multifunctional nature of one specific type of open space – parks (in the CLERE model of community, landscape, ecology, recreation and economy).

In practice, planners and landscape architects are working with the government's definition of open spaces, provided in *Planning Policy Guidance 17* (ODPM, 2002). This government policy adopts a division between green and civic spaces, with green spaces being defined as parks and gardens; natural and semi-natural green space, including urban woodland; green corridors, outdoor sports facilities; amenity green space; provision for children and young people; allotments, community gardens and urban farms; and cemeteries, disused churchyards and other burial grounds. Civic spaces are deemed to include 'civic and market squares and other hard surfaced areas designated for pedestrians' (ODPM, 2002).

One approach which combines both physical and social understandings of open space is that open spaces can be identified as domestic, neighbourhood and civic, and that different types of spaces within these themes might be used socially at different times of life (Woolley, 2003a). Thus, *domestic open spaces*, identified as spaces in housing areas, private gardens, community gardens and allotments, are considered to be used throughout life. *Neighbourhood open spaces*, defined as parks, playgrounds, playing fields and sports grounds, school playgrounds, streets, city farms and incidental spaces, are physically further from home and provide opportunities for new and different social encounters for a range of individuals and groups. For children and young people in particular, the neighbourhood spaces are often part of the developing home range which has traditionally come with increasing age. This increase in home range for young people then, of course, leads them to using *civic open spaces* – particularly the commercial ones in city centres.

So it can be seen that open space and public space can be understood by different people to have different meanings, perhaps depending upon their academic or professional background or their experiences of and context in life. For the purposes of this chapter I will consider that *public open space* is open space which may be domestic, neighbourhood or civic open space *and* which can be used publicly – that is, theoretically, by anyone. Thus, spaces in housing areas are public open spaces but private gardens are not. Similarly, parks are public open spaces, as are streets. School playgrounds, funded by taxpayers, should be public open spaces but are increasingly being treated as private or semi-private spaces, a debate about which could take a chapter of its own. Civic open spaces include hospital grounds, recreation open spaces such as municipal golf courses and civic spaces in city centres. All of these could be considered as public open spaces, and yet there are many instances in practice where such spaces are not being treated as public and the boundaries between public and private are being challenged (Madanipour, 2003).

Children and young people's use of public open spaces

Some 40 years ago concerns were expressed by Lady Allen of Hurtwood, a renowned landscape architect and campaigner for children's welfare, about children's environments in England. She stated:

> Children and young people living in the so-called civilized countries probably enjoy better living conditions than ever before: good hygiene, good food, better schools and better housing. But there still remains immense emotional poverty and privation. There may be less direct hardship, but we are aware of more depression, more mental illness, more violence, more delinquency and more drug taking. (Allen of Hurtwood, 1968: 11)

Much of this statement remains true today, although the good food might be questioned, with concerns about the amounts of 'fast' and often unhealthy food eaten, and also the physical states of many schools being less than they might be, due to years of poor maintenance. Perhaps one of the starkest issues is that of mental illness. One in ten children under 16 in the UK is thought to have a clinically diagnosed mental health disorder (British Medical Association, 2006). Today many of society's issues in the UK about children and young people are also expressed as concerns about physical health, particularly obesity (and potential subsequent health matters of diabetes and heart problems), and mental health, including depression and behavioural disorders, among them Attention Deficit Hyperactivity Disorder (ADHD).

Children and young people are often demonised for issues such as the fact that they do not play out enough or walk to school or do enough exercise; and yet often it is adults who are controlling the potential for children and young people to undertake these and other activities in open spaces. For instance, decisions to reduce the length and even the existence of school playtimes (Pelligrini and Blatchford, 1993), which provide opportunities for play in the broad definition of the word (see, for example, NPFA, 2000; Bishop and Curtis, 2001; Woolley et al, 2005), are taken by adults in schools, not by the children.

Despite the transport White Paper of over 10 years ago (DETR, 1997) and the subsequent introduction of interventions such as School Travel Plans, which can include the provision of 'walking buses' and safer routes to schools, many children are still going to school in England by car, rather than walking. Over this period there has been a year-on-year decrease in numbers of children walking to school. The latest published figures show that 46% of 5- to 16-year-olds walked to school in 2006 (National Statistics and Department of Transport, 2008), compared to 49% in 1999–2001 and 56% in 1989–91 (National Statistics and Department for Transport, 2003). Is this perennial decline in the number of children walking to school a result of children's choices? One suspects that it is a result of the desire of parents to travel by car, possibly on their way to work, and of the parental choice of schools. In addition, children have expressed that they would like to play outside more often and yet this is also constrained by adults' fears of cars and of other people (McNeish and Roberts, 1995).

Often, activities in which children and young people participate in open spaces are called 'play'. There are many adult definitions of this word with respect to children (more of which later). However, these many definitions lead me increasingly to think that the word 'play' is, in fact, an adult construct – partly because children often talk about going outside, doing things or doing stuff. Perhaps a discussion about this would be appropriate elsewhere, and so for the purpose of this chapter I continue to use the word 'play'.

Play in which children and young people participate in open spaces can take many forms. In the same way that academics, policy makers and practitioners have tried to define open space, these different groups have tried not only to define play but also to categorise it. Thus, Sutton-Smith (1997) identifies as play a list of activities which include: mind or subjective play; solitary play; playful behaviours; informal social play; vicarious audience play; performance play; celebrations and festivals; contests (games and sports); risky or deep play. From a play-worker practice point of view, the most generally accepted categorisation is that of Hughes (1996). This typology has fifteen categories: symbolic play; rough and tumble play; socio-dramatic play; social play; creative play; communication play; dramatic play; deep play; exploratory play; fantasy play; imaginative play; locomotor play; mastery play; object play; role play (NPFA, 2000).

In the setting of school three main forms of play have been identified: physical, intellectual and social/emotional. Such forms are identified as having subdivisions of: gross motor, fine motor and psychomotor for physical play; linguistic, scientific, symbolic/mathematical and creative for intellectual play; and therapeutic, linguistic, repetitious, empathic, self-concept and gaming as social/emotional play (Moyles, 1989). More recently, a wider range of play has been identified as taking place in primary school playgrounds and this has been categorised as play with high verbal content; play with high imaginative content; play with high physical content; and less structured play, including walking, talking, sitting and watching (Woolley et al, 2005). Perhaps more significant than any definitions or categorisations of play is that play is important, and that this has been incorporated into a *Charter for Children's Play* (Children's Play Council, 1998; Play England, 2007):

> Play is an essential part of every child's life – vital to his or her development. It is the way that children explore for themselves the world around them; the way that they naturally develop understanding and practise skills. Play is essential for healthy physical and emotional growth, intellectual and educational development, and for acquiring social and behavioural skills. (Play England, 2007: 2)

Various types of children's and young people's play[1] can take place in different open spaces. Individuals or groups of children and young people may be differently attracted to these different types of open spaces (and there may be great variety in how they interpret these spaces and in what they want to do with them). The discussion will now focus on two specific situations in public open spaces: first, skateboarders and the way in which they are dealt with; and second, the design and provision of playgrounds for children. I will then reflect on whether these situations are an expression of 'respect' towards children and young people in public open spaces.

Adult control of skateboarders' use of public open space by social, legal and physical constraints

One group of children and young people who have increasingly been identified as being under-provided for in public open spaces is that of teenagers (Dunnett et al, 2002). In recent years this has led to a resurgence in the provision of MUGAs (Multi Use Games Areas) and the introduction of 'teen shelters' in locations such as parks. These are elements within open spaces which are provided specifically for young people to use and they are fairly standard in the way in which they appear in the landscape. Visually, some of the 'teen shelters' which are being provided look as if they have landed from outer space, because they are put into a space with little or no thought for the landscape, physical or social context of that space.

One group, skateboarders – predominantly teenagers (although not exclusively so – see also Millie, Chapter Eight) – do not necessarily use open spaces designed for them, but use the urban fabric as they see an opportunity. Skateboarders use public open spaces in the urban fabric in a way few other groups do.[2] Not only do they use it, but they observe in order to identify how they might use it, looking for the affordance of any particular open space. Reasons why skateboarders choose certain open spaces have been identified as accessibility, trickability, sociability and compatibility (Woolley and Johns, 2001). The activity of skateboarding has been shown to have both physical and social benefits for the participants. The physical benefits derive from participants' noticing and using aspects of the urban environment, such as steps, walls, curbs and ramps (see for example Borden, 2001). The social benefits relate to supporting each other, being creative within the activity and encouraging development of skills for skateboarding, as opposed to being competitive and bound by rules in the way that many organised sports are (see for example Beal, 1995; Karsten and Pel, 2000).

Yet the activity of skateboarding, and sometimes even the presence of skateboarders, gives rise to concern for some people who are not participants in the activity. Thus, over time a series of social and physical concerns has been raised by non-participants about the activity of skateboarding (Woolley, 2008a). The social concerns relate to the fact that there is a perception that skateboarding is not compatible with other users or activities. This is especially the case where the open space being used is a civic one in the centre of a city and is surrounded by commercial, retail or civic buildings (Nemeth, 2006; Woolley, 2008a). In these situations office workers have not liked even to look out on skateboarders (Flusty, 2002), and policy makers have decided that skateboarding is an anti-social activity and not appropriate in certain open spaces (Woolley, 2008a). Apart from the visual concern of actually seeing skateboarding, other sensory concerns have included people finding skateboarding to be 'noisy' (Flusty, 2002). The other social concern is that of compatibility, or perceived compatibility, with other users. The little evidence there is on this aspect gives rise to an understanding that the major issue here is one of perception rather than reality (Woolley, 2008a). Physical concern relates to the fact that sometimes skateboarding causes damage to the urban fabric. Such damage can include gouges and scratches and wax deposits being left on benches, steps and handrails (Borden, 2001; Woolley and Johns, 2001).

Overall, these concerns about social and physical issues have led some people to believe that skateboarding is not an appropriate activity for certain open spaces, considering the activity to be a 'social incivility' or 'public disorder' (Oc and Tiesdell, 1997), or 'anti-social' and 'disrespectful'. This can result in skateboarders' being treated as being on the margins of acceptability in civic open spaces, in the same way that homeless people often are (Borden, 2001). As a response to these concerns, society as a whole has decided to exclude skateboarders from certain open spaces. These tend to be civic open spaces, predominantly in central business districts of towns and cities. Although young people who are not skateboarders can also be made to feel unwelcome in these urban centres (see for example Woolley et al, 1999), the focus now turns to the methods used specifically to exclude skateboarders from using civic open spaces.

A series of measures is used to exclude skateboarders from open spaces, the methods being social, legal and physical (Woolley, 2006). Exclusion by social methods includes the use of security guards. Legal exclusion is underpinned by the use of, for instance, Dispersal Orders or by-laws prohibiting the activity of skateboarding in a particular open space (or in an area of town or city centre, thus including a series of open spaces). The physical domain of excluding skateboarding has been explored more recently, with the result that, apart from the provision of skateboard parks, two different approaches have been identified, which can be labelled as either reactive or proactive (Woolley, 2008a).

- Reactive approaches include those where some open spaces have details added onto elements – such as benches, walls and handrails – in order to prevent skateboarders from using them. This approach sometimes happens after the construction or regeneration of a public space. It is not necessarily a new approach, in that it was observed as a method of exclusion at least 20 years ago.
- Proactive approaches involve a design philosophy, to include elements and details that exclude skateboarding as part of the design process, rather than adding them on. The evidence recorded so far (Woolley, 2008a) reveals that this proactive approach results in details which are more aesthetically pleasing to the eye, although this is not the place to open up a discussion about the subjective nature of the aesthetics of open spaces.

In one location the proactive approach was driven by both politicians and council officers. Their concern was that a multimillion-pound redevelopment of public civic spaces might result in both social and physical issues arising from skateboarders' using the open spaces. However, in this same location not only physical control is used. Both legal and social controls are used, in the form of a by-law outlawing skateboarding in the city centre, and the use of City Centre Ambassadors who patrol the main civic open spaces for most of the day and night. The research revealed that other locations have also been identified as using more than one of the three of social, legal and physical controls. Some are using two of these controls, and further research is required to investigate whether all three controls are necessary for one location and whether this is value for money. In the location where the proactive approach to design is being taken, this is a response to concerns about skateboarders' use of certain open spaces over a period of years (Woolley, 2003b). The skateboarders have been moved on from space to space during this time, with social, physical and legal controls being used at different times, the proactive approach to design being the culmination of the process of exclusion. In this particular city the skateboarders have been offered a skateboard park on the edge of the city centre, constructed on what was previously a barely used games area. However, there is conflict between users in this space, in that BMXers appear to be dominant users, rather than skateboarders (Thompson, 2003). And indeed, it is clearly understood that many skateboarders like to use the 'found space' in urban areas for their activity, rather than to be confined to the 'constructed space' of skate parks (Borden, 2001; Woolley and Johns, 2001; Woolley, 2008b).

Adult control of children's use of public open space through design

Skateboarders are, in the main, a minority male group in civic open spaces, and the focus now turns to children of a younger age range. This is a larger group of users of open spaces, those who use what are called playgrounds, often provided in the neighbourhood open spaces of parks. There is now plenty of evidence about 'play' and the many benefits it has for individual children and society as a whole, with the benefits being experienced both at the time of play and later in life (for example NPFA, 2000). Play is something that children do as a natural instinct. An all-encompassing definition is one given by sociologists, who declare that play is the 'nature of childhood' (Prout and James, 1997). However, play is described in various other ways by other academics. Thus some have declared it to be 'a continually creative process' (Aaron and Winawer, 1965) and others as 'scientific research conducted by children' (Eibl-Eibesfeldt, 1970). Broader definitions, which are not focused on the direct activity but on the underlying drivers, include those which state that play is 'an approach to action, not a form of activity' (Moyles, 1989), and that it is an 'imitation of adults' activities bringing children closer to the adult world' (Noschis, 1992). From the practice and policy perspectives, other definitions exist. Thus, a widely accepted contemporary definition within the field of play-workers in England is that 'play is freely chosen, personally directed, intrinsically motivated behaviour that actively engages the child' (NPFA, 2000). The policy approach from the government defines play as 'what children and young people do when they follow their own ideas and interests' (DCMS, 2003).

These many definitions of play all seem to imply that it is a creative, moveable feast, primarily directed by children themselves. So let us spend a little time considering the open spaces which are called playgrounds. For many years now in England, specific provision for outdoor play for children has been in the form of playgrounds. So, despite the fact that Opie and Opie (1969: 10) – renowned for their work investigating children's play – clearly understood that 'where children are, is where they play', England as a society has chosen to provide for children's outdoor play in, mainly, enclosed spaces called playgrounds.

The origins of enclosed spaces for play in the western world can be traced back to the introduction of 'outdoor gymnasia' in America in 1821 (Frost, 2006), where gymnastic apparatus was placed in the outdoor environment. The use of apparatus of this sort was followed by the development of what is now called fixed play equipment (Frost, 1992). The Playground Association of America then sought to introduce playgrounds across the whole of America (Gagen, 2004). This desire to physically contain children was a result of social and moral reformers' desires to keep children away form the 'bad influences' of the street (Hart, 2002). Towards the end of the nineteenth century the approach of providing enclosed play spaces was accompanied by an overall process of specialisation of land use (Aaron and Winawer, 1965). In England the first playground came later, in 1877, with the opening of the Burberry Street Recreation Ground in Birmingham (Heseltine and Holborn, 1987). Play parks, parks, playing fields and adventure playgrounds (Allen of Hurtwood, 1968; Heseltine and Holborn, 1987; Woolley, 2008b) all took their place in the way that adults provided for and thus controlled where children should play in the outdoor environment.

This approach of adults controlling the nature of the open spaces they deem suitable for children to play in has become increasingly evident in England. For the last 40 or so years playgrounds in England have included fixed play equipment the design, style and colour of which changes to some extent, but not fundamentally. Surfacing within the space has moved away from being predominantly tarmac – on which no doubt many a reader will remember grazing their knees – to rubber synthetic surfacing which is mistakenly called 'safety surfacing'. It can quite properly be called safer surfacing, as the former name implies that no injuries, even minor ones will happen. Such surfacing was originally derived from synthetic athletic track surfaces and was, and still is, available in both tile and wet-pour form for use in playgrounds. What has changed is that in the early years it was only available in black, whereas now it is available in any colour, and so some play spaces have multicoloured surfacing, or colours representing the sea and sand of a beach. The fixed equipment and synthetic surfacing are enclosed by fencing, usually about a metre high and often with a bow top. Initially, such fencing was supposed to keep dogs out, but increasingly it appears to be to keep children in, though this time not from the 'bad influences' of the street mentioned by Hart (2002), but from the perceived social and physical dangers which adults fear (Moore, 1989). Such playgrounds therefore comprise a 'Kit' of fixed play equipment, a 'Fence', and a 'Carpet' of surfacing – referred to as KFC playgrounds (Woolley, 2007; 2008b). These open spaces also tend to be flat in topography and without contact with vegetation or other elements of nature – indeed, they can be considered to be bland open spaces. They are the ultimate of adult control of children's outdoor play environments. Yet do they allow for a range of the creative, moveable feast of child-initiated play? Observations and evidence would suggest not, although there is at this time no easily accessible research evidence to support this. There is, however, plenty of evidence that landscape elements such as landform, vegetation, water, sand and loose parts and equipment can provide many benefits and play opportunities for children (for a fuller discussion of this see Woolley, 2007; 2008b). Yet adults continue to use this physical control of the way in which play spaces are designed to preclude children from having richer play environments and experiences. The possible reasons for this have been explored elsewhere (Woolley, 2008) and include interpretation of standards and legislation (Frost, 2005), parental fear about children's safety (McNeish and Roberts, 1995; Jutras, 2003), fear of litigation from the provider's perspective (Moorcock, 1998) and fear of accidents and risk (Ball, 2004). In addition, Hendricks (2002) has suggested that there is not enough design competence, designing for children has little prestige, society does not prioritise good quality space for children, children have no political power, and adults are too busy dealing with their own issues. Tim Gill (2008: 27–8), formerly Director of the Children's Play Council, has stated that the design approach of some providers

> has in turn largely been driven by the concerns of providers to minimise three elements: capital cost, the risk of liability and the costs of ongoing management and maintenance. There has been little regard for what children and young people need or value in a playful space.

Do relevant policies facilitate respect of children and young people in public open spaces?

In order that children and young people can be supported to develop their citizenship it has been suggested that they need to have trust in the city and that this, in turn, involves having trust in the street, trust in peers, trust in parents, trust in strangers and trust in traffic (Woolley et al, 2001). Such trust could be seen as an understanding of respect, which has been described as resulting in successful collaboration, which is responsive to other people (Sennett, 2003). So how can trust and respect happen in public open spaces, for children and young people? The approaches to skateboarders and children who use playgrounds, which have been discussed above, clearly exhibit ways in which adults are not trusting and respecting children and young people. Quite the opposite: adults are controlling children's and young people's use of public open space by use of social, legal and physical means. Such controls do not appear to be negotiated with the young people in a respectful manner, as Sennett (2003) suggests that respect can be. Instead, these controls seem to be imposed on the young people without discussion with them, or even an explanation as to why certain controls are introduced and implemented. Some have commented that the politics of Respect are not promoting inclusion (for example Stephen, 2008). The treatment of children and young people in the ways outlined in this chapter are one expression of such exclusion. Others might understand this control of children and young people in open spaces as part of a 'return of state agencies as governors of social control' (Flint, 2002: 246).

Yet there are ways in which children's and young people's presence in public open spaces can be treated with respect. It has been identified that there is a range of policies in place which could help to support children's and young people's use of open spaces in the built environment (Woolley, 2006) in a constructive and positive way. These include, to name a few, policies about housing and home zones, travelling to school, Sure Start and children's centres, health, open spaces and, increasingly, play. But policy needs to be expressed in practice in order to make it come to life, and it needs to be expressed, as far as children and young people are concerned, in a manner which demonstrates respect.

One way, and only one way, in which policy is sometimes supported by government is in funding programmes, and this is very relevant for the subject of children's and young people's play. In recent years play has been not only on the policy agenda but also on the funding agenda, with a series of national announcements. Thus, following a government review as to how money might be spent (DCMS, 2004), the BIG Lottery fund allocated £155 million 'to improve more children's lives through play' (BIG Lottery website). Some of this money has funded Play England for a period of five years and is providing funds for play-workers and both indoor and outdoor play facilities. More recently the government launched its 10-year *Children's Plan* in December 2007. This included the announcement that the government will spend £225 million, increasing to £235 million in April 2008, over a period of three years to provide local authorities with capital to rebuild or renew 3,500 playgrounds across the country, together with the creation of 30 new adventure playgrounds (DCSF, 2007).

Thus, trying to provide for children of all ages within the urban framework is on the government's agenda, now confirmed by the 10-year *Children's Plan*. However, just because policy is in place, and supported by some initial funding at a national level, there is no guarantee that the outputs in practice at a local level will be different from what has been provided for the last 40 years, nor that the change in attitudes which is required to facilitate the provision of change in practice will occur. Only time will tell whether skateboarders will be allowed to use spaces they find affordance in, rather than being confined to skate parks. Similarly in 10, possibly even 5, years' time we will know whether the social imperative to enclose children in 'KFC' playgrounds has become more enlightened, providing more playful landscapes with access to 'natural' elements supporting play opportunities.

Instead of primarily seeing children and young people as needing control by social, legal and physical means (thus disrespecting them), might adults decide that children and young people should be provided for in a more meaningful way in public open space, with children and young people themselves often involved in the process of providing opportunities? Will the tables be turned and social, legal and physical *respect* be shown to children and young people, rather than their use of public open spaces being increasingly controlled by adults?

Notes

[1] Adults, no doubt, also take part in play in open spaces, sometimes in the form of sports such as football or bowls; but adult play in open spaces is not the focus of this discussion – nor is a debate about the difference between play and games.

[2] Other groups with a similar interest and use of public open spaces include BMX-riders and those practising *Parcour*, otherwise known as 'free runners' (for example Millie, 2008).

References

Aaron, D. and Winawer, B. (1965) *Child's Play*, New York and London: Harper and Row.

Allen of Hurtwood, Lady (1968) *Planning for Play*, London: Thames and Hudson.

Ball, D.J. (2004) 'Policy issues and risk-benefit trade-offs of "safer surfacing" for children's playgrounds', *Accident Analysis and Prevention*, 36(4), 661–70.

Barber, A. (2005) *Green Future: A Study of the Management of Multifunctional Urban Green Spaces in England*, Reading: GreenSpace.

Beal, B. (1995) 'Disqualifying the official: an exploration of social resistance through the subculture of skateboarding', *Sociology of Sport Journal*, 12(3), 252–67.

Bishop, J. and Curtis, M. (eds) (2001) *Play Today in the Primary School Playground*, Buckingham: Open University Press.

Borden, I. (2001) *Skateboarding, Space and the City: Architecture and the Body*, London: Berg.

British Medical Association (2006) *Child and Adolescent Mental Health: A Guide for Healthcare Professionals*, London: BMA Board of Science.

Carr, S., Francis, M., Rivlin, R. and Stone, A. (1992) *Public Space*, Cambridge: Cambridge University Press.

Chief Secretary to the Treasury (2003) *Every Child Matters*, Cm 5860, London: HMSO.

Children's Play Council (1998) *New Charter for Children's Play*, London: Children's Society.

Cranz, G. (1982) *The Politics of Park Design: A History of Urban Parks in America*, London: MIT Press.

DCMS (Department of Culture, Media and Sport) (2004) *Getting Serious About Play*, London: Department of Culture, Media and Sport.

DCSF (Department for Children, Schools and Families) (2007) *The Children's Plan: Building Brighter Futures*, London: Department for Children, Schools and Families.

DETR (Department for Environment, Transport and the Regions) (1997) *A New Deal for Transport: Better for Everyone – The Government's White Paper on the Future of Transport*, London: The Stationery Office.

Dunnett, N., Swanwick, C. and Woolley, H. (2002) *Improving Urban Parks, Play Areas and Green Spaces*, London: Office of the Deputy Prime Minister.

Eckbo, G. (1969) *The Landscape that We See*, New York, NY: McGraw-Hill.

Eibl-Eibesfeldt, I. (1970) *Ethology, the Biology of Behaviour*, New York, NY: Holt, Rinehart and Winston.

Flint, J. (2002) 'Return of the governors: citizenship and the new governance of neighbourhood disorder in the UK', *Citizenship Studies*, 6(3), 245–64.

Flusty, S. (2002) 'Trashing downtown: play as resistance to the spatial and representational regulation of Los Angeles', in M. Dear and S. Flusty (eds) *The Spaces of Post Modernity: Readings in Human Geography*, Oxford: Blackwell, pp 334–46.

Frost, J.L. (1992) *Play and Playscapes*, Albany, NY: Delmar Publishers Incorporated.

Frost, J.L. (2005) 'How playground regulations and standards are messing up children's play', *Today's Playground*, 5(7), 14–19.

Frost, J.L. (2006) *The Dissolution of Children's Outdoor Play: Courses and Consequences*, copyright Joe Frost 11 May 2006.

Gagen, E.A. (2004) 'Making America flesh: physicality and nationhood in turn-of-the-century New York schools', *Cultural Geographies*, 11(4), 417–42.

Gibson, J.J. (1986) *The Ecological Approach to Visual Perception*, Mahwah, NJ: Lawrence Erlbaum Associates.

Gill, T. (2008) *Supplementary Planning Guidance: Providing for Children and Young People's Play and Informal Recreation*, London: Greater London Authority.

Gold, S.M. (1980) *Recreation Planning and Development*, New York, NY: McGraw-Hill.

Hart, R. (2002) 'Containing children: some lessons on planning for play from New York City', *Environment and Urbanization*, 14(2), 135–48.

Hendricks, B.E. (2002) *Designing for Play*, Aldershot: Ashgate.

Heseltine, P. and Holborn, J. (1987) *Playgrounds: The Planning, Design and Construction of Play Environments*, London: Mitchell.

Hughes, B. (1996) *A Playworker's Taxonomy of Play Types*, London: PLAYLINK.

ILAM (Institute of Leisure and Amenity Management) (1996) *Policy Position Statement No 15, Nature Conservation and Urban Green Space*, Reading: ILAM.

Jutras, S. (2003) 'Go outside and play! Contributions of an urban environment to the developing and wellbeing of children', *Psychologie Canadienne*, 44(3), 257–66.

Karsten, L. and Pel, E. (2000) 'Skateboarders exploring urban public space: Ollies, obstacles and conflicts', *Journal of Housing and the Built Environment*, 15(4), 327–40.

Llewelyn-Davies Planning (1992) *Open Spaces Planning in London*, London: London Planning Advisory Committee.

Lynch, K. (1981) *A Theory of Good City Form*, Cambridge MA: MIT Press.

McNeish, D. and Roberts, H. (1995) *Playing it Safe: Today's Children at Play*, London: Barnardo's.

Madanipour, A. (1999) 'Why are the design and development of public spaces significant for cities?' *Environment and Planning B: Planning and Design*, 26(6), 870–91.

Madanipour, A. (2003) *Public and Private Spaces of the City*, London and New York: Routledge.

Mean, M. and Tims, C. (2005) *People Make Places: Growing the Public Life of Cities*, London: Demos, supported by the Joseph Rowntree Foundation.

Millie, A. (2008) *Anti-social Behaviour*, Maidenhead: Open University Press.

Moorcock, K. (1998) *Swings and Roundabouts: The Danger of Safety in Outside Play Environments*, Sheffield: Sheffield Hallam University Press.

Moore, R. (1989) 'Playgrounds at the crossroads', in I. Altman and E. Zube (eds) (1989) *Public Places and Spaces* (Human Behaviour and Environment 10), New York, NY: Plenum, pp 83–120.

Morgan, G. (1991) *A Strategic Approach to the Planning and Management of Parks and Open Spaces*, Reading: ILAM.

Moyles, J. (1989) *Just Playing: The Role and Status of Play in Early Childhood Education*, Maidenhead: Open University Press.

National Statistics and Department for Transport (2003) *Travel to School: Personal Travel Factsheet*, London: National Statistics and Department for Transport. Available at: www.dft/pgr/statistics. [Accessed 6 May 2008.]

National Statistics and Department for Transport (2008) *Travel to School: Personal Travel Factsheet*, London: National Statistics and Department for Transport. Available at: www.dft/pgr/statistics. [Accessed 6 May 2008.]

NPFA (National Playing Fields Association) (2000) *Best Play: What Play Provision Should Do for Children*, London: National Playing Fields Association, Children's Play Council and PLAYLINK.

Nemeth, J. (2006) 'Conflict, exclusion, relocation: skateboarding and public space', *Journal of Urban Design*, 11(3), 297–318.

Noschis, K. (1992) 'Child development theory and planning for neighbourhood play', *Children's Environments*, 9(2), 3–9.

Oc, T. and Tiesdell, S. (1997) *Safer City Centres: Reviving the Public Realm*, London: Paul Chapman Publishing.

ODPM (2002) *Planning Policy Guidance 17: Planning for Open Space, Sport and Recreation*, London: Office of the Deputy Prime Minister.

Opie, I. and Opie, P. (1969) *Children's Games in Street and Playground: Chasing, Catching, Seeking, Hunting, Racing, Duelling, Exerting, Daring, Guessing, Acting, Pretending*, Oxford: Clarenden Press.

Pelligrini, A.D. and Blatchford, P. (1993) 'Time for a break', *The Psychologist*, 63, 51–67.

Play England (2007) *Charter for Children's Play*, London: Play England.

Prout, A. and James, A. (1997) *Constructing and Reconstructing Childhood: Contemporary Issues in the Sociological Study of Childhood*, London: Routledge.

Sennett, R. (2003) *Respect: The Formation of Character in an Age of Inequality*, London: Penguin Books Limited.

Shonfield, K. (1998) 'The richness of cities: urban policy in a new landscape', *Working Paper 8: At Home with Strangers: Public Space and the New Urbanity*, London: Comedia with Demos.

Stephen, D.E. (2008) 'The responsibility of respecting justice: an open challenge to Tony Blair's successors', in P. Squires (ed) *ASBO Nation: The Criminalisation of Nuisance*, Bristol: The Policy Press, pp 319–35.

Sutton-Smith, B. (1997) *The Ambiguity of Play*, Cambridge, MA: Harvard University Press.

Tankel, S. (1963) 'The importance of open spaces in urban pattern', in L. Wing (ed) *Cities and Spaces: The Future Use of Urban Spaces*, Baltimore: Hopkins.

Thompson, H. (2003) 'Be a pedestrian ... or be a skateboarder', *Sheffield Online Papers in Social Research (SHOP)*, special edition on skateboarding, July. Available at: www.shef.ac.uk/socstudies/Shop. [Accessed 22 April 2008.]

Walzer, M. (1986) 'Public space: pleasures and costs of urbanity', *Dissent*, 33(4), 470–5.

Woolley, H. (2003a) *Urban Open Spaces*, London: Spon Press.

Woolley, H. (2003b) 'Excluded from streets and spaces?', *Sheffield Online Papers in Social Research (SHOP)*, Special edition on skateboarding, July. Available at: www.shef.ac.uk/socstudies/Shop. [Accessed 22 April 2008.]

Woolley, H. (2006) 'Freedom of the city: contemporary issues and policy influences on children and young people's use of public open spaces in England', *Children's Geographies*, 4(1), 45–59.

Woolley, H. (2007) 'Where do the children play? How policies can influence practice', *Municipal Engineer*, 160(ME2), 89–95.

Woolley, H. (2008a) 'Adult control of children's play environments', Paper for IAPS Conference 'Urban Diversities, Biosphere and Well-being: Designing and Managing out Common Environment', Rome, August.

Woolley, H. (2008b) 'Watch this space: designing for children's play in public open spaces', *Geography Compass*, 2(2), 495–512.

Woolley, H. and Johns, R. (2001) 'Skateboarding: the city as a playground', *Journal of Urban Design*, 6(2), 211–30.

Woolley, H., Gathorne-Hardy, F. and Stringfellow, S. (2001) 'The listening game', in C. Jefferson, J. Rowe and C. Brebbia (eds) *The Sustainable Street*, Southampton: WIT Press, pp 109–32.

Woolley, H., Armitage, M., Bishop, J., Curtis, M. and Ginsborg, J. (2005) *Inclusion of Disabled Children in Primary School Playgrounds*, London: National Children's Bureau and Joseph Rowntree Foundation.

Woolley, H., Dunn, J., Spencer, C., Short, T. and Rowley, G. (1999) 'Children describe their experiences of the city centre: a qualitative study of the fears and concerns which may limit their full participation', *Landscape Research*, 24(3), 287–301.

Worpole, K. and Greenhalgh, L. (1995) *Park Life: Urban Parks and Social Renewal*, London: Comedia and Demos.

Part Three
Respectful families and communities

FIVE

Disciplining women: anti-social behaviour and the governance of conduct

Judy Nixon and Caroline Hunter

Introduction

Our interest in women and anti-social behaviour stems from a long-standing research partnership. As sociolegal scholars, we have sought to combine our focus on legal instruments and on the processes of governance. Towards the end of the 1990s we published a report detailing social landlords' responses to the growing problem of anti-social behaviour (ASB) (Hunter et al, 1999). As part of this study we analysed data from a sample of 67 nuisance case files drawn from 10 case study landlords, which we subsequently combined with scrutiny of reported Court of Appeal ASB cases. The findings provided a stark indication of the way in which ASB was emerging as a gendered issue; over half the sample of landlord cases involved women heads of households, the majority of whom were single parents; the Court of Appeal cases showed a similar bias. Critically, in both sets of data, in two out of three cases, the complaints focused not on the woman's behaviour but rather on her inability to control the behaviour of teenage (mostly male) children and/or the violent and disruptive behaviour of male partners (Hunter and Nixon, 2001). Since this work was published, the issue of ASB has continued to attract widespread media and political interest, but there has been a marked silence on the disproportionate use of technologies to control behaviour of women-headed households. It is our intention in this chapter to focus attention once again on the compelling evidence that suggests that ASB is indeed a gendered issue.

Policy discourses on ASB reflect notions of self-regulation, active citizenship and communitarian-informed rights and responsibilities. It is also apparent that within such discourses – as exemplified by the government's Respect campaign – the family is located as an important site of control, with a focus on individual deficiencies associated with dysfunctional families and bad parenting (see for example Youth Taskforce, 2008, ch 3). While gender plays a pivotal role and is implicit in such discourses, scant attention has been paid by either policy makers or academic commentators to the impact of disciplining interventions on women. In trying to make visible the hidden within these ASB discourses, we draw on two key sources of data collected by us over the period 2004–07.

First, we present findings from a three-year evaluation of six Family Intervention Projects (FIPs) which were established in 2003 to provide services to families who were under threat of homelessness as a result of complaints of anti-social behaviour (Nixon et al, 2006; Nixon and Parr, 2006; 2008; Parr and Nixon, 2008). The FIPs included in the study were pioneering a 'new' form of ASB intervention which involved providing families at risk of eviction with intensive support to help them address behavioural and other problems. In addition to the provision of outreach support in order to help families maintain their existing tenancy, a small number of families were moved into core residential accommodation where they were required to adhere to strict rules and regulations and were subject to daily supervision and observation. Over the course of the evaluation quantitative and qualitative data were collected in relation to 256 families living in disparate geographical locations in the north of England. The study represents one of the first large-scale pieces of work to explore the lived realities of anti-social behaviour from the perspective of alleged 'perpetrators' (see also Dillane et al, 2001; Stephen and Squires, 2004; Squires and Stephen, 2005; Jones et al, 2006). The research findings are fascinating and highlight the contradictory and contested ways in which ASB is gendered. It is a site where women are simultaneously characterised as victims and villains, responsible adults and dysfunctional parents, active citizens and outsiders, subjects and objects of abuse.

Second, we contrast the discourses of the women in the FIPs with those of the (almost always male) judges of the Court of Appeal when considering cases involving anti-social behaviour. The cases are those where possession was the primary application of the landlord and which went to a full hearing. The analysis identified all those cases appealed in the period from 2001–07 (thus updating our earlier analysis, which covered the period 1996–2000 (Hunter and Nixon, 2001)). Fourteen cases were included in the current analysis, of which seven involved tenancies where the woman was the sole tenant and had dependent children. This did not necessarily mean that there was no adult male involved – in two of the cases a male partner was living at the premises (at least at the time of the alleged ASB, if not in one case at the time of the possession proceedings), and in one it was not clear whether the partner lived at the property as opposed to just visiting it. But in each of these three cases it was the woman tenant who risked losing her home with her children, and in each case the behaviour complained of included that of the male partner. It is striking that it was only in the cases where there was no male partner that it was solely the behaviour of the women's children that formed the basis of the complaints.

The chapter is divided into three sections. The first section provides a summary of the framework for analysis that has been used. Here attention is drawn to the locales of conflict, in which the public and private spheres are clearly interconnected. Policy interventions which stress the importance of self-regulation and responsible citizenship are saturated with a normalising moral discourse. Unpicking this discourse reveals that the frequent calls for increased 'parental responsibility' are underpinned by a clearly gendered rhetoric in which mothers rather than fathers are held to be primarily responsible for the conduct of their children. In the second section we turn to an examination of the lived material realities of ASB, as evidenced by the experiences of lone-parent women who are referred to Family Intervention Projects. The third section focuses on recent Court of Appeal ASB judgments, highlighting the ways in which judgments have been informed by the use of moralising binary divides to apportion culpability. The chapter concludes with a number of observations on the contradictions inherent in the formation of women as gendered welfare subjects, which in turn emphasises the need for the development of a more finely nuanced gendered analysis in this under-theorised field.

The role of the state in the gendering of ASB

A number of researchers have sought to understand and articulate the social and political consequences of discursive practices in relation to the control of conduct (Papps, 1998; Hastings, 1999; 2000; Jacobs et al, 2003; Squires and Stephen, 2005; Flint, 2006; Nixon and Parr, 2006; Prior, 2007). One of the dominant features of ASB discourses is the ubiquitous call for increased self-regulation, reinforced by the use of a demonising rhetoric about those who fail to regulate their behaviour in line with normalised standards. The use of binary divides serves as a form of cultural essentialism or 'othering' in which the 'anti-social' are clearly distinguished from the self-regulating 'decent majority'. Young (2007) identifies two distinct modes of 'othering'. One is a relatively straightforward conservative version whereby negative attributes are projected onto the other, with difference manifested as a perversion, or a pathological fault. At the same time Young recognises the recent development of a more nuanced, liberal form of 'othering' in which deficits are explained in terms of the negative impacts of 'deprivations of material or cultural circumstance or capital'. While these two modes of cultural essentialism are linked to different political rationalities they share a distinctive feature in that the subjects of 'othering' are always constituted as a 'homogeneous residuum underclass whose actual experiences are rendered invisible' (Young, 2007: 5). The effect is to create an effective divide in which the voices of those deemed to constitute the underclass are silenced. The lack of voice given to those labelled as 'anti-social' (or 'disrespectful') illustrates Young's point. It is a site in which gender plays a pivotal role and yet remains a hidden facet of the construction of the problem, revealed only in the return to Victorian notions that a 'violent' husband or 'anti-social' child is the result of poor mothering (Carr, 2006). Equally, there is no acknowledgement of the incoherence and complexity that typifies the enactment of community safety and ASB/'respect' policies on the ground – for example, people can be simultaneously both 'victims' and 'perpetrators' of anti-social acts (Stephen and Squires, 2004; Jones et al, 2006; Nixon and Parr, 2006).

In the wider context of ASB policy discourses which vilify particular segments of the population, it is striking that a majority of families defined as anti-social are headed by single mothers. The empirical evidence clearly illustrates how women-headed households have become the target group for disciplining technologies such as FIPs. For example, in our study, just over two-thirds (68%) of families working with FIPs, most of them containing three or more children, were headed by lone-parent women. This finding reflects a very consistent pattern confirmed by other evaluations of intensive support interventions (see, for example, Dillane et al, 2001; Jones et al, 2006; Parr, 2007; 2008), although, as with broader policy issues regarding parenting, the policy language obscures this through the use of gender-neutral terminology (Gillies, 2005; Lister, 2006). Recognition of the gendered nature of ASB raises interesting questions as to how responsibility and culpability are apportioned and the ways in which the construction of the problem informs the choice of intervention. In order to begin to address these issues we turn briefly to the wider role of the family.

Feminist analysis has long established the pivotal role of the family as a site both of welfare consumption and of production (Barrett and McIntosh, 1982). As an institutional basis of welfare, the ideal family form – namely that of two married parents with children – has been privileged to the detriment of alternative forms of living arrangement. In particular, families headed by lone-parent women have been the focus of a demonising discourse, with the lone-parent woman constructed as being 'feckless and wilfully responsible for the poverty in which she is confined to live and thus undeserving of either public sympathy or economic support' (Phoenix, 1996: 175). Phoenix argues that such pervasive discourses serve as justification for punitive policies, which are rationalised as necessary for the deterrence of others. Thus, negative discourses of lone mothers can be seen to constitute a 'regime of truth' (Foucault, 1991) in which lone-parent motherhood is defined as a deviant family form. This is exemplified in the work of Carr (2007), when considering two Court of Appeal decisions on ASB. She concludes that 'A woman alone with children is not sufficient for the court. Her resistance to conventional family structures cannot be tolerated' (Carr, 2007: 130).

The extension of controls into the private sphere

Since the early 1980s feminist researchers have been highly critical of the constructed dichotomy between the public sphere of citizenship and the private spheres of family and personal relations (Lister, 2000). The feminist project of re-gendering issues deemed to be private into legitimate concerns of public policy is well illustrated by reference to domestic violence, which has been transformed from a hidden, private matter to one that is a legitimate concern for a wide range of welfare agencies. Anti-social behaviour has also been constructed as a problem which bridges the public and private divide (Walklate, 2002), but with very different consequences. Here, rather than focusing attention on very real material deprivations and structural constraints underlying troublesome behaviour, the 'anti-social' are presented as threatening the wider community, thus legitimising the introduction of punitive interventions to control behaviour in private as well as in public spaces. For example, the terms of many Anti-Social Behaviour Orders (ASBOs) prohibit association with named individuals, criminalise everyday behaviour and exclude individuals from their family home and surrounding area (Burney, 2005).

Two further themes can be seen to underpin legislation to control behaviour in the private and public spheres: the twin concepts of 'parental responsibility' and the move from 'private to public patriarchy'. Across a range of policy fields the active promotion of parental responsibility by successive neoliberal governments has been highlighted as a prerequisite for the creation of a suitable moral climate in which the introduction of disciplining technologies can be justified (Gillies, 2005; Fox-Harding, 1996). Eekelaar (1991) points out how the principles of 'responsiblisation', noted by Garland (2001) and others in relation to responses to the 'crime control complex' of late modernity, are equally evident in moves to promote parental responsibility as being pre-eminently an individual responsibility, thus absolving the state from a wider duty of care. At the same time Walby (1990) notes a movement away from private patriarchy, in which the individual man controls women and excludes them from public spheres, to public patriarchy, in which the state assumes the mantle of protecting the public interest by enforcing sexual controls in the public sphere. Thus, she argues, as women have struggled to escape from private patriarchy and have become more active in the labour force their *exclusion from the state* has been replaced by their *subordination to the state*, which is of itself essentially patriarchal. This process is particularly evident in relation to lone mothers:

> While they lose their own individual patriarch, they do not lose their subordination to other patriarchal structures and practices. Indeed they become even more exposed to certain of the more diffused public sets of patriarchal practices. (Walby, 1990: 197)

The shift from private to public patriarchy is, we believe, critical to understanding state responses to ASB, where responsibility and culpability are implicitly or explicitly gendered, and is one which is well illustrated by reference to the role of the court. Carr and Cowan (2006) point out how, in ASB cases, there is a clear mapping of the spaces of deviance and agents of deviance, as well as the security fears of others residents. Drawing on Valverde (2003), they describe this as 'ventriloquizing the national community'. Part of the ventriloquism, we suggest, is of public patriarchy.

On the other hand, others have noted how women may sometimes be privileged in welfare systems. They may be treated more leniently, as they are seen as more deserving of assistance from the state. For example, Cramer (2005) identifies how local authority homelessness officers treat homeless women as a special group, tending to favour them. They are treated as more deserving because they are closer to the 'moral community of housing officers', more likely to be the sole carers of children, seeking to maintain a stable family life. Likewise Pilcher (1999), examining the criminal justice system, where women were constructed as being vulnerable, passive, unassertive and remorseful, found they were more likely to be treated leniently. The down side of such constructions of women is that those who do not conform to these constructions – who do not perform their gender correctly (Butler, 1990) – are more likely to be treated harshly. As Cramer puts it (2005: 745), 'for a claimant to behave outside gender norms, was to potentially jeopardise claims to homelessness'.

In the remaining sections of the chapter we explore the contradictory, multilayered reality of ASB, focusing on two key themes which emerged both from women's accounts of why they had been referred to Family Intervention Projects and from the Court of Appeal judgments:

- women as victims, both inside and outside the home
- resistance and the role of remorse.

The lived material realities of ASB

As outlined earlier in the chapter, although within the official ASB discourse there is a clear emphasis on dysfunctional families and bad parenting, the discourse is silent on the gendered nature of the construction of the problem and little account is taken of the stark, lived material realities of ASB. The problem is never put in a social context or conceptualised as a manifestation of outcomes generated by wider economic, social and political forces (Gillies, 2005; Lister, 2006). As women told us their stories it was clear that they resisted and contested the dominant demonising analysis apparent within official discourses, where morally deficient families are attributed causal primacy in explaining the behaviour of young people.

Women as victims inside and outside the home

In listening to women we were struck by the complexity and contradictions inherent in their accounts. While families were reported as being the subject of numerous and sometimes very serious complaints of ASB, they also reported that they had been exposed to very high levels of victimisation and retaliation. Further, the evidence suggests that those who are constructed as the object of technologies to control behaviour are also vulnerable to becoming the subjects of family violence, and it is to the issue of violence within the home that we now turn.

Family violence was found to be prevalent among families referred to FIPs. In just under half (47%) of families women either were suffering from a history of, or were currently subject to, intimate partner violence and/or intergenerational violence involving physical, mental or sexual abuse. In some instances there had been a long history of violence within the family, involving children as well:

> Q: 'Were the kids causing any trouble or …?'

> A: 'It's not the kids that are causing trouble, it's their dad that causes trouble because he loses it. And he's had tendency to sock 'em. And hit 'em…. Now I'm one that's always said, if anything happens, then tell the Social Services. Tell your teachers at school and they'll get in contact with Social Services…. I was sexually abused when I were little, I was raped when I was 17.'

As well as the direct impacts on health and well-being, domestic violence is closely associated with alcohol misuse and can impact on neighbour relations in a number of ways, resulting in complaints of noise nuisance and disorderly behaviour, as one woman explained:

> 'Yeah he was coming a lot of time, I mean, it wasn't fair on the neighbours. It really wasn't. If he wasn't drunk, he wouldn't come anywhere near and as soon as he's drunk he was putting me windows through, me front door, banging the door, shouting, screaming. It wasn't fair, it was anti-social behaviour, it wasn't fair on me but I wasn't causing it, he was actually coming and I was asking him to go away. I must have called the police from last Christmas to New Year seventeen times.'

The issue of intergenerational violence between teenage sons and their mothers was also raised by a number of lone mothers. The language used to describe this type of violent conflict tended to be hesitant, with the issue raised in an 'off-hand' way, as if it was of no real importance; for instance, as one mother stated, 'I was having a lot of trouble with my children and like my son was hitting me – and mental abuse'. Lone-parent women in particular reported finding it hard to access help to deal with the violence, as one mother explained:

> 'It was like when I first phoned up Social Services, I said to them "it's going to be him [her son] or me" because he had a knife up at me at one point, just it's going to be a case of him or me, that's how it was going next with things getting

that bad and he was that violent towards me ... but even then ... they [Social Services] didn't want to know.'

Such reports are reminiscent of responses to domestic violence prior to the 1970s (Dobash and Dobash, 1979), and they caused us to reflect on why, 40 years later, women continue to experience such difficulty in accessing support to deal with violence in the home. One possible explanation is that, once families are labelled as 'anti-social', the disciplinary gaze effectively prevents the development of a more subtle and nuanced understanding. For example, scrutiny of individual families' project case records revealed that references to family violence were presented as secondary, peripheral issues, with little causal primacy attributed to the impact of violence *within* the family on behaviour *outside* the family home.

Examination of the lived experiences of ASB reflects the ways in which women were also vulnerable to becoming victims outside the home. For example, in our study we found that, in addition to being 'perpetrators' of ASB, in 60% of families one or more members of the household were also victims of ASB. Many women reported that they had been subjected to repeat attacks and other forms of victimisation, and had made complaints to either the police, housing and/or local councillors about the behaviour of their neighbours.

'Well I'd say that were anti-social what they all used to do, chucking mud at the windows and everything like that, do you know, I thought that were anti-social behaviour. Kicking all the door in, setting on fire the front door, do you know what I mean? I said "Listen I, I, we are the victims, not them." They could say they are the victims because I told them to "fff" down the path, do you know what I mean? And cos I'd done that and told them to stay away they didn't like it, so they were retaliated that way so then that meant we ended up being the victims.'

Frequently women felt powerless to prevent the anti-social behaviour, and often took avoidance action rather than confront the 'perpetrators' about their behaviour:

'I have been a victim, yeah. At the beginning, when I first moved in there I had, because I were having a lot of trouble about the balls banging against this garage and I kept going out. And they were like 16-, 17-year-old lads these, there were about 18, 19 of these hanging around on the street, just where I lived ... I had spray paint on me door, things being put through me letterbox, all me washing pulled off me line, all ripped.... Yeah. I were on antidepressants and everything from doctor. Put everything in [to the landlord] and said "Look I need a move" and that. [The landlord] weren't interested. Never, so I just kept me gob shut, let them carry on doing what they're doing, just kept the kids in.'

For a small number of interviewees, the alleged anti-social behaviour they had endured was serious in nature and included racial harassment and threats of violence, and had resulted in families being rehoused. The severity of the behaviour had contributed to health problems among family members. One woman, a single mother with three sons, all subject to ASBOs and all of whom had been the subject of local publicity campaigns, described how the local community had undertaken a course of harassment against her family in order to force them from their home. The police believed that the family was indeed at considerable risk of harm and recommended that the family be rehoused, which it subsequently was:

'We had the curtains closed 24 hours a day. We didn't go outside. If we had to go shopping, doctor's surgery, it was always in a taxi, cos we always got, you know, people calling us, racial harassment names and stuff. So, so I ended up seeing a counsellor, cos I can't sleep you know, at nights, and stuff.'

The issue of victimisation led some interviewees to consider that complaints of ASB were a product of personal vendettas or intolerant neighbours. This resulted in people feeling that they were the ones who were being harassed, not the complainants, but their views were not taken seriously. The experience of not being heard was directly related to being labelled 'anti-social' and it was strongly felt by many families that, once labelled, no one would be prepared to hear their side of the story. These experiences left many women feeling further marginalised and powerless to defend themselves against the damaging consequences of the demonisation process. These families did not fall within the conventional frame of victimhood as constructed within policy responses to community safety (see further Walklate's (2006) useful discussion of who is the victim within community safety discourses).

Resistance and remorse

Issues of powerlessness and lack of control featured strongly in women's accounts of why they had been referred to FIPs. Nonetheless, women were also resistant to the label being put on them, which they found to be 'humiliating', 'upsetting' and 'embarrassing'. Stephen and Squires' work on contemporary constructs of marginalised youth illustrates the way in which judgements about appropriate behaviour are commonly made by reference to perceived norms of behaviour in a neighbourhood (Stephen and Squires, 2004). We also found that people assessed the severity of behaviour by reference to relative norms. Women were aware of the binary oppositions that are employed to distinguish the 'anti-social' from the 'responsible' neighbour and were anxious to affirm that they and their children conformed to norms of conduct, making clear distinctions between their own behaviour and their constructions of behaviour which could legitimately be described as anti-social:

> 'What I say's anti-social is like, say if like, a neighbour, neighbours have got disputes, so that you're going onto their property shouting, screaming, banging doors, causing trouble and things like that.... If you are playing music really loud and things like that, fair enough, that is anti-social behaviour. But I know for a fact I don't do that. I won't expect someone to do it to me, so I don't do it to them. I expect to be treated the way I treat people. I always have, I were brought up like that.'

> 'I know they are no angels, I know that for a fact but like there's kids round here, really, really naughty kids that have got ASBOs against them. I know they have and then, when we went to that meeting and they threatened them with an ASBO, I thought God you're putting my kids in the same category as that, they are nowhere near as bad as that, nowhere near.'

Further evidence of resistance was apparent in discussions about the extent to which women felt that the complaints that had been made against them were justified. Many disputed the legitimacy of either all or at least some of the claims being made. Typically, it was held that the behaviour being complained about did not happen, was exaggerated, or was simply behaviour that is common to many families. Particularly where the alleged behaviour involved children, mothers felt that the complaints were largely a result of personal vendettas or a lack of tolerance of the natural tendency for young people to challenge boundaries. These perceptions engendered a strong sense of unfairness and it was common for women to describe feelings of being victimised, and confused as to why they had been singled out as the target of complaints, as Teresa, a mother of three teenage children explained:

'They're good kids. They've never been in trouble with the police ever. They do know right from wrong but I think when they are out with their friends they try and show off a bit, but they are just normal kids and they're not, they're not really bad. I know they are not angels, no kids are but they're not as bad as half of them round here and I can't understand why it's us. I really can't.'

As women told us their stories it was clear that narratives of struggle were interwoven with examples of resistance and personal agency. A common theme emerging from interviews was the need to stay strong in the face of numerous adversities, as one woman with six children explained:

'When it's all going on and like when you're actually stood there and you're in shock and you're panicking because nobody believes you.... I've got six kids. I can't afford to like breakdown or anything else and then the kids are going to get took off me, so I just have to stay strong.'

The neighbourhoods in which women were living were typically among the poorest in the country, with high levels of unemployment, deprivation and social exclusion. Ongoing concerns about personal safety dominated women's accounts of their lives. In seeking to protect themselves and their children, many women disputed the allegations made by neighbours and felt they had been unfairly targeted and singled out for intervention. Such responses sit uneasily with the requirement that, in order to protect themselves and their children from eviction, women are required to exhibit remorse, and it is to this issue that we now turn.

The court realities of anti-social behaviour

In the Court of Appeal judgments there are a number of striking counterpoints to the analysis of the discourses of the women. As in the preceding section, first we consider how women are constructed as victims and then we move on to explore how far women can resist being labelled as anti-social.

Women as victims

While it is true that not all the women were portrayed as vulnerable in the judgments, this was a strong theme. Such vulnerability was relevant to their ability to control the behaviour of their children. In *Manchester CC v Higgins* [2006] HLR 14, possession was sought against a single mother with a 13-year-old son who had been subject to an ASBO for his behaviour, particularly towards an immediate neighbour. The mother is described as being depressed and having to look after a much younger child with a hole in the heart. In another case (*Knowsley HT v McMullen* [2006] HLR 43) it was clear that the woman was not in a position to take responsibility for the actions of her 19-year-old son, because of her low IQ, which meant that she could not read or write and had to be represented in court through a litigation friend. However, an outright order was still upheld. Here the court stated that (para [23]):

> There is no express restriction on the making of an order
> for possession ... simply because the tenant, for whatever
> reason, cannot control that other person's behaviour.

But it was not just that it was clear that some of the women could not control the behaviour of their children or partners; some too were seen to be victims. Thus, in *London & Quadrant HT v Root* [2005] HLR 28, the defendant tenant is described as a 'somewhat passive lady'. The primary behaviour complained of is that of her partner, who is the father of one of her three children. As with the women we interviewed, there is a casual and passing reference to the domestic violence she suffered from the partner (para [30]):

> this is a very bad case, although ... it was Mr Barnes who
> caused the case to be so very bad and that to some extent
> Miss Root would have been influenced by his character
> – and indeed the judge found that she had been subjected

to violence – there is a limit to which the courts can be willing to tolerate behaviour of this kind out of the kindness of their hearts to a woman and three children when their neighbours have suffered as much as they have ...

In *Higgins* the judgment starts (at para [1]) with a description of the area of Manchester in which Ms Higgins lived and in particular, the young people, in the following terms: 'When not loitering idly on street corners, young vandals damage cars, kick down fences, smash windows and are generally foul mouthed and abusive to all and sundry'. It continues that the defendant tenant says:

> she and her family have suffered such damage and such abuse. That may well be true, but what this case is about ... is the appalling misbehaviour of her 12-year-old son.

Thus the experiences of the woman are immediately dismissed, she was the one who had been labelled and whose conduct was before the court. Thus, the court experience mirrors and reinforces those described by the women we interviewed.

Like Ms Root, Ms Higgins is also described as passive: 'she has a rather non-assertive personality'. Here we see the conundrum that women defendants face in performing their gender. Unlike in some of the studies discussed above (Pilcher, 1999; Cramer, 2005), here passivity is not the appropriate way to perform their gender. Vulnerability is not a marker of deserving motherhood, but a failure. Rather, they are required to be assertive in their control of their children and partners. Yet the wrong form of assertiveness, denial, is to be punished. There is no exploration of the limits of their ability to assert control over their children or partners, or of their victimhood in any of the relationships.

Resistance and remorse

We have set out above how many women sought to resist the label put on them of being anti-social. What the court discourses show is that, unless women accept that they are responsible and wish to change (themselves, and more particularly their children), they can expect to lose their home. This requirement of responsibility emerged in our earlier analysis (Hunter and Nixon, 2001), but here it was allied in particular to the need to show remorse. Time and again the cases refer to the tenant mother needing to show remorse. Thus, in *Higgins*, where the Court of Appeal changed a suspended possession order to outright possession, the court (adding the emphasis) stated (at para [43]) that the:

> Recorder found that 'the defendant did have a *significant* personal responsibility'.... She was herself without remorse and at all time totally indifferent to the effect her children's behaviour was having on her neighbours.

Similarly, in *New Charter Housing (North) v Ashcroft* [2004] HLR 36, where the tenant's 17-year-old son had received an ASBO for property damage, harassment, threats to neighbours and attempted breaking and entering, a suspended order was changed into an outright one. The court said (at para [10]) that:

> While the defendant [mother] was aware of her need to control the behaviour of her son, the threat of the possession proceedings have not caused her to seek to modify his behaviour and neither prior to, nor in the course of, the proceedings has she expressed any desire or intention to do so.

In *Sheffield CC v Fletcher* [2007] HLR 26, the single-parent mother was seeking to set aside an order for outright possession. The complaints were primarily as to her behaviour – in particular verbal abuse of neighbours. She too failed to accept that she was in the wrong and needed to change her views (para [10]):

> The evidence which Miss Fletcher placed before [the judge] contained no expression of remorse at all. It contained nothing which gave any hope of any change in her behaviour for the future. The burden of her evidence was that the incidents complained of never took place, or if they did, they were not as serious as the Council alleged. Even now, despite the fact that Miss Fletcher has made a second witness statement ... there is still no expression of remorse, no assurances for the future.

It is striking that in none of the cases where the women did have partners was the failure to control the children ascribed to the men. It is the women who have to perform the remorse for their children's behaviour. In the one case (*Castle Vale HAT v Gallagher* (2001) 33 HLR

810), where the behaviour was of adult children rather than of children under the age of 18, is it significant that the tenant was successful in her appeal? Here the daughter and her boyfriend had been able to move out of the property. In overturning the outright possession order and replacing it with a suspended one, the court stated that a number of factors were relevant, including (para [34]):

> that Mrs Gallagher's sin is essentially one of omission, her inability or unwillingness to prevent her daughter and Christopher from causing a nuisance or a noise to others ... [T]he chances of this occurring in the future must be much reduced now that ... Sarah has a home of her own.

Could it be said that at this point her responsibility for her child was lessened by the fact that the daughter was an adult who had chosen to move out of the property?

These performances of gender by women were clearly not correct. They needed to be both assertive in their control of their children, but also remorseful for what had gone before – for their failure of parenting. In some ways, women are in double jeopardy, because they are also required to perform remorse because of their status as tenants. Thus evidence of remorse may be required of sole male tenants for their behaviour (see, for example, *Lambeth LBC v Howard* [2001] HLR 58 and *Sheffield CC v Shaw* [2007] HLR 25), but it is only the women tenants who have to be remorseful for the behaviour of others, or rather for their failure to control the behaviour of others.

What is clear is that the impulse to resistance, illustrated by the interviews with women in the project, is entirely the wrong response to any court proceedings for possession of their home. The courts ventriloquise the expectations of our society as to the role of mothers, without any consideration of the ability of those mothers living in the types of neighbourhoods described in *Higgins*.

Conclusions

While there is now a growing body of work examining technologies to control behaviour in both the private and public spheres, to date little attention has been paid to the way in which such interventions have had a disproportionate impact on women-headed households. In contrast to the highly politicised constructions of domestic violence, anti-social behaviour discourses remain largely ungendered, which facilitates a return to Victorian notions of womanhood, where the failure of women to control the behaviour of members of their families is presented as a failure of parenting and citizenship. When framed in these ways, women become the villains and are thus the legitimate targets of state intervention. Equally, while the rationalities informing Court of Appeal judgments are highly gendered, women's lack of remorse and their inability to control the behaviour of children and partners serve as the prime justification for the loss of home.

Despite the rhetoric of 'respect' promoted by the now defunct Respect Taskforce, the empirical evidence indicates just how little 'respect' is actually accorded to women subject to ASB interventions. Rather than the moralising and paternalistic discourses reflected in the government's ASB and 'respect' policies, and in Court of Appeal judgments, there is an urgent need for increased recognition of the complex material lived realities of ASB. What both ASB/'respect' policies and Court of Appeal judgments share is a construction of the problem that denies complexity. That lone-parent women can be simultaneously both 'victims' and 'villains' has not been recognised by New Labour politicians or the media who predominantly portray perpetrators of ASB in negative and demonising ways.

Scrutinising ASB discourses and interventions through a feminist lens reveals the hidden but nonetheless compelling ways in which technologies to control conduct disproportionately affect women. It is, we believe, a site worthy of greater exploration by feminist scholars, for a number of reasons. First, it illustrates the enduring interdependency between the public sphere of citizenship and the private spheres of family and personal relations. Second, it provides further evidence of the wide-ranging ways in which the family home is often a site of conflict and discord rather than security and safety. Third, an examination of the processes by which the control of conduct has emerged as a legitimate area of policy concern highlights the different ways in which concepts of culpability and responsibility are employed in relation to women. Finally, the empirical findings presented in this chapter highlight some of the enduring contradictions inherent in the formation of women as gendered welfare subjects and indicate the importance of developing more finely nuanced gendered analysis in this under-theorised field.

References

Barrett, M. and McIntosh, M. (1982) *The Anti-social Family*, London: Verso.

Burney, E. (2005) *Making People Behave: Anti-social Behaviour Politics and Policies*, Cullompton: Willan Publishing.

Butler, J. (1990) 'Gender trouble, feminist theory and psychological discourse', in L.J. Nicholson (ed) *Feminism/Postmodernism*, London: Routledge, pp 324–40.

Carr, H. (2006) 'The look of love – performance, spectators and anti-social behaviour', paper to the European Network for Housing Research Conference 2006.

Carr, H. (2007) 'Womens work: locating gender in the discourse of anti-social behaviour', in H. Lim and A. Bottomley (eds) *Feminist Perspectives on Land Law*, London: Routledge-Cavendish, pp 121–34.

Carr, H. and Cowan, D. (2006) 'Labelling: constructing definitions of anti-social behaviour', in J. Flint (ed) *Housing, Urban Governance and Anti-social Behaviour: Perspectives, Policy and Practice*, Bristol: The Policy Press, pp 57–78.

Cramer, H. (2005) 'Informal and gendered practices in a homeless persons unit', *Housing Studies*, 20(5), 737–51.

Dillane, J., Hill, M., Bannister, J. and Scott, S. (2001) *Evaluation of Dundee Families Project*, Edinburgh: Scottish Executive.

Dobash, R.E. and Dobash, R. (1979) *Violence Against Wives: A Case Against the Patriarchy*, Shepton Mallet: Open Books Publishing Ltd.

Eekelaar, J. (1991) 'Parental responsibility: state of nature or nature of the state', *Journal of Social Welfare and Family Law*, 13(1), 37–50.

Flint, J. (2006) (ed) *Housing, Urban Governance and Anti-social Behaviour: Perspectives, Policy and Practice*, Bristol: The Policy Press.

Foucault, M. (1991) 'Governmentality', in G. Birchell (ed) *The Foucault Effect: Studies in Governmentality*, Hemel Hempstead: Harvester Wheatsheaf, pp 87–104.

Fox-Harding, L. (1996) 'Parental responsibility; the reassertion of private patriarchy?' in E.B. Silva (ed) *Good Enough Mothering? Feminist Perspectives on Lone Motherhoods*, London: Routledge, pp 130–47.

Garland, D. (2001) *The Culture of Control: Crime and Social Order in Contemporary Society*, Oxford: Oxford University Press.

Gillies, V. (2005) 'Meeting parents' needs? Discourses of "support" and "inclusion" in family policy', *Critical Social Policy*, 25(1), 70–90.

Hastings, A. (1999) 'Analysing power relationships in partnerships: is there a role for discourse analysis?' *Urban Studies*, 36(1), 91–106.

Hastings, A. (2000) 'Discourse analysis: what does it offer housing studies?' *Housing Theory and Society*, 17(3), 131–9.

Hunter, C. and Nixon, J. (2001) 'Taking the blame and losing the home: women and anti-social behaviour', *Journal of Social Welfare and Family Law*, 23(4), 395–410.

Hunter, C., Nixon, J. and Shayer, S. (1999) *Neighbour Nuisance, Social Landlords and the Law*, Coventry: Chartered Institute of Housing.

Jacobs, K., Kemeny, J. and Manzi, T. (2003) 'Power, discursive space and institutional practices in the construction of housing problems', *Housing Studies*, 18(4), 429–46.

Jones, A., Pleace, N., Quilgars, D. and Sanderson, D. (2006) *Shelter Inclusion Project: Evaluation of a New Model to Address Anti-social Behaviour*, York: Centre for Housing Policy, University of York.

Lister, R. (2000) 'Gender and the analysis of social policy', in G. Lewis, S. Gewirtz and J. Clarke (eds) *Rethinking Social Policy*, London: The Open University/Sage, pp 22–36.

Lister, R. (2006) 'Children (but not women) first: New Labour, child welfare and gender', *Critical Social Policy*, 26(2), 315–35

Nixon, J. and Parr, S. (2006) 'Anti-social behaviour: voices from the front line', in J. Flint (ed) *Housing, Urban Governance and Anti-social Behaviour: Perspectives, Policy and Practice*, Bristol: The Policy Press, pp 79–98.

Nixon, J. and Parr, S. (2008) *The Longer-Term Outcomes Associated with Families who had Worked with Intensive Family Support Projects*, London: DCLG.

Nixon, J., Hunter, C., Parr, S., Whittle, S., Myers, S. and Sanderson, D. (2006) *ASB Intensive Family Support Projects: An Evaluation of 6 Pioneering Projects*, London: DCLG.

Papps, P. (1998) 'Anti-social behaviour strategies – individualistic or holistic?' *Housing Studies*, 13(5), 639–56.

Parr, S. (2007) *The Signpost Family Intervention Project: An Evaluation*, Sheffield: CRESR, Sheffield Hallam University.

Parr, S. (2008) 'Family intervention projects: a site of social work practice', *British Journal of Social Work*, Advance Access, published 29 April 2008, 1–18.

Parr, S. and Nixon, J. (2008) 'Rationalising family intervention projects', in P. Squires (ed) *ASBO Nation: The Criminalisation of Nuisance*, Bristol: The Policy Press, pp 161–77.

Phoenix, A. (1996) 'Social constructions of lone motherhood', in E.B. Silva (ed) *Good Enough Mothering? Feminist Perspectives on Lone Motherhoods*, London: Routledge, pp 175–90.

Pilcher, J. (1999) *Women and Gender: Sociological Perspectives*, London: Routledge.

Prior, D. (2007) *Continuities and Discontinuities in Governing Anti-social Behaviour*, Birmingham: Institute of Applied Social Studies, University of Birmingham.

Squires, P. and Stephen, D. (2005) *Rougher Justice: Anti-social Behaviour and Young People*, Cullompton: Willan Publishing.

Stephen, D. and Squires, P. (2004) 'They are still children and entitled to be children: problematising the institutionalised mistrust of the marginalised youth in Britain', *Journal of Youth Studies*, 7(3), 351–69.

Valverde, M. (2003) *Law's Dream of a Common Knowledge*, Princeton, NJ: Princeton University Press.

Walby, S. (1990) *Theorising Patriarchy*, Oxford: Blackwell.

Walklate, S. (2002) 'Gendering crime prevention; exploring the tensions between policy and process', in G. Hughes, E. McLaughlin, and J. Muncie (eds) *Crime Prevention and Community Safety: New Directions*, London: Sage, pp 58–76.

Walklate, S. (2006) 'Community safety and victims: who is the victim of community safety?', in P. Squires (ed) *Community Safety, Critical Perspectives on Policy and Practice*, Bristol: The Policy Press.

Young, J. (2007) *The Vertigo of Late Modernity*, London: Sage.

Youth Taskforce (2008) *Youth Taskforce Action Plan: Give Respect, Get Respect – Youth Matters*, London: Department for Children, Schools and Families.

SIX

'The feeling's mutual': respect as the basis for cooperative interaction

Peter Somerville

This chapter reviews our understanding of mutual respect and recognition, identifying it as a general form of cooperative interaction, underpinning practices of civility, sociability and intimacy. It distinguishes between 'thin' and 'thick' variants of civility and sociability, and throws new light on the nature of solidarity. It makes a connection between disrespect and social inequality, and attempts to show how the latter leads to the former. It criticises governmental approaches to respect, specifically the *Respect Action Plan*, arguing that these approaches are inherently disrespectful and therefore counterproductive. It explores the issue of 'informal social control' as an alternative to governmental approaches, arguing that this is better understood as a type of self-governance. It concludes with suggestions on how mutual respect and recognition may be better promoted in contemporary communities.

Respect, recognition and styles of interaction

Respect is about 'how people value themselves and others' – what Sayer (2005: 948) has called 'lay normativity' or 'lay morality'. Sayer elaborates on this point as follows:

> We are normative beings, in the sense that we are concerned about the world and the well being of what we value in it, including ourselves. The most important questions people tend to face in their everyday lives are normative ones of how to act, what to do for the best, what is good or bad about what is happening, including how others are treating them. The presence of this concern may be evident in fleeting encounters and conversations, in feelings about how things are going, as well as in momentous decisions such as

whether to have children, change job, or what to do about
a relationship which has gone bad. (Sayer, 2005: 949)

Respect therefore means valuing, caring about and being concerned
for oneself and others. Such valuing and concern assumes a prior
identification of the self and others that are valued – otherwise, the
respect would have no object or focus. Respect, then, is not action in
itself but a disposition to judgement. The action of paying or giving
respect is *recognition*, that is an act of attributing value to a person.
Recognition goes beyond respect in clearly signalling a degree of
participation in social or public life.

This chapter is concerned with *mutual* respect, that is where
individuals respect and are respected by others. Strictly speaking,
however, since mutuality involves acts of exchange, this is really mutual
recognition (the exchange of respect). Mutual recognition is a form
of cooperative interaction, which depends upon what Burns (1992:
74) calls a 'capacity for interpersonal concordance ... which comes
directly not so much from a propensity to identify with others as from
an ability and readiness to assume their point of view and interpret
their intentions'.

In most cases, if respect is shown to someone who has the capacity
for interpersonal concordance, they will return that respect. In this way,
as Sennett (2003) and many others have noted, respect is maintained,
reproduced and reinforced. For example, the civil inattention that I
give to strangers tends to be returned by them; if I look at them and
happen to catch their eye, I look away – and if they look at me and
catch mine, they look away. Here, mutual recognition, even though
unregistered in the sense that neither of us acknowledges the presence
of the other (Harris, 2006: 7), reinforces a particular form of mutual
respect, namely respect for each other's privacy.

As Burns (1992: 248), following Goffman (1961; 1974), explains, all
cooperative interaction requires a shared agreement on the 'frame' of
the moment, with a frame being a set of assumptions about how the
world works in situations of a particular kind, together with normative
expectations about how people should behave in such situations. For
cooperative interaction to work, each participant has to *trust* the other,
with trust being understood, in Luhmann's (1986) terms, as a willingness
to assume risk – here, the risk that another participant may be using
a different frame from one's own. People use different strategies and
tactics to maintain such trust, which depend partly on the nature of
the situation and partly on the roles available for them to play (cf
Bourdieu's (1984) concept of habitus). Goffman (1961) points out that

the more roles there are available, the more freedom the actor has in selecting the style or form of interaction and, consequently, the greater the facility for shifting frames and the larger the space for informality (by the same token, the greater the risk and, correspondingly, the trust required). Misztal (2000) relies, in part, on Goffman's (1961) concept of role distance (the distance between the person and the role she or he adopts in an interaction) to arrive at a classification of styles of interaction, with civility, sociability and intimacy signifying large, medium and small distances respectively. She argues that each of these styles is a way of balancing the informality and formality of interactional practices, so that interaction is neither too rigid nor too loose, neither too structured nor too formless, neither too solid nor too liquid.

Civility involves the paying of respects in everyday accidental and momentary encounters and is therefore a form of recognition – it is social action contributing to the (re)production of civil society, and therefore different from respect, which is a psychological disposition of individuals. Arguably, civility is the practice or habit of recognition, whether this is registered or unregistered, and whether this is of strangers or of those who are familiar to us. It recognises people's right to privacy, and so protects their autonomy, their ability to develop and realise their projects in their own ways. According to Misztal (2000: 78), being civil means striking a balance

> between the demand not to violate others' privacy and the demand for the articulation of individual desires and opinions ... [or between the] freedom to shift frames to avoid the empty routinisation of manners [and] the necessity of some restraints to avoid 'incivil' society, that is, society suffering from the deficit of respect.

Boyd (2006) makes an important distinction between 'formal' and 'substantive' civility. According to Boyd, *formal* civility refers to practices of everyday life, involving conventional manners and courtesy, which form part of a shared moral community or public. This is close to Misztal's conception of civility, but entirely misses the dimension of informality (for example, in shifting frames) that is so crucial for civility as a style of interaction. It also appears to tie civility too closely to specific kinds of community or society – specifically, bourgeois or 'respectable' society. In reality, the *everyday* mutual monitoring that is characteristic of civility has a *universalising* character. This means at least two things:

- first, civility is potentially cosmopolitan, extendable to all of humanity, not restricted to any particular moral or political community (an idea explored further by Andrew Millie in Chapter 8);[1]
- second, civility is not unique to encounters between strangers but is required for cooperative interaction of all kinds.

Substantive civility, on the other hand:

- first, involves mutual recognition between people in their role as citizens;
- second, signifies commitment to a common set of rules that describe their mutual rights and obligations.

These rules are developed internally in the process of interaction, and trust relationships help to monitor and sanction them (Ostrom, 1990: 185–6). For Boyd, substantive civility is a weak form of solidarity (where 'solidarity' is defined as 'commitment that subordinates individual interest to a larger social whole' (Misztal, 2000: 116)).[2] The role distance is shorter than in Misztal's concept of civility, meaning that Misztal's (everyday) civility is relatively 'thin', while substantive civility is relatively 'thick'. To simplify, therefore, I shall call these styles of interaction 'thin' civility and 'thick' civility. 'Thick' civility goes beyond the mutual but non-solidaristic recognition associated with 'thin' civility, to the extent that it involves forms of popular self-organising based on trust in the specific performance of other citizens beyond all accidental, momentary encounters. It assumes the existence of constitutions and institutions of various kinds, and it combines the formality of these with the informality of trust in fellow citizens.[3]

A similar distinction is made by Dobson (2006) between 'thin' and 'thick' cosmopolitanism. 'Thin' cosmopolitanism refers to the obligations we owe to one another as members of a common humanity – that is, we recognise one another as having equal value as human beings. This is effectively equivalent to 'thin' civility, because it does not commit us to act in any particular way apart from being polite and considerate towards one another. Here, however, it is conceived as a (weak) moral obligation rather than as a style of interaction. In contrast, 'thick' cosmopolitanism requires us to overcome the 'tyranny of distance' (Linklater, 2006) that separates us from one another, and Dobson argues that this is to be done by recognising our 'causal responsibility' (Dobson, 2006: 172) for one another – that is, we recognise the obligations we have to one another as a consequence of the foreseeable effects of our actions upon one another. Like 'thick' civility, this is a form of weak solidarity, but it goes beyond everyday interactional practices in committing participants to a variety of courses of action in pursuit of a programme for global social justice (Dobson examines the particular issue of global warming). Yet it seems to be a logical development of the universalising character of everyday mutual recognition.

One way of transforming thin into thick cosmopolitanism could be through deepening *sociability*. For Bourdieu, sociability is the ability and disposition to sustain networks (of 'more or less institutionalised relationships of mutual acquaintance and recognition'), and is the constitutive element of social capital (Bourdieu and Wacquant, 1992: 119). Sociability involves reciprocity, understood as a continuing relationship of exchange that 'involves mutual expectations that a benefit granted now should be repaid in the future' (Putnam, 1993: 172). It involves a balance between informality, with partners having freedom to choose, shape and model the main features of their particular relationships, and formality, with reliance on universal and more or less codified norms such as ethical codes and occupational rules (Misztal, 2000: 81). Boyd argues that civility actually promotes sociability because it makes interaction more pleasant (Boyd, 2006: 865), and so can lead to mutual granting of favours (in the case of thin civility) or to the formation of civil associations (in the case of thick civility). Whether pleasant or not, it does seem that 'dense iterative social situations' (Pennington and Rydin, 2000) characterised by thick civility can foster sociability. Misztal (2000: 83) emphasises the importance of sociability in expressing both instrumental and non-instrumental motivations, thus contributing to the collaboration and integration of society; sociability is 'capable of creating a feeling of belonging and providing people with social acceptance and position' (Misztal, 2000: 94), and is essential for collective action because of its role in the formation of identity and public opinion. Sociability therefore both is facilitated by and informs and makes possible thick civility as a style of interaction.[4]

Like civility, sociability has 'thin' and 'thick' variants, which can be understood as involving forms of weak and strong solidarity, respectively. At the thin end, we have rudimentary forms of exchange and reciprocity, while at the thick end we have Habermas's concept of civic solidarity, with its associated notion of 'thick communicative embeddedness' (Habermas, 2001: 108–9). An example of thin sociability is neighbourliness. A neighbour can be understood not only as someone living in the same area as me (whom I recognise as such) but anyone with whom I interact sociably, that is have communication and action that involve exchanges that go beyond the interactions of civility (whether thin or thick). Neighbourliness is produced by 'repeated informal encounters over time' (Harris, 2006: 54), which could apply to any kind of space where communication networks (whether face to face or through media such as the Internet) can develop – for example, not only a residential neighbourhood but also a school or workplace or shop, or virtually, in the space of the World Wide Web. Neighbourliness therefore seems to represent a first step towards a deeper level of involvement than the payment of respect to strangers: in becoming neighbours, people cease to be strangers to one another. This involves a stronger form of solidarity than that associated with civility, though it is more limited in scope. It leads to communitarian (sociability networks as 'in-groups') as opposed to cosmopolitan perspectives (based on notions of generalised interdependence).

Thick sociability is perhaps more controversial and difficult to define. What I have in mind is something like Ratner's (2007: 14) concept of 'co-operativism', where 'people work toward a common goal that benefits the participants, and that expresses common interests which they impart to the collective, co-ordinated action'.[5] This goes beyond neighbourliness but remains a form of sociability. It represents a stronger form of solidarity, in which cooperative interaction is more extensive and intensive, and communicated through more extensively and intensively shared values and identity. Such solidarity can be forged in a number of ways, for example, through participation in an association; belonging to the same community; working with others towards a common purpose; or having substantive interests in common – for example, working for the same organisation, in the same occupation or belonging to the same social class or ethnic group. Neighbourhood itself can form a focus for such thick sociability, where local people identify common issues relating to local services, particularly housing (Watt, 2006; Livingston et al, 2008).

With apologies to Tönnies (1988), two kinds of thick sociability can perhaps be distinguished, corresponding roughly to whether the solidarity concerned is identified with *Gemeinschaft* (an imagined moral or political order of mutual rights and obligations) or with *Gesellschaft* (understood as shared experience of action and struggle). There is a degree of overlap between these kinds of solidarity, but the former goes beyond interactional practices (it involves imagined forms of interaction), while the latter is nurtured through the actual organisation of interactional practices. *Gesellschaft* or *associational solidarity* seems to be rooted in everyday experience, while *Gemeinschaft* or *community solidarity* suggests imagined ties among people who are largely strangers to one another but are presumed to hold the same substantive values, norms, culture, way of life, and so on. In practice, there is often a symbiotic relationship between the two, with mutual aid and community identity/attachment being mutually reinforcing.[6] Interestingly, associational solidarity can be fragile and fragmented, split as it is among different associations, many of which are changeable, transient and divided within themselves; while community solidarity, despite its imagined character, can be stronger and more durable.[7]

The strongest bonds of solidarity are those between members of the same family, in other words love ties of different kinds between sexual partners, between parents and children, between siblings, and so on. Such ties can be so strong that they subsist even in the absence of frequent interaction or acts of mutual recognition (for this reason, civility is less important in such relationships). In this respect, they have some of the character of community solidarity – indeed, community solidarity can to some extent be understood as an extension of family solidarity to a wider group of people with whom one is not so familiar. This has implications for the role of civility, and its precise nature is important for understanding the issue of mutual respect in the community.

To simplify what are very complex interactional processes, Table 6.1 shows different realms of interaction, based on the work of Misztal (2000: 71). Interactions range from accidental encounters through to *pure* relationships. What is important to observe, however, is that mutual respect is crucial for all styles of interaction (civil, sociable or intimate). Mutual respect also implies democracy, at least in principle (equality among persons and recognition of the value of each person's contribution), whether these persons be recognised as fellow human beings, citizens, neighbours, members of the same association or community, or one's own kith and kin. On the other hand, democracy requires mutual respect; as Harris (2006: 124) has noted: 'We expect a society that is civil to have a democratic culture that has pertinence for all citizens and reflects an unspoken principle of the respectful recognition of others as its basis.' Democracy requires a capacity to respect different views and interests in order to arrive at a sense of the common interest. In a democracy worthy of the name, therefore, citizens have a right to be respected and an obligation to respect their fellow citizens.

Disrespect and shame; incivility and false civility

If respect is the valuing of oneself and others, then disrespect must be the devaluing of the same. Mutual respect presumes equality of persons, so perhaps the commonest cause of disrespect is the existence of

Table 6.1: Realms of interaction

	Accidental encounters	Non-accidental encounters	Exchange	Organisation	Pure relationships
Style of interaction	Thin civility	Thick civility	Thin sociability	Thick sociability	Intimacy
Partners' identity	Persons	Citizens	Network members	Co-producers	Individuals
Motivation	Self-presentation	Self-governance	Individual goals	Collective goals	Co-identification
Normative regulation	Non-codified general rules	Frames, some codified rules	Rules and norms, some codified	Rules and norms, many codified	Individualised rules
Content of relation	Respect	Interest	Reciprocity	Association or community	Responsibility
Quality of relational tie	Recognition only	Instrumental trust	Weak or thin obligations	Strong or thick obligations	Commitment

Source: Adapted from Misztal (2000: 71)

inequality. Inequality leads to the devaluing of some people in relation to others, in that they are seen as being of lower status, less deserving (of respect). As Sennett (1998) eloquently argues, a meritocracy, for example, in which those who succeed are deemed to be the most deserving, creates a pattern of mutual disrespect: first, those who are less successful lose respect for themselves and consequently disengage; later on, their children disrespect the social practices and institutions that so disrespected their parents.

Sayer (2005: 954) argues that: 'The worst kind of disrespect, the kind that is most likely to make one feel shame, is that which comes from those whose values and judgments one most respects.' As noted in Chapter Three by France and Meredith, in a society dominated by the work ethic, for example, the person who cannot find suitable employment is likely to feel shame, which is a sense of failure to live according to one's values or commitments. Disrespect from society is reflected in disrespect for self, in the sense of believing oneself to be of lower value than others. However, this happens only if one agrees with the judgements made by the disrespecters. Those who are said to be 'shameless' reject these judgements, even though this rejection increases others' disdain or contempt for them (Bourdieu, 1984). This helps to explain why practices such as 'naming and shaming' cannot work in relation to people who already feel disrespected by the very authorities who are proposing to 'name and shame' them.

The labelling of people as capable or incapable of shame (what might be called 'shameful' and 'shameless', respectively) echoes traditional class-based divisions between so-called 'respectable' and 'rough' or 'disreputable' people. Broadly speaking, 'respectables' are those who adhere or aspire to dominant or conventional norms, values and modes of behaviour. They believe that in this way they will be more highly respected and thereby distinguish themselves from people in 'lower' classes. In contrast, 'roughs' are those who frequently flout the rules, show lack of consideration for others, let their children run riot and appear to reject dominant values such as the work ethic, or at least to be unable to live up to them (for more detail, see Watt, 2006). Evidence of both 'respectable' and 'rough' behaviour is considerable, but the identification of distinct groups of people has never been clear cut, with the boundaries between the two groups being highly contestable – see Watt (2006) for examples from Camden in London; or Reynolds' (1986) earlier, unsuccessful attempts to identify the 'problem tenants' on one council estate. By exaggerating the inequality between groups of people, the drawing of this distinction is itself disrespectful because it devalues one group in relation to another.

In striving for and maintaining respectability (for oneself), civility can be used as a weapon for disrespect (of others). In general, civility can function as a veneer or mask (Misztal, 2000: 74), concealing a lack of respect for those seen as 'uncivilised'. More specifically, it can be part of an elite culture, an instrument of social control that works not only by constructing differences (like that between 'respectables' and 'roughs'), but also by instituting 'the regularity, predictability and sameness that makes society possible under conditions beyond the level of the primary group' (Boyd, 2006: 869). Among equals, therefore, civility tends to be positive, but among unequals, or among those attempting to make themselves valued more highly than others, civility can reinforce both the inequality of the relationship and the social order in which such inequality is embedded. Civility among unequals therefore tends towards false civility, with the double emphasis on sameness ('people like us') and difference ('people like them') (see Butler, 1997) producing and sustaining forms of social inclusion and exclusion. Those who are disrespected by this false civility, and who recognise it as false, are liable to become angry, and their anger may be expressed in acts of rebellion (Boyd, 2006: 870).

The nature of false civility is well described by Sen (2007: 54):

> [In a society or community ruled by norms of 'civility'] there is − by definition − little or no room for deviants, for sections that do not follow the rules of being civilised, which is a rule that is in turn also set by those who consider themselves to be civil and civilised. To the contrary, the civilised feel threatened by those who do not conform (and who they therefore term 'anti-social', 'deviant', 'wild', and 'uncivil') and by the very existence of the uncivil, and so they seek to subjugate it, convert it, tame it, civilise it; if it becomes sufficiently docile and domesticated, then to ignore it; and on the other hand, if it is too assertive, to attempt to destroy it, exterminate it. (Only in the most civilised of ways, of course.) In short, it is − in their understanding − the historical task of those who arrogate this term to themselves, to 'civilise' society and to establish a civil order − which most centrally means to establish hegemony over all those who (and all that) they consider to be uncivil.

What Sen is exposing here is the false claims of the powerful to be civil (false because they are seriously disrespectful of the powerless). However, he also draws an interesting distinction between two groups:

the 'incivil' and the 'uncivil'. Both groups are disrespected by the so-called 'civilised' and attempt to combat this, but in different ways. The incivil build insurgent associations, challenging power structures dominated by the civil, while the uncivil are far more limited in their activity, being generally 'criminal and exploitative' (Sen, 2007: 60). This distinction, however, seems to risk reproducing, on a global scale, the traditional distinction between the 'respectable' and the 'disreputable' working class, with the former struggling to advance the interests of the downtrodden, while the latter are simply reciprocating disrespect with disrespect. It is also concerning that Sen has nothing to say about the nature of the civility that might be required of the incivil.

This argument concerning false civility can be extended to sociability and even to intimacy. Differences of class and status become organised into contrasting and conflicting networks of associations, with accompanying mutual obligations and commitments, so that people become sociable and intimate only with others who seem like themselves (see, for example, Blokland, 2003). In this way, social differences become stabilised and institutionalised. False sociability, however, can occur even among equals, where one person pretends to be interested in or concerned about the affairs of another, with no serious intention to enter into a relationship of exchange. Similarly, one could identify relationships of false intimacy, where people are bound together by, for example, jealousy, fear, emotional blackmail, and so on.

Governmental approaches to respect

The government's *Respect Action Plan* states that: 'Respect cannot be learned, purchased or acquired, it can only be earned' (Respect Task Force, 2006: 30). As Harris (2006: 6) points out, this is 'a theoretically disempowering premise'. Arguably, its most serious flaw is that it devalues, and therefore disrespects, all those who have not managed, for whatever reason, to 'earn' the respect of others. Further, the Plan has nothing to say about the government's responsibility in 'earning' the respect of others, and particularly of those whom it is precisely disrespecting by its policy approach. Consequently, there is simply no basis here for a principled development of mutual respect between the government and its citizens. Instead, what we have is a patronising, top-down and arbitrarily punitive approach that ignores the causes of disrespect and attempts to appease the feelings of what could be called the 'respectable' classes ('decent, law-abiding, hard-working people', and so on). Whatever may be the merits of particular policies drafted in pursuit of this approach, we can be sure that the approach itself is doomed to failure.

Harris (2006) lists at least four other, more specific, problems with the government's approach in relation to respect in the neighbourhood alone:

1) *Civic absence*, that is, in some poorer areas, the lack of visible state authority, poor quality of services and lack of response to calls and complaints. Consequently: 'Residents feel disempowered and they are subject to systematic and legitimised disrespect, but it goes unregistered' (p 13).
2) Its emphasis on *shaming*. Basically, as argued above, 'Shaming doesn't work because it's not based on respect' (p 14). Public shaming in particular is just legitimised disrespect.
3) It ignores 'the sanctioned disrespectful behaviour of "respectable" citizens' (p 14). On top of the institutionalised disrespect already heaped onto people by patterns of inequality, 'respectable' people add to this disrespect in at least two ways: first, through self-indulgent and socially and environmentally damaging *consumption*: 'Our officially sanctioned respectable way of life – consume more, only engage with others at your own discretion – seems to work in precisely the opposite direction to the trumpeted intentions of the respect agenda' (p 16); and second, what Harris calls '*professional disrespect*': 'People with power and responsibility within society are routinely abusing it in minor ways by not showing respect to those in their charge' (p 16).
4) It ignores the role of *informal support systems* (p 123), particularly in setting standards and managing the behaviour of children (Barnes, 2006: 19), and relies solely on a mixture of legal enforcement and enforced 'support' such as parenting classes. The problem with this is that 'Norms of behaviour are being asserted from the top down without acknowledgment that they need to be mutually accepted and owned at local level' (Harris, 2006: 123).[8]

One could add that the Respect Agenda actually encourages disrespectful behaviour by people who believe themselves to be respectable. The Respect Agenda is part of a wider culture and politics that encourages people to complain about others, report their transgressions to the authorities, 'take a stand', and so on, rather than attempt to communicate, mediate, negotiate, and so on. In short, it encourages people to adopt the status of a victim rather than a citizen. It is perhaps no accident, therefore, that it has been found that: '"Respectable" people such as the middle-aged and elderly were the most likely perpetrators of an everyday incivility, not minority youth' (Phillips and Smith, 2006: 898).[9] Indeed, Bannister et al (2006: 923) suggest that the respectable city (with its zero tolerance of anti-social behaviour) and the revanchist city are closely related. They argue further, that the purification of the public realm, in eliminating the possibility of engagement with the 'other', results in increasing fear and intolerance, though it is by no means clear why this should be so (Bannister et al, 2006: 932; see also Bannister and Kearns, Chapter Seven, this volume).[10]

There is one final, and general, problem with governmental approaches to respect. This is that mutual respect requires equality of persons, whereas government demands compliance. The basic inequality between a government and its citizens can make it very difficult to achieve a respectful relationship between the two. The emergence of community and contractual governance (see for example, Flint and Nixon, 2006) does not change the fundamental asymmetry of the relationship. Contractual governance binds citizens by means of specific performance contracts instead of by law or general employment conditions, and community governance binds citizens through their roles as parents, tenants, service users, and so on.[11] The main point, however, is that they are bound by government rules and regulations. Whether it is only a 'passive desistance from incivility' that is required or 'a series of positive actions' (Flint and Nixon, 2006: 952), the intended effect is that citizens should be what Althusser (1970) called 'interpellated' (or 'hailed into place') as subjects of governmental authority. Being required to act positively is actually more demanding of citizens, and therefore potentially more oppressive (in the sense of an unjustified restriction of freedom), even though (and perhaps especially because) it is intended to be for their own good.

Informal social control – or self-governance?

Mutual respect and recognition is therefore crucial for all forms of cooperative interaction. It is stimulated by the general desire among human beings to get on with one another, assisted by what Dean (2003) calls 'cultural parenting'. It is fragile and finely balanced, however, and can be undermined by any one of a myriad of factors: misunderstandings, mistakes, misrepresentations, harmful acts of commission and omission, and accidental combinations of circumstances, as well as more systematic injustices and institutionalised disrespect. This section considers how mutual respect and recognition, and the order to which it gives rise (which Goffman called the 'interaction order'), is or can be maintained in the face of such threats.

Much of the literature in this area talks of 'informal social control' as a mechanism by which such order is produced and reproduced. On closer examination, however, what is called 'informal social control' turns out not to be completely informal, nor does it seem necessarily geared towards social control. Atkinson and Flint (2004: 335), for example, describe informal social control as involving collective norms and values within a 'community', and the ability of the community to regulate its members and realise collective goals. The terms 'norms' and 'regulate', however, suggest the existence of codes and rules, which are formal, and the term 'social control' raises questions of who is in control and what they are in control of, which are not explicitly addressed.[12] The focus here, therefore, seems to be on a mechanism (or set of mechanisms) that allows people to organise or regulate or govern themselves in ways of their own choosing. People may, however, choose to organise themselves in ways that involve disrespect of various kinds,[13] so it is not clear what this approach contributes to our understanding of how mutual respect (as opposed to disrespect) is maintained.

Mechanisms to support mutual respect are, of course, to be found in the cooperative interactional practices discussed in earlier sections of this chapter. Civility, sociability and intimacy are all of key importance in securing such so-called 'informal social control'. These styles of interaction all involve action that occurs spontaneously, according to the free will of individuals. They therefore correspond with a particular kind of social order maintenance that Kooiman (2003: 83) calls 'self-governance'. Self-governance in the case of a collectivity is essentially democratic, because it implies that each member is able to contribute freely and equally towards producing the order of the collectivity as a whole.

At one level, self-governance can be equated with the shaping of civility, particularly thick civility. Indeed, it is a key motivation for non-accidental encounters between citizens. It represents a development or deepening of the capacity for interpersonal concordance discussed earlier, which requires mutual judgement, or weighing in the balance, of the needs, interests, dispositions, expectations, and so on, of the various parties in any particular interaction. It derives, in Sayer's (2005: 952) terms, 'from the ongoing mutual and self-monitoring that occurs in everyday interactions with others, imagining what our behaviour implies for others and how it will be viewed by others, and generalising from one kind of moral experience to other situations which seem similar' (see also Jacobs, 1961). It is, first of all, governance of the self, and then governance of one another through the development of codes of behaviour and mutual monitoring of one another's behaviour.[14]

Self-governance therefore involves a balance between the formality of codes of behaviour (for example, queuing – see Misztal, 2000: 121) and the informality of everyday processes such as those of Sayer's or Jacobs' mutual monitoring and surveillance or 'the grapevine' (informal dissemination of information).[15] This conception suggests that the term 'self-governance' can be applied to the shaping of sociability (and, by extension, intimacy) as well as civility, depending upon the nature of the codes and the content of the communication concerned. However, the deepening interdependence that accompanies increasing sociability tends to be associated with a diminishing scope of the self-governing 'community' – that is, the circle of people with whom one is sociable is, perhaps inevitably, smaller than that with whom one is civil. Self-governing collectivities, therefore, where sociability is the dominant style of interaction, tend to be small in comparison with civil society, where civility predominates. Indeed, and unsurprisingly, deepening levels of mutual involvement correspond with shrinking numbers of involved people: from thin civility at one end of the continuum, involving the whole of humanity, through thick civility (members of the same civil society), to sociability (members of the same network or association or community), to intimacy (members of the same primary group). Self-governance therefore operates on a number of different levels, according to the style of interaction and the size of the self-governing collectivity. Each level has its own codes and communication content, its own combination of formality and informality.

A key disposition for self-governance is the willingness and readiness to intervene where an uncivil (or possibly anti-civil) or unsociable (or anti-social) act occurs. What is required is a deliberate encounter that results in a restoration of the balance of mutual respect that has been disturbed by the act. Harris (2006: 65–6) emphasises the importance of *opportunities* for encounter generally, especially in situations where one is required to interact cooperatively, such as shopping areas and meeting places. Such spaces are not only essential for thick civility but are important for promoting sociability. Readiness to intervene, however, is related to many different factors (see Harris, 2006: 63), such as whether the perpetrators of the uncivil act are known to the witness or whether the witness is known to them,[16] whether it occurs in the witness's own immediate neighbourhood (Harris, 2006: 64), whether fellow bystanders are seen as people like them (Levine et al, 2002: 3),[17] whether the authorities are perceived as responsive, supportive or trustworthy, the perceived risk of harm to themselves, and the perception of one's own responsibility/duty or of the value of intervening (Barnes and Baylis, 2004: 101).

Interestingly, most, if not all, of these factors relate to sociability, not just civility.[18] This strongly suggests that civility in itself, no matter how 'thick', is not self-supporting. Civility sets conditions that are necessary for sociability to flourish but, at the same time, sociability seems to be required for reasonably stable and enduring self-governance. One result of this, however, is that self-governance is limited by the boundaries of particular social networks rather than, as with civility, being extendable to large political communities, and even to global society. Different networks may operate by different norms and have different values (for example on what counts as a fair or legitimate exchange), rather than the universalising norms and values required for civility. This raises the question of which particular group norms and values might be more supportive of mutual respect generally.

This question is perhaps not as difficult to answer as some people have suggested. Sociability can indeed create divisions between in-groups and out-groups, leading to the disrespect of the latter. However, if people respect one another's beliefs, opinions, modes of appearance, ways of communicating, and so on, then there does not seem to be any good reason why they should not be able to be sociable with one another, even if they disagree on major issues of politics, religion and morality. For example, in relation to the care and control of children, Barnes (2006: 31–2) concluded, from a study of four English neighbourhoods, that self-governance was more likely where people felt that parents were effectively monitoring their own children in a way they agreed with; there were shared norms about parenting and discipline; and there was greater sociability generally, in the sense that parents knew more of their neighbours and supported them in small ways, sharing information, looking after keys, and so on, or otherwise socialised with them. Sociability and shared norms of everyday sociable interaction are therefore key to effective self-governance.

Problems arise, however, where people hold to contradictory norms of interaction and do not respect one another sufficiently to negotiate compromises. The disrespectful behaviour that results is displayed by a wide variety of people: not only people whose behaviour can be described as arrogant, rude, tactless, uncaring, prejudiced, bigoted, and so on, but also by people in positions of power, authority or status whose behaviour devalues other people. In the context of such wider social inequality and disrespect, sociability tends to encourage more particularistic forms of self-governance that reinforce existing social divisions based, for example, on class or ethnicity or 'tribe'. In this context, there is a risk that the universalising character of civility can become lost.

The concept of *cohesion* is useful here, understood as 'a collective ability to manage the shifting array of tensions and disagreements among diverse communities' (Gilchrist, 2004: 6), because it recognises that, in practice, disrespectful behaviour will occur, both within communities and across communities, but the problems it causes can, in principle, be resolved through self-governance. Cohesion across networks therefore has the potential to universalise sociability and produce less particularistic forms of self-governance, in which diversity itself is respected and valued. 'The challenge ... is to think about "difference" in ways in which it becomes the basis of affinity rather than antagonism' (Brah, 2007: 136).

An acute but unfortunately not uncommon example of lack of sociability at the neighbourhood level, giving rise to failure of self-governance, is provided by Barnes (2006). Her research findings appear to indicate that people's willingness to intervene to protect their neighbours' children or correct their misbehaviour was strongly associated with confidence that such intervention would not result in retaliation from the children's parents. Fear and distrust of other parents was therefore a key feature of the unsociability of interaction in certain areas. Barnes (2006: 32) suggests that this has developed partly because governmental policies have had the effect of putting most parents on the defensive, making them feel that 'the child is now more often someone to be defended at all costs'. In this respect, governmental approaches (along with other factors such as housing market changes) have contributed to the weakening of community solidarity and the undermining of self-governance.[19]

In general, current forms of state intervention do not effectively promote self-governance, not least because they do not understand the bases of self-governance. They favour enforcement approaches to encouraging mutual respect and recognition, without appreciating that such approaches may in themselves be disrespectful and without attempting to ensure that the enforcers themselves are respected. They strengthen hierarchical governance, for instance through the 'extended policing family' (that is, the extension of policing from the public police to include agencies such as police community support officers, neighbourhood wardens and private security companies), new technologies of surveillance, new forms of court order, new kinds of contract, multi-agency partnerships, and so on,[20] but without attempting in advance to gauge what the effects of these innovations might be on forms of self-governance. They fail entirely to heed the warning of Jacobs (1961: 32) that 'No amount of police can enforce civilisation where the normal, casual enforcement of it has broken down'.

Two other kinds of government policies, however, appear to hold out more promise. First, there are policies that involve supporting and conferring powers on community associations such as parish councils, neighbourhood policing panels and Neighbourhood Watch organisations. The style of interaction in such associations is that of sociability (of various degrees of thickness) and, insofar as they are inclusive of the whole community, they have the potential to be genuine forms of cohesive self-governance. In practice, however, most of them fall short of this ideal, so they need to be guided and assisted in their development.

This leads to the second kind of policy, where the government (as it usually is) works in partnership with the community as a whole in forms of *co-governance*[21] – for example, through reassurance/neighbourhood policing (eg Millie and Herrington, 2005) where the sociability tends to be thin, based on forms of reciprocity between certain community members and individual representatives of the state (such as community support officers and neighbourhood wardens); similarly, in community cohesion or intercultural initiatives, between members of different ethnic groups in processes orchestrated by the state – for example, interculturalism (eg Hussain et al, 2006; see also Chapter Eight by Millie). The readiness to intervene found in self-governance situations is echoed here in the readiness to summon assistance from enforcement agencies, with the degree of readiness being an inverse function of the effectiveness of self-governance and a direct function of the trust placed in the agencies concerned. Each form of reciprocity has to be considered on its own merits, but the main point is that it has to be allowed to work with the grain of existing mechanisms of self-governance, insofar as those mechanisms are broadly supportive of processes of mutual recognition. If they are not so supportive, co-governance cannot work, and old-style policing approaches may be required, along with a panoply of interventions of other kinds.

It can be concluded, therefore, that mutual respect and recognition are supported and sustained in a complex variety of ways, which can be summarised in terms of processes of self-governance and co-governance. Self-governance involves the spontaneous mutual shaping of styles of interaction, through a balance of formal codes and informal communications operating on different scales. Effective self-governance requires sociability but, paradoxically, sociability can reinforce social divisions that result in mutual disrespect. To counteract this, measures are required to reduce social inequality and to increase cohesion and solidarity across sociability networks. To some extent, these measures can be developed spontaneously, through specific learning processes that result in more liberal and outward-looking forms of self-governance. In addition, however, there is considerable scope for forms of co-governance in which different self-governing associations work together or in which hierarchical organisations such as governments learn to work cooperatively with self-governing associations of different kinds.

Promoting respect

As Pahl (2006: 184) says, 'the important goal is to provide the social framework in which a culture of mutual respect may take root and flourish'. There are problems with attempting to stimulate respect directly, through legislation or enforcement or other hierarchical means, since these are all based on assumptions of moral superiority (for example, 'I show respect but you do not' or 'I am respectable but you are not') which devalue and disrespect the other (see further discussion in Boyd, 2006: 875–6; see also Sennett, 2003). In general, approaches that seek to control the behaviour of others are disrespectful insofar as they deny people's freedom to make their own choices as they see fit and reject the democratic principle of equality of voice. To be controlled means that one follows a rule or obeys an order because one cannot perceive an alternative, or because the hazards associated with non-compliance or disobedience are seen to be too great. A 'respectful' society, however (see Sennett, 2003), is one whose rules are followed by the people because they respect their authority, which, in a democratic society, derives from the people themselves. Such respect for authority is earned through showing that it is authorised by the people and exercised fairly, impartially, accountably and transparently.

Misztal (2000: 230–1) concludes that there are basically two ways in which people's desire for a 'respectful' society can be realised. The first is through an expansion of formalisation, conventionalisation and rationalisation, and the second is through reliance on trust. Policy to promote respect, therefore, needs to focus on strengthening the 'right' norms of civility, sociability and intimacy, and on acting in such a way that trust is created and nurtured rather than diminished and undermined. This means a wide range of policies, from community development to wealth redistribution, that on the one hand encourage, extend and deepen sociability in particular and, on the other hand, ensure that policy decisions enjoy the support of the people and are implemented in a respectful manner. In promoting respect, the government needs to take a lead in *showing* respect.

Policy to promote respect may focus on civility, sociability or intimacy, and on building self-governance or developing co-governance. For example: 'Fostering [thin] civility may be more related to enhancing the conditions, both physical and social, that allow people to co-exist and interact through promoting tolerance and respectful indifference amongst loosely connected strangers' (Crawford, 2006: 974). Encouraging sociability, in contrast, needs something more richly detailed – for example, Harris (2006: 122) has suggested something similar to the Highway Code for a wide variety of types of (thin) sociable interaction. For thick sociability, people need to value one another for their intrinsic human worth, irrespective of whatever partial identities they may hold related to gender, ethnicity, sexuality, and so on. Indeed, to see someone *only* in terms of such a partial identity is itself disrespectful, because it diminishes their value as a human being. Social constructions such as patriarchy, neocolonialism, heteronormativity, disablism and ageism can therefore all be viewed as disrespectful insofar as they devalue or oppress certain human beings in relation to others (see Spalek, 2008). Rules for intimacy are something else again, and traditionally have been left to be negotiated by the parties concerned, with intervention occurring only in cases of bodily harm and neglect – although intervention has also occurred in support of oppressive norms, such as heteronormativity.

With regard to restoring sociability in neighbourhoods in particular, Harris (2006: 116–22) has proposed a principled way forward for government. He emphasises the need to generate:

- trust among neighbours (for self-governance)
- trust in the authorities (for co-governance).

According to Harris, trust among neighbours will be achieved through:

- ensuring neighbourhood stability, with the neighbours becoming a community of choice rather than a community of fate;
- maintaining a walkable, orderly local environment;
- promoting social networks, for example, around the use of local facilities.

Trust in the authorities is further developed by ensuring that there is both 'engaged formality' (Harris, 2006: 120) and 'detached formality' (Harris, 2006: 121). This means that there should be formal opportunities for community engagement, on the one hand, and on the other, 'civic presence' (that is, visible, responsible and accountable policing) and an accessible justice system, with local people participating in its governance.[22]

Where sociability and intimacy overlap, as in the case of norms relating to childcare, particular difficulties can arise. For example, in some neighbourhoods different parents have different and conflicting norms, such as on 'playing out', swearing, noise levels, road safety, ball kicking, entering other people's homes and so on, and in some cases parents will always take the word of their child against that of their adult neighbours. In such cases there is no real substitute for efforts to improve the sociability of the parents concerned. Such efforts can include a variety of forms of support, such as parenting advice, nursery care and a range of opportunities for parents to come together with and without their children. Thin sociability may be sufficient here, but it would also need to involve willingness not to judge other people according to oppressive norms, in other words, norms that unjustifiably restrict the freedom of the individuals concerned.[23]

Prior et al (2005, cited in Brannan et al, 2006: 1003–4) found a large measure of agreement by both communities and officials on the way forward in achieving more respectful communities. This involved practices such as enforcing the existing and agreed rules relating to anti-social behaviour; working with and supporting young people and their families to develop skills, capacities and self-esteem; building community capacity and investing in physical infrastructure; and developing better multi-agency working. The challenges for official agencies are to be sufficiently flexible to recognise and adapt to different types and levels of social capital in different neighbourhoods, and to support and facilitate activities of local volunteers while not being threatened by or seeking to subordinate them.

Such findings confirm both the necessity for co-governance and the extraordinary difficulties in making it work. Standardised approaches from government agencies and professionals simply do not connect with the sociability networks of particular communities, yet ways have to be found of working together if mutual respect is to be nurtured in communities where it is currently lacking. Official agencies have to rethink their approaches in order to become more relevant and more effective. Beyond that, decision makers generally need to examine more carefully the sometimes arrogant claims and demands of the 'respectable' and consider the full implications of these for their fellow citizens before taking action. Just as the government expects to be trusted by its citizens, so it is reasonable for citizens to expect to be trusted by their government.

Notes

[1] The obligation to give hospitality to strangers, for example, appears to be common to all societies, binding on all members of those societies, and applied to all strangers, wherever they come from.

[2] Based on a Hayekian model of market relations, with a civil society being seen as one in which people do not have to agree on ends but only on means that can serve a variety of ends that, hopefully, include their own (Hayek, 1976: 3).

[3] Misztal (2000: 126) comments as follows: 'The development of self-organising and self-governing forms of collective action needs, for example, to overcome problems such as "lack of predictability, information, and trust as well as high levels of complexity and transactional difficulties" (Ostrom, 1990: 25–6).' Also: 'Studies of the development of self-organising and self-governing forms of collective action suggest that … all of them require the removal of institutional obstacles to open deliberation and the establishment of institutional support for their creation. Moreover, all these positive solutions demand the recognition of collectivities based on people's reinterpretation of themselves and their history in such a way as to make trust the natural outcome of their common experience' (Misztal, 2000: 126–7).

[4] This can be explained in terms of Hirschman's (1986) distinction between horizontal and vertical voice. Recognition of one another as citizens involves vertical voice (more audible socially, for example public communication, complaint, petition, protest), while horizontal voice involves informal exchange of information and opinion (spontaneous conversation, gossip, criticism, 'murmuring of the people'). The sociability of the latter can develop into the 'thick' civility of the former: 'By fostering opinion formation, invention and self-reliance, horizontal voice transcends purely social, spontaneous contacts into public dialogues about rules and standards of fairness, excellence and common sense' (Misztal, 2000: 95).

[5] One could also cite Habermas (1992: 244), where solidarity is said to be rooted in people's experiences of taking responsibility for one another because 'all must have an interest in the integrity of their shared life context the same way'.

[6] See, for example, Dekker and Van Kempen (2004) or Robertson et al (2008) (particularly noting the gendered character of this relationship). For a more wide-ranging discussion of solidarity, see Crow (2002).

[7] There remains considerable uncertainty about the extent to which associational (or material) solidarity might be a basis for community (or moral) solidarity – or vice versa. As Sennett (2003: 219) suggests, 'Reciprocity is the foundation for mutual respect,' but it could also be the other way round, that is, mutual respect could be the basis for reciprocity. Just as it is unclear whether market relations are a basis for civility, or neighbouring is a basis for neighbourliness (although contact theory, for instance, refers to meaningful contact in a shared space (Hewstone et al, 2007)), there does not appear to be any straightforward relationship between, for example, being a waged worker in a capitalist society and expressing solidarity with other (unknown) waged workers in the same society – that is, between a class-in-itself and a class-for-itself.

[8] The same point has been made by many other writers. For example, Buonfino and Mulgan (2006: 4): 'Again and again policy makers either failed to notice, or chose to ignore, the webs of informal mutual support that are decisive in helping people get by, to live, learn, or be healthy.' Or Sennett (2003: 260): 'Treating people with respect cannot occur simply by commanding it should happen. Mutual recognition has to be negotiated.'

[9] Admittedly, this was in Australia, but maybe the UK is not so very different.

[10] A good example of this was reported in *Inside Housing* of 7 September 2007, where the chief executive of an organisation providing supported housing for ex-offenders and drug users was told by local residents that he should 'leave the country' after his organisation rehoused a client in their neighbourhood. Such residents may even regard themselves as 'respectable'.

[11] The government's policy on 'active citizenship' tends to confuse these different roles, and also does not adequately link the responsibilities of the active citizen to the responsibilities of government itself.

[12] Though see Flint (2002), where the 'informal' control exercised by drug dealers is contrasted with the 'formal' control exercised by the state.

[13] For example, in the drug-dealing neighbourhood, where Flint (2002: 259) talks of 'an imposition of particular morals and norms of

behaviour on the majority of residents by a powerful few'. Here the 'informal rules' include those of anti-grassing and non-cooperation with official agencies.

[14] This terminology, of course, derives from Foucault (see, in particular, his lectures on ethics – Foucault, 1997), but the content of the argument can be traced back to Adam Smith's concept of the impartial spectator in his *The Theory of Moral Sentiments* (1759). Most recently, I have used the term 'public self-policing' to refer to this development (Somerville, 2009).

[15] The grapevine is 'the mechanism by which the local moral economy is socially disseminated' (Brewer et al, 1998: 580).

[16] Harris and Gale (2004: 27) note the importance of 'neighbour clout' for the effectiveness of interventions.

[17] Levine et al (2002) concluded that bystanders play a vital role in encouraging or discouraging violent attacks, not just because of intervening or not intervening, but because by their action or inaction they communicate to both victim and perpetrator their approval or disapproval of what is taking place.

[18] In her research on neighbourliness, for example, Richardson (2006) found that the three most important factors affecting people's willingness to take action against anti-social behaviour were their perception of the authorities, their fear of retaliation, and the level of sociability itself, in terms of their general participation in neighbourhood life, including helping out neighbours and going to meetings. This link appears to go both ways, since, in her research on 'distressed' neighbourhoods, Dekker (2007) found that residents with social networks in the neighbourhood who rejected deviant behaviour and had a strong neighbourhood attachment were more likely to participate in neighbourhood life, including activities to tackle deviant behaviour. One suspects that the argument may be circular, ie willingness to take action against deviant behaviour is caused by the holding of norms that prescribe just such action. How such norms come to be held, and how they relate to all the other factors involved (social, psychological and situational), remain unknown.

[19] At the urban level, Ellison and Burrows (2007), for example, also point to problems of declining sociability or 'urban fragmentation' (p 298) and attempt to outline the dynamics of 'social politics' (involving complex processes of engagement and disengagement) associated with this decline. As in Watt (2006), social class and space appear to emerge

as key factors in this 'social politics'. The exacerbation of class divisions on this level, revealed by their analysis, suggests once again that the prospects for self-governance are poor.

[20] See, for example, Brown (2004) for an account of developments in mesh thinning, net widening, etc in relation to the control of anti-social behaviour.

[21] Co-governance is 'where a collectivity works co-operatively with other collectivities in a process of mutual shaping and mutual representation' (Somerville and Haines, 2008: 62).

[22] Richardson (2006: 39), among others, has found that the perception of authorities is improved by having a more visible presence of authority figures, who make a difference by enforcing rules, maintaining environments, reassuring, etc.

[23] For example, a proposal to introduce a child curfew in an area might be viewed as oppressive in this sense, but not if it was justified in terms of the benefits for the children concerned, agreed by their parents and accepted by the children.

References

Althusser, L. (1970) 'Ideology and ideological state apparatuses', in *Lenin and Philosophy and Other Essays*, trans B. Brewster, Monthly Review Press. Available online at: www.marxists.org/reference/archive/althusser/1970/ideology.htm.

Atkinson, R. and Flint, J. (2004) 'Order born of chaos? The capacity for informal social control in disempowered and "disorganised" neighbourhoods', *Policy & Politics*, 32(3), 333–50.

Bannister, J., Fyfe, N. and Kearns, A. (2006) 'Respectable or respectful? (In)civility and the city', *Urban Studies*, 43(5/6) 919–37.

Barnes, J. (2006) 'Networks, intervention and retaliation: informal social control in four English neighbourhoods', in K. Harris (ed) *Respect in the Neighbourhood*, Lyme Regis: Russell House Publishing, pp 19–33.

Barnes, J. and Baylis, G. (2004) *Place and Parenting: A Study of Four Communities*, London: Institute for the Study of Children, Families and Social Issues, University of London.

Blokland, T. (2003) *Urban Bonds*, Cambridge: Polity Press.

Bourdieu, P. (1984) *Distinction: A Social Critique of the Judgement of Taste*, London: Routledge.

Bourdieu, P. and Wacquant, L. (1992) *An Invitation to Reflexive Sociology*, Cambridge: Polity Press.

Boyd, R. (2006) 'The value of civility', *Urban Studies*, 43(5/6) 863–78.

Brah, A. (2007) 'Non-binarized identities of similarity and difference', in M. Wetherell, M. Laflèche and R. Berkeley (eds) *Identity, Ethnic Diversity and Community Cohesion*, London: Sage pp 136–45.

Brannan, T., John, P. and Stoker, G. (2006) 'Active citizenship and effective public services and programmes: how can we know what really works?' *Urban Studies*, 43(5/6) 993–1008.

Brewer, J.D., Lockhart, B. and Rodgers, P. (1998) 'Informal social control and crime management in Belfast', *British Journal of Sociology*, 49(4), 570–85.

Brown, A. (2004) 'Anti-social behaviour, crime control and social control', *Howard Journal of Criminal Justice*, 43(2), 203–11.

Buonfino, A. and Mulgan, G. (2006) 'Porcupines in winter: an introduction', in A. Buonfino and G. Mulgan (eds) *Porcupines in Winter: The Pleasures and Pains of Living Together in Modern Britain*, London: The Young Foundation, pp 1–14.

Burns, T.R. (1992) *Erving Goffman*, London: Routledge.

Butler, T. (1997) *Gentrification and the Middle Classes*, Aldershot: Ashgate.

Crawford, A. (2006) '"Fixing broken promises?" Neighbourhood wardens and social capital', *Urban Studies*, 43(5/6), 957–76.

Crow, G. (2002) *Social Solidarities: Theories, Identities and Social Change*, Buckingham: Open University Press.

Dean, K. (2003) *Capitalism and Citizenship: The Impossible Partnership*, London: Routledge.

Dekker, K. (2007) 'Social capital, neighbourhood attachment and participation in distressed urban areas. A case study in The Hague and Utrecht, the Netherlands', *Housing Studies*, 22(3), 355–79.

Dekker, K. and Van Kempen, R. (2004) 'Large housing estates in Europe: current situation and developments', *Tijdschrift voor Economische en Sociale Geografie*, 95, 570–7.

Dobson, A. (2006) 'Thick cosmopolitanism', *Political Studies*, 54, 165–84.

Ellison, N. and Burrows, R. (2007) 'New spaces of (dis)engagement? Social politics, urban technologies and the meaning of the city', *Housing Studies*, 22(3), 295–312.

Flint, J. (2002) 'Return of the governors: citizenship and the new governance of neighbourhood disorder in the UK', *Citizenship Studies*, 6(3), 245–64.

Flint, J. and Nixon, J. (2006) 'Governing neighbours: anti-social behaviour orders and new forms of regulating conduct in the UK', *Urban Studies*, 43(5/6), 939–55.

Foucault, M. with Rabinow, P. (1997) *Ethics: Subjectivity and Truth*, trans R. Hurley, London: Allen Lane.

Gilchrist, A. (2004) *Community Cohesion and Community Development: Bridges or Barricades?* London: Community Development Foundation.

Goffman, E. (1961) *The Presentation of the Self in Everyday Life*, Harmondsworth: Penguin.

Goffman, E. (1974) *Frame Analysis: An Essay in Face-to-Face Behaviour*, New York, NY: Anchor.

Habermas, J. (1992) *Autonomy and Solidarity: Interview with Jurgen Habermas*, ed R. Dews, London: Verso.

Habermas, J. (2001) *The Postnational Constellation: Political Essays*, Cambridge: Polity Press.

Harris, K. (ed) (2006) *Respect in the Neighbourhood: Why Neighbourliness Matters*, Lyme Regis: Russell House Publishing.

Harris, K. and Gale, T. (2004) *Looking Out for Each Other: The Manchester Neighbourliness Review*, London: Community Development Foundation.

Hayek, F. (1976) *Law, Legislation and Liberty: Vol 2, The Mirage of Social Justice*, Chicago, IL: University of Chicago Press.

Hewstone, M., Tausch, N., Hughes, J. and Cairns, E. (2007) 'Prejudice, intergroup contact and identity: do neighbourhoods matter?', in M. Wetherell, M. Laflèche and R. Berkeley (eds) *Identity, Ethnic Diversity and Community Cohesion*, London: Sage, pp 102–12.

Hirschman, A. (1986) *Rival Views of Market Society*, New York, NY: Viking.

Hussain, A., Law, B. and Haq, T. (2006) *Engagement in Cultures: From Diversity to Interculturalism*, Leicester: Institute of Lifelong Learning, University of Leicester.

Jacobs, J. (1961) *The Death and Life of Great American Cities*, London: Pimlico.

Kooiman, J. (2003) *Governing as Governance*, London: Sage.

Levine, M., Reicher, S., Cassidy, C. and Harrison, K. (2002) *Promoting Intervention against Violent Crime: A Social Identity Approach*, Swindon: Economic and Social Research Council.

Linklater, A. (2006) 'Cosmopolitanism', in A. Dobson and R. Eckersley (eds) *Political Theory and the Ecological Challenge*, Cambridge: Cambridge University Press, pp 109–28.

Livingston, M., Bailey, N. and Kearns, A. (2008) *People's Attachment to Place: The Influence of Neighbourhood Deprivation*, York: Joseph Rowntree Foundation.

Luhmann, N. (1986) *Love as Passion: The Codification of Intimacy*, trans J. Gaines and D.L. Jones, Cambridge: Polity Press.

Millie, A. and Herrington, V. (2005) 'Bridging the gap: understanding reassurance policing', *Howard Journal of Criminal Justice*, 44(1), 41–56.

Misztal, B. (2000) *Informality: Social Theory and Contemporary Practice*, London: Routledge.

Ostrom, E. (1990) *Governing the Commons: The Evolution of Institutions for Collective Action*, Cambridge: Cambridge University Press.

Pahl, R. (2006) 'On respect: the social strains of social change', in A. Buonfino and G. Mulgan (eds) *Porcupines in Winter: The Pleasures and Pains of Living Together in Modern Britain*, London: The Young Foundation, pp 55–60.

Pennington, M. and Rydin, Y. (2000) 'Researching social capital in local environmental policy contexts', *Policy & Politics*, 28(2), 233–49.

Phillips, T. and Smith, P. (2006) 'Rethinking urban incivility research: strangers, bodies and circulations', *Urban Studies*, 43(5/6), 879–901.

Putnam, R. (1993) *Making Democracy Work: Civic Traditions in Modern Italy*, Princeton, NJ: Princeton University Press.

Ratner, C. (2007) 'The co-operative manifesto: social philosophy, economics and psychology for co-operative behaviour', *Journal of Co-operative Studies*, 40(3), 14–26.

Respect Task Force (2006) *Respect Action Plan*, London: Home Office.

Reynolds, F. (1986) *The Problem Housing Estate*, Aldershot: Gower.

Richardson, L. (2006) 'Incentives and motivations for neighbourliness', in K. Harris (ed) *Respect in the Neighbourhood*, Lyme Regis: Russell House Publishing, pp 34–46.

Robertson, D., Smyth, J. and McIntosh, I. (2008) *Neighbourhood Identity: People, Time and Place*, York: Joseph Rowntree Foundation.

Sayer, A. (2005) 'Class, moral worth and recognition', *Sociology*, 39(5), 947–63.

Sen, J. (2007) 'The power of civility', *Development Dialogue*, 49, 51–67.

Sennett, R. (1998) *The Corrosion of Character*, New York, NY: W.W. Norton.

Sennett, R. (2003) *Respect: The Formation of Character in an Age of Inequality*, London: Penguin.

Smith, A. (1976) [1759] *The Theory of Moral Sentiments*, Oxford: Oxford University Press.

Somerville, P. (2009, forthcoming) 'Understanding community policing', *Policing: An International Journal of Police Strategies and Management*.

Somerville, P. and Haines, N. (2008) 'Prospects for local co-governance', *Local Government Studies*, 34(1), 61–79.

Spalek, B. (2008) *Communities, Identities and Crime*, Cambridge: Polity Press.

Tönnies, F. (1988) *Community and Society (Gemeinschaft und Gesellschaft)*, New York, NY: Transaction Publishers.

Watt, P. (2006) 'Respectability, roughness and "race": neighbourhood place images and the making of working-class social distinctions in London', *International Journal of Urban and Regional Research*, 30(4), 776–97.

Part Four
Respectful city living

SEVEN

Tolerance, respect and civility amid changing cities

Jon Bannister and Ade Kearns

Introduction: Tolerant Britain?

Britain has a reputation for tolerance (see, for example, Paxman, 1999). In the first half of the twentieth century, tolerance was regarded as one of several British virtues experienced by foreign travellers, compared to the alternative characteristics of other nationalities. International socialites such as Odette Keun (1934) described the 'adorable things' she liked about the English as including 'courtesy, kindness, obligingness and tolerance'. In the post-war period, the creation of the myth about the virtues of the British that had both helped us to achieve victory in the war and also justified our ascendancy, included proclamations about British tolerance, in contrast to the less attractive virtues of both our erstwhile enemies and our allies (Calder, 1991).

In the early twenty-first century, New Labour has, at one level, adopted the language of tolerance as part of its attempts to promote multicultural Britain and shore up British identity in the face of inter-ethnic tensions and working-class disaffection. Tony Blair, in December 2006, argued that tolerance was 'what makes Britain, Britain', that Britain's 'hallmark' was its 'common culture of tolerance'. Tolerance was one of the 'essential values' that minorities had to share in order to integrate. Blair's successor, Gordon Brown, in the early stages of his crusade about Britishness in March 2007, said that 'When people are asked what they admire about Britain, they usually say it is our values: British tolerance; the British belief in liberty.'

Reputation and rhetoric, therefore, support the notion that Britain is a tolerant place. The realities of public opinion and public policy, however, suggest otherwise, as we show in the next section. But while policy uses the language of tolerance and respect, it does not offer a clear definition or understanding of these terms: in the second and third sections, we seek to define tolerance and specify its relationship to respect and civility. While we argue that active engagement with others is an essential foundation of tolerance, we go on to show in the following two sections that such engagement and tolerance are less likely to arise as a result of a purified public realm, and that tolerance is very context specific. In the final two sections we look at how a combination of global forces, which increase the need for tolerance, and a public policy response which emphasises 'otherness' and which seeks to support a preference for privatism through increasing regulation of 'inappropriate behaviours', serve to create a 'cycle of intolerance' in which thresholds of tolerance are in a downward spiral. We conclude that the pursuance of a form of cohesion that stresses consensus and conformity is counterproductive, since it serves to highlight social differences and to frame those differences as undesirable and unacceptable, rather than to promote tolerance.

Public opinion and public policy: intolerant realities

Having briefly set out how Britain trades on its tolerant reputation, here we look at how public opinion and public policy portray a growing intolerance, first through anxieties about incivility, and second through the imprecise framing of more and more behaviours as things 'not to be tolerated'.

Anxiety about anti-social behaviour

Official measures of crime and anti-social behaviour have remained stable, if they have not fallen, in recent years. However, the majority of the population believe that crime is rising (Nicholas et al, 2007), while a significant minority believe that anti-social behaviour is also getting worse (Wood, 2004). How might we begin to explain these apparent contradictions? To an extent, general anxieties about crime and anti-social behaviour reflect our thoughts about the qualities of urban life, our perception of the values and intentions of others with whom we share the city. Perhaps, our current indices of crime and anti-social behaviour are failing to grasp all that now annoys and upsets us about the behaviour of others. Perhaps we are less tolerant of those with whom we do not appear to share common values. As Bunting (2008) suggests when writing in *The Guardian*, 'crime may be falling, but something more intangible and just as important is moving centre stage: a pervasive anxiety about a deterioration in the everyday interaction between strangers'.

Certainly, there are those who believe we are less considerate, less respectful, of the sensibilities of others when pursuing our own goals. A recent editorial in the *Daily Telegraph* (2007: 27) portrayed this as a collapse of public manners and located the expression of bad manners in a range of settings and situations:

> Bad manners are like a virus spreading through all society. Neighbours' loud music in the garden is unmannerly. So are aggressive drivers, casually drunk office workers in Friday-night streets, idiots who leave chewing-gum for our shoe soles, pedestrians who barge through doors without holding them for fellow shoppers. In the building of an orderly society, a bus queue was a glory of our national character. Now it is on the verge of extinction. Manners make the nation. Without them, as we see, it becomes nasty and brutish.

At the heart of this account is a belief that we no longer hold the means, or public manners, to negotiate the shared use of public space. Moreover, it is assumed that we occupy public space with selfish intent; in other words, with little regard for others. Endeavours to probe generic perceptions of crime and anti-social behaviour may thus be tapping into a rising intolerance of the behaviours of others that are seen to impinge upon our own use of public space. This public intolerance is supported by official policy.

Tolerance and the Respect Agenda

The long-standing fight against anti-social behaviour is framed by a rhetoric of (in)tolerance and respect. Thus, leading up to the launch of the *Respect Action Plan* (Respect Task Force, 2006), we were told that 'anti-social behaviour ... will not be ignored or tolerated any longer' (Scottish Executive, 2003: vii), and similarly that 'disrespect and yobbish behaviour will not be tolerated anymore' (Blair, 2005). Instead, a 'no tolerance approach to anti-social behaviour' (Home Office, 2004: 10) would be adopted in an endeavour to 'bring back a proper sense of respect' (Home Office, 2003: 6). What is striking is the lack of attention (perhaps deliberately) given to the meaning of these various terms.

The *Respect Action Plan* refers to respect as being based on 'values that almost everyone in this country shares' and as relying 'on a shared understanding and clear rules', but the precise nature of these values and rules remains unspecified. What is clear, however, is that a minority of society is regarded as acting in a disrespectful manner towards the majority. Moreover, that minority requires to adopt the values and rules of the majority or risk expulsion. Certainly, the *Respect Action Plan* contains a toolkit that enables the exclusion of those deemed to be acting in an anti-social manner. In this way, and for Burney (Chapter One, this volume), the Respect Agenda does not convey a message of mutual tolerance. Rather, it affords primacy to the values of some over others. The Respect Agenda is about forcing a minority to adopt the code of conduct of the majority, to demonstrate their respectability. Intolerance or a lack of mutual tolerance thus sits at the heart of the Respect Agenda, this despite the Home Office (England and Wales) identifying (though also failing to qualify) the creation of 'a safe, just and tolerant society' to be its core aim.

There is a paradox, then, between, on the one hand, public declarations of the virtue of and desire for tolerance and, on the other hand, a policy thrust that demands compliance and respect from others (rather than offering tolerance to others), and supports a social trend towards growing intolerance. In order to explore this dilemma further, we need to define tolerance and its relationship to respect, something policy has failed to do.

Defining tolerance

From its sixteenth- and seventeenth-century roots as a principle to resolve and avoid religious conflict in Europe, tolerance is now described as 'a liberal virtue' (Knowles 2001: 100), as 'a core concept and value in the formation of modernity and modern societies' (Karstedt, 2007), and as an 'underpinning of democracy' (Sullivan and Transue, 1999). But despite its centrality to our conception of modern, liberal, western societies, commentators' accounts of tolerance reveal that there are many different ways of conceptualising the processes involved. There is a need, therefore, to clarify the different versions and perspectives on tolerance, which can be seen, for example, as positive or negative, and as moral or practical, as well as in many other ways.

Karstedt (2007) characterises tolerance as something which 'can only be defined in a negative way' and as involving passivity, the absence of action and of strong emotions. These elements are debatable, as these two shorthand definitions illustrate:

> Toleration ... requires one not to interfere in conduct which one believes to be morally wrong. (Knowles, 2001: 102)

And:

> The working definition of 'tolerance' which is widely used
> is: 'The deliberate choice not to interfere with conduct
> or beliefs with which one disapproves'. (Hancock and
> Matthews, 2001: 99)

It is immediately apparent from these definitions that both the object
of tolerance and the response to it can vary. Thus, let us explicate the
key components of tolerance: the objects of tolerance, the assessment
of those objects, and the response.

The object(s) of tolerance

The object of tolerance, the thing to be tolerated, can be an action (or
'conduct'[1]), a life-style or behaviours (or a 'set of conducts'), or a set
of beliefs (or a 'culture') (Table 7.1). Residing behind these immediate
objects of tolerance, though, may lie a dislike of an individual (the
perpetrator) – thus making tolerance personal; or a concern about
the consequences or impacts of the action. Thus, we may feel that we
are tolerating the perpetrators, their actions, and/or the consequences
of their actions.

Many years ago, Cavan (1961) identified public attitudes to
negatively judged conduct[2] as ranging from tolerance with approval,
through tolerance without approval, to disapproval and condemnation,
depending upon their degree of threat to the smooth running of
social organisation. Others, for example Mendus (1989), declared that
permitting something to happen, without the presence of disapproval,
is not tolerance so much as liberty. However, Newey (1999) identified
the fact that the disapproval at the heart of tolerance can be on either
moral or non-moral grounds.

Table 7.1: The objects of tolerance

Object of tolerance	Examples of things people may feel they tolerate
Conduct	Spitting in public; passive smoking
Life-style	Large families living long-term on benefits; Travellers
Culture/beliefs	Islamic practices
Social group	Single parents; students
Impacts	Untidy gardens; streets with reduced visual amenity

So, in facing any unwanted or unfavoured situation, we first make an assessment of the object of tolerance, based upon our own interests and/or those of wider society; this defines those things that we feel we are tolerating. We may *dislike* something because it offends our tastes and preferences. We may *object* to something because it infringes our privacy or quiet enjoyment of private or public space. We may be *offended* by something because it contravenes our moral code. We may *disapprove* of something because we consider it to be harmful to the individual concerned. Finally, we may *condemn* something because we believe it to be a threat to social organisation or accepted social norms (Table 7.2).

Table 7.2: Tolerant assessments (of unfavoured behaviours)

Assessment	Rationale
Dislike	Offends our taste or preferences
Object	Infringes our privacy or quiet enjoyment
Offended	Goes against our moral code
Disapprove	Harmful to the perpetrator
Condemn	Threat to social norm or organisation

Tolerant responses

We then make choices about how to respond to the objects of tolerance. It is important to remember that tolerance is not the same thing as indifference, acquiescence, or 'situations where there may be no real choice over whether to take action or not' (Hancock and Matthews, 2001: 99). Tolerance is 'necessarily selective', 'purposeful and intentional', and 'a rational and conscious act even if it is expressed through inaction' (Hancock and Matthews, 2001: 100). Other 'reasons for non-interference such as indolence or cowardice ... are quite distinct from, and sometimes antithetical to, toleration' (Horton and Nicholson, 1992: 3).

Thus, having formed a view about the object of tolerance, we then opt for one of several responses.

- Our response may take the form of 'pure tolerance', namely, non-intervention about those things we do not agree with, despite our abhorrence of the conduct and its impacts. Alternatively, we may adopt one of several other tolerant responses.

- We may adopt a cognitive response whereby we do not intervene, by virtue of a reduced propensity to disagree with the conduct; this may be due either to a shift in our moral perspective, or to an increased understanding of the causes of, or the perpetrator's 'need' or 'right' to engage in, the conduct, that is, we think about it differently and see it as 'less wrong' than previously. However, for Seligman (1999), people become increasingly tolerant more through self-restraint (more often opting not to intervene) than through normative adjustment (judging behaviours as less wrong).
- We may respond behaviourally, raising our threshold of tolerance – our ability to cope with the conduct – through an adaptation of our own behaviour in order to lessen the impact of the disfavoured conduct, for example through avoidance tactics.
- We could also raise our threshold of tolerance psychologically, coaching ourselves to be less irritated or angered by the conduct.
- Last, we may choose to willingly coexist with the unfavoured conduct while at the same time attempting to moderate the behaviour of the 'perpetrator'.

The first response we would call 'static tolerance' and the others 'dynamic' or 'developmental tolerance' (Table 7.3).

Having developed this broader understanding of tolerance, we can realise that public policy and its associated public discourse can influence three crucial things: what sorts of things (objects) we identify as potentially intolerable; how serious or fundamental we consider such 'intolerable conducts' to be (our assessments); and what kinds of

Table 7.3: Tolerant responses

Response	Content
Static	
Pure tolerance	Disapproval plus non-intervention
Dynamic	
Cognitive	Reduction in disapproval through changed moral code or via understanding
Behavioural	Raised threshold of tolerance through behavioural adaptation, eg avoidance
Psychological	Raised threshold of tolerance through improved coping mechanisms
Ameliorative coexistence	Toleration plus attempted moderation of the perpetrator's behaviour

responses we contemplate. In our view, both public policy and public discourse have served to broaden the scope of objects of intolerance while at the same time narrowing the spectrum of our assessments and responses, contributing to a 'cycle of intolerance' (see below).

The foundations of tolerance: engagement, respect and civility

Underpinning the type of response we offer to unfavoured conduct (as outlined above) – that is, whether or not to tolerate the conduct and if so, what form of tolerance to offer – is engagement with others and its potential products of civility, respect and empathy, as shown in Figure 7.1.

Figure 7.1: The foundations of tolerance

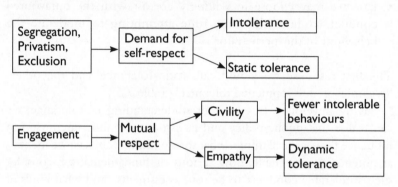

Intolerance and static tolerance are the product both of spatial trends towards segregation and exclusion and of a citizen's preference to censure that which s/he dislikes and to prioritise his or her own self-respect, that is, to demand that others respect their rights (for example, to privacy).

Engagement

Engagement with others is a foundation of the other, dynamic versions of tolerance. Even a limited level of engagement can generate two-way respect (not only demanding respect but offering respect). By engagement we are referring to meaningful and purposeful social interaction and collective activity, not simply co-presence in space along with casual, unintended, ephemeral contact.

Engagement can also support the development of empathy with others: acknowledging that others may have a right or a need to act as they do, given their backgrounds or circumstances, and showing a willingness to see things from the other's point of view (Burns, 1992). In turn, mutual respect and empathy can result in further engagement, through which tolerance becomes developmental, with increased understanding of the other, as well as opening up opportunities to seek moderation in the other's behaviour.

Respect

> Every action done in company, ought to be with some sign
> of respect, to those that are present. (George Washington's
> First Rule of Civility and Decent Behaviour)

By respect, we mean giving attention, regard, consideration and esteem to others: valuing them as human beings and as co-citizens. Our actions should promote social harmony, avoid unnecessary hurt and offence to others, and protect the dignity and quality of life of individuals and groups. Respect is both given and received, and some would say that people need self-respect in order to offer respect to others. In his consideration of respect, Sennett (2003) identifies two barriers to its attainment and transfer, namely inequality and dependence. In addition to Sennett's consideration of inequality and dependence, we have argued, above, that a third pillar of respect for others is engagement, through which familiarity and understanding may develop, feeding into respect and opening the door to empathy.

Respect of the other has two important consequences. On the one hand, it increases our willingness to show empathy for others, thus enhancing the chances that we will seek to tolerate that conduct of others which we dislike. On the other, it supports the civility of our own conduct, thus reducing the chances that our behaviour should become the object of others' tolerance.

Civility: proximate and diffuse

The other product of respect for others is our own civility, which serves to reduce the need for our own conduct to be tolerated by others. Like Somerville's idea of 'thin' and 'thick' civility (Chapter Six), we similarly conceive of two forms of civility. The first we term *proximate civility*, wherein civility is most commonly understood as politeness, or the absence of rudeness in our interactions with others, and the observance of common courtesies and conventions with others. This includes verbal and non-verbal communication, the words and gestures aimed at others or used in the presence of others. This may be similar to Somerville's 'thin civility', but it may also involve elements of Boyd's (2006) 'substantive civility', since our willingness to be courteous or civil, in an everyday sense, towards others depends on recognising them not only as human beings, but also as citizens with an equal right to occupy the space we are in: this is, in turn, contingent upon the nature of the space in question which we are expected to share (see below).

But civility can be broadened, as it often implicitly is in discussions of 'incivility' and anti-social behaviour, to embrace a wider spectrum of behaviours that impact upon others – which we term *diffuse civility*. To be civil in this sense is to have regard for the effects of our actions and use of space on others with whom we share that space, without the condition of direct interaction or of co-presence at a point in time (to some extent akin to Somerville's 'thick civility'). This type of civility is a tougher challenge, since without interaction or co-presence our conduct is less easily regulated by the approbation or sanction exercised by others.

Again, this second version of civility is not straightforward and is dependent upon three types of awareness and sensitivity on the part of citizens. First, we need to be aware of how public venues and spaces are used by other groups at different times of the day and week, in order to know whether our own behaviour might be problematic for others. Second, we need a cultural and social awareness to realise whether behaviours and forms of expression might be offensive to, or reinforce the stereotyping of, others (minority groups of whatever sort). As Parekh (2000) argues, for example, art cannot be exempt from moral and social responsibility, and some communities that are vulnerable to stereotyping and discrimination deserve protection. But third, we also need an awareness of the right to freedom of expression on the part of cultural subgroups – as Millie examines in Chapter Eight, one person's offensive and damaging graffiti is another person's artistic endeavour and identity formation. These things need to be negotiated and discussed, not predetermined as right or wrong. They also depend on a public disposition to be open to the legitimate presence and inclusion of others. Unfortunately, the nature of modern, urban society often works against such a reality.

Tolerance and the city

The relationship between aspects of civility (including tolerance) and qualities of the urban realm has provoked the attention of scholars for some considerable time. The relationship between the city and civility, however, is equivocal. Thus, 'celebrations of civility and the city have existed alongside deep anxieties about the incivility of urban life' (Fyfe et al, 2006: 854). The city, it seems, holds the potential to bring out the best and the worst in us.

Elsewhere (Bannister et al, 2006), we have argued that the endeavour to cleanse the city of all its incivilities, of all that we regard as different to us, is counterproductive. Public spaces in our cities can enable us to encounter the tastes, preferences and beliefs of all those with whom we 'share' the city. Though confronting differences may be uncomfortable or even unpleasant, interaction with others enables us to develop mutual trust and solidarity. Our differences become less threatening because they are understood and we are able to determine common values and intentions. Seeking to purify public space may seem appealing in the short term, but will ultimately accentuate our distrust of others.

The presupposition, however, that interaction brought about by co-presence, interaction that is not framed by a pre-existing mutual distrust, will serve to illuminate and bind us together is problematic. Our capacity and willingness to tolerate the behaviours of others is not an innate quality. It is something that we need to promote through engagement, as described earlier.

In *All That Is Solid Melts into Air*, Marshall Berman (1982) draws upon the writing of Baudelaire, in particular a story entitled 'The Eyes of the Poor', to illustrate the impact of modernity on the public sphere. Baudelaire's story takes place during Haussmann's reconstruction of Paris, following the building of the great boulevards, of the public spaces that enabled an intermingling of classes to take place as never before. In this story, two lovers meet in a newly constructed cafe on one of the boulevards. Engaged in a private moment, they become aware of a poor family gazing at the cafe scene. Though there is no malice in the behaviour of this family (and none ascribed to them by the couple); their observed presence, the mere meeting of eyes, make the couple feel uncomfortable. The man in the story feels uneasy about being able to enjoy the splendours of the cafe when the poor family cannot afford to do so. In contrast, the woman feels her privacy invaded and says to the man, 'those people with their great saucer eyes are unbearable! Can't you tell the manager to get them away from here?'. Bringing people together in public space, therefore, can raise our awareness of others, but it does not necessarily mean than we will tolerate their presence if our purposes are entirely private rather than to any extent social, and if we do not view the presence of others as legitimate or justified. Tolerance in the city is also very context specific: it depends in which part of the city one is operating.

Placing tolerance in context

While trends in modern urban society both make us more likely to engage in behaviours that are problematic for others, and less likely to find common purpose with our fellow citizens, it is also the case that our response to unfavoured conducts is very context specific. The sociospatial situation in which we find ourselves both influences our predisposition towards tolerance and determines a set of other drivers of the tolerant response, so that our thresholds of tolerance are situationally specific and spatially variant.

We can illustrate this by considering some of the urban arenas in which we may exercise tolerance, or operationalise our thresholds of tolerance. In town and city centres we are more likely to tolerate unfavoured conduct(s) because we expect it to happen, and we also expect regulatory agencies to deal with it. At the same time, however, widespread behavioural regulation may cause us to increasingly dislike nonconformist conduct. However, as long as unfavoured conduct does not prevent us from pursuing our intended activity, we may tolerate that which we dislike; and also because we do not have to suffer it for too long. Further, since we are likely to be unfamiliar with the perpetrators, and thus uncertain of the consequences of their response to any regulatory efforts we might make ourselves, we are also more likely to tolerate things rather than to intervene.

As we move around the city on public transport we may also come across behaviours that we dislike, disapprove of or object to. Here we often tolerate things we would rather not have to, but are deterred from intervention by a mixture of unfamiliarity and exposure (through fixed durations and confined spaces). If we choose to act, we are unsure of the degree of support we would get from our fellow passengers, especially as silence and the absence of any form of interaction is the norm on public transport in the UK. Thus, we do not know what other people think about the conduct in question, or would do about it were they to disapprove, and we do not favour acting alone. Exposure may be short but it is of a fixed duration, that is, the key being exposure to the perpetrator rather than to the conduct; we cannot easily escape, in space or time, if the perpetrator turns nasty in response to our objections. So, more often than not, we do nothing and tolerate the conduct.

In residential neighbourhoods a different set of considerations is at play, and the stakes are higher. Our threshold of tolerance is lowered by the prospect – in the place where we live – of repeated and regular exposure to the unfavoured conduct. Our inclination to intervene is supported, in relatively stable residential situations, by familiarity with our neighbours (both perpetrators and potential allies); and by the frequent absence of official or effective agencies of regulation – many people, for example, have come to think that the police are uninterested in everyday nuisances and anti-social behaviour (in people's day-to-day complaints) because the prospects of securing a criminal conviction are low. Tolerance is lowered by the perceived serious consequences of doing nothing: an area may gain a negative reputation, or at the very least lose status; property values may fall if social or visual amenity is eroded, or due to a perception of area decline; unfavoured behaviours may be seen to put one's own family and children at physical risk or to potentially impact upon their social or educational development. Of course, these responses are all equally dependent upon the expectations and interests of the resident group, which can vary from place to place.

Public policy, therefore, rather than having a one-size-fits-all approach, should consider to what extent our tolerance or intolerance of certain behaviours, in different urban contexts, is either harmful for the individual concerned and/or harmful for society if unchecked. Policy then needs to understand what the drivers of our (in)tolerance are in the context in question, in order to work out how to intervene so as to shift our thresholds of tolerance up or down. Policies for tolerance in different contexts may prove more useful than policies which merely regulate behaviour on the basis of demands for respect. This is because the general circumstance facing society and policy is one of rapid change and increasing intolerance.

Tolerance and changing urban society

In 2007 the Joseph Rowntree Foundation (JRF) undertook a public consultation in which it asked the question 'What are today's social evils?' (Watts, 2008). Respondents to this exercise expressed concern about a decline of community, with neighbours thought to be increasingly isolated from one another. Similar concerns were expressed about a decline in the role of the family in modern Britain. In place of these social structures, respondents perceived others as tending to act in a selfish and insular manner, driven by consumerism and greed. Cumulatively, the findings of this study suggest the nature of urban society in Britain to be changing, or at least to be perceived as changing.

The findings of the JRF consultation have a strong resonance with the insights of those who have probed the consequences for urban living of globalisation in late modernity. Migration, individualism (particularly as embodied in consumer culture) and economic uncertainty have all been suggested as contributing to the fracturing of traditional social structures, creating conditions in which we have little consideration for the sensibilities of others. Rather, the splintering of society brought about by these forces (see inter alia, Graham and Marvin, 2001) leads social groups to retreat from engagement with others in the public realm (Sennett, 1996) and to segregate dynamically into privatised enclaves (Atkinson and Flint, 2005).

Diversity itself may pose a significant challenge to the exercise of tolerance. This is ironic, given that the formalisation of the principles of tolerance was based on the moral and practical need to accommodate difference. However, the co-presence of multiple identities (as embodied in different cultures, subcultures, religions and so forth), on a scale and of a nature made possible by the globalisation of peoples and markets, can act to overwhelm the traditional societal mechanisms of accommodation and engagement. Taking the perceived consequences of migration as an example, it is of little surprise, though of much concern, that the 2006 Scottish Social Attitudes Survey found that half of those questioned thought that Scotland would lose its identity if any more Muslims came to the country, and almost one-third believed that there is sometimes a good reason to be prejudiced (*The Herald*, 2007).

As for the emergence of multiple subcultures, identity is closely bound to consumption and always has been. Yet, 'what may be new is that consumers are more sophisticated in their awareness of this and more self-consciously collusive in the face of the expanding range of alternatives produced by a global market' (Jenkins, 1996: 8). In other words, we are able to express ourselves, our uniqueness in relation to those with whom we share the city, in more ways than ever before. Finally, a growing economic uncertainty, that which reminds us of our interconnected vulnerability (such as in the recent credit, fuel and food crises) also serves to drive us apart. Young (2007: 12), in *The Vertigo of Late Modernity*, suggests that our recognition of the insecurity of economic position and of growing inequalities fosters 'feelings of resentment both in those looking up the class structure and those peering down'.

Taken as a whole, the diversity embodied in the globalisation of peoples and markets, as framed by economic uncertainty, serves to overwhelm and/or damage the capacities of our traditional social structures to accommodate and engage with difference. It is not surprising, if this process remains unchecked, that the social fabric becomes torn, that we withdraw into a privatised existence. However, we are not always able to fulfil our goals without recourse to the public realm. This presents us with a significant dilemma, as 'there is no longer a set of shared values to guide behaviour', according to the respondents of the JRF consultation (Watts, 2008: 1). Our response, made with the support of public policy, is to engage in a process of 'othering'. By this we mean to engage in the act of labelling the other as threatening and/or deficient, thus providing a justification for their exclusion from the public realm. As Ellickson (2001: 21) contends, for a space 'to be truly public, a space must be orderly enough to invite the entry of a larger majority of those who come to it'. It is this logic that we use to justify the exclusion of those identities we perceive as impeding our own. In this way, contemporary urban society can be characterised as exhibiting 'a lack of tolerance, compassion and respect' (Watts, 2008: 1).

A cycle of intolerance?

Different approaches to tolerance are being played out across the city, and people's thresholds of tolerance are sensitive to the context in which they find themselves sharing space with others. What, then, is the trajectory of tolerance in Britain? Does tolerance remain a resilient virtue? In this section we question whether current approaches to tolerance, framed by the forces shaping urban living, are in fact serving to fuel a cycle of intolerance, where our thresholds of tolerance are spiralling downwards. And, if so, what might we expect of an intolerant Britain?

Are social encounters increasingly qualified by uncivil as opposed to civil qualities? Certainly, it is difficult to conceive of a thoughtfulness for, or considerateness of, others as a defining characteristic of social interactions in contemporary Britain. Moreover, public perception that crime and anti-social behaviour are worsening appears to be indicative of a lack of respect for others being embedded in face-to-face interaction. Responding to this perceived challenge to civility, the rhetoric underpinning the Respect Agenda (as we indicated earlier) suggests that those identified as acting in a disrespectful manner have stretched our tolerance to breaking point.

Drawing on Young (2007), the *Respect Action Plan* (Respect Task Force, 2006) serves to 'other' the perceived perpetrators of disrespect, to create a 'them' and 'us' situation. It conceives of those engaged in anti-social behaviour as being different from the majority of the population, it accuses them of not possessing the 'clear value system' shared by us. 'Othering' can be framed in both liberal and conservative terms. 'Others', qualified through a liberal gaze, are identified as lacking the characteristics that would make them like us; and qualified through a conservative gaze, as possessing negative attributes that set them apart from us. Liberal agendas stress reformation, whereas conservative agendas demand expulsion. Examination of the *Respect Action Plan* reveals initiatives (though not necessarily a balanced strategy) informed by both liberal and conservative perspectives.

But can we lay the blame for incivility at the feet of 'others'? Do the rest of us really share common values? Do we always act in a civil manner towards others in the urban realm? Hunter (1995) identifies an emerging asymmetry in public space between the expression of public rights and public duties, with our rights perceived to outweigh our duties. By extension, we believe it is our right to use public space as we see fit and without being impeded by others. In so doing, we express lower regard for, and a decreasing awareness of, the effect of our own behaviour on others. We endeavour to use public space in an increasingly privatised, selfish fashion. For Watson (2006), the expression of private behaviours in public spaces feeds animosity towards others. She states that:

> Underlying some of the resistances to rubbing along in public, encountering others who are different, is a distaste towards others who behave in ways that are deemed inappropriate and unacceptable, often because they are designated as 'private', and that this produces and legitimates hostility in the self to others who are different. (Watson, 2006: 161)

If we are all tending to act in such an individualistic fashion, is not the anti-social behaviour of others rooted in the general qualities of urban living rather than the deficient or negative attributes of the other, the qualities of the many, rather than the qualities of the few? Bunting (2008), taking up the case of the negative labelling of young people's activities in public space, for example, suggests: 'Antisocial teenagers are simply playing out their own version of the aggression and indifference that has been meted out to them.'

The preference for privacy, then, has permeated our use of public space and impacted on the frequency and nature of the social interactions in which we engage. Consider the last time you talked to a stranger. Even when occupying public space, it is rare to engage in conversation with another member of the public. Quite simply, there is little reason or justification to do so. We endeavour to support our privatised use of public space through designing or regulating it to be mono-functional, to support a single activity (such as shopping) or to allow multiple private endeavours that do not require physical or verbal social interaction. The physical spaces and social purposes for interaction in the public realm are being eradicated.

This simplification or purification of space may seem attractive in an age of uncertainty but, perversely, it holds the potential to fuel that uncertainty yet further, and in so doing to lower our thresholds of tolerance. In line with Sennett (1996), if we withdraw from social interaction with others in the public realm, if we always mix with the like-minded and similar, we will lose our ability to negotiate the shared use of space. Rather, we will come to rely on what we see and hear indirectly to form a judgement of other people's intentions, of their values. Stereotyping, rather than learning about others through direct interaction, encourages us to err on the side of caution. It is safer to assume the worst. Our growing anxieties are more comfortably processed when projected onto the perceived flaws of others, rather than being rooted in our collective frailties. If left unchecked, increasingly minor (perceived) infringements will tend to breach our tolerance threshold, leading to increased demands to regulate the behaviour, or exclude the presence, of those regarded as different from us. Not only this, but with

> so little tolerance of disorder in their own lives, and having shut themselves off so that they have little experience of disorder as well, the eruption of social tension becomes a situation in which the ultimate methods of aggression, violent force and reprisal, seem to become not only justified, but life preserving. (Sennett, 1996: 44–5)

In this sense, the recursive relationship between social withdrawal, social anxiety and regulatory demands produces a cycle of intolerance.

Conclusion: urban (in)tolerance

> No man born with a living soul, can be working for the
> clampdown. ('Clampdown', Strummer/Jones –The Clash,
> 1979)

The launch of the Youth Taskforce in 2007 effectively saw the end of the
Respect Action Plan, although elements of the Respect Agenda survived.
At the time, government ministers expressed concern that their own
intense focus on the anti-social behaviour of young people had 'brought
about a negative image of British youth' when 'most young people
contribute to society' (*The Guardian*, 2007: 4). A year earlier, Louise
Casey, the civil servant charged with delivering 'Respect', appeared
to have offered a change of tack. She suggested that we should strive
to promote good manners: 'we need a greater sense that it's ok to be
decent ... you're the person who's making Britain the country that
we want to live in' (Sylvester and Thomson, 2007: 1). But how should
we define good manners? And who are deemed to have good and bad
manners? Does it remain a case of 'us' and 'them'?

Our regard, use and regulation of public space are a barometer of
tolerance in urban Britain. As the forces shaping urban living in late
modernity serve to promote difference and dynamic segregation, we
have become trapped in a cycle of intolerance. Attempting to address
our anxieties by withdrawal to private enclaves, by adopting a privatised
use of public space and by striving to exclude the 'other', we have only
served to fuel our anxieties and lower our threshold of tolerance. The
spectrum of unfavoured behaviours becomes concertinaed; more and
more (minor) actions are perceived to threaten our social norms, and
consequently demand to be condemned. 'Others' should show respect
to 'us' by adopting a code of conduct that we see fit.

Watson (2006) contends that it is (ultimately) counterproductive to
endeavour to bring people together with a common identity. The more
that we strive to impose a common code of conduct, the more we
will become aware, and anxious, of the differences between us. Rather,
'engagement across differences, a mutual respect for those who are
different from oneself, and a space for them to be so, is a precondition
for space to be public' (Watson, 2006: 171). The challenge remains to
explore the mechanisms by which tolerance, respect and civility can
be reinvigorated (in all of us) in the city, rather than solely developing
strategies designed to confront growing intolerance, disrespect and
incivility.

Here, the pursuance of a form of cohesion that stresses consensus and conformity is counterproductive, since it serves to highlight social differences and to frame those differences as undesirable and unacceptable. Such an approach denies the diversity of society, rather than embracing it. Social progress, alongside social harmony, can only come from an approach which acknowledges social differences, affords those differences legitimacy and seeks to develop our mutual respect and tolerance of each other, both generally and in specific contexts; rather than an approach which simply demands that various minority social groups 'show respect' to the moral majority and the more powerful in society. Neither tolerance nor respect will flourish and survive if they evidently involve only one-way traffic. Current public policies and their associated public discourses are, unfortunately, fostering both the sociospatial conditions and the public attitudes which feed a climate of intolerance (with, at best, a complement of static tolerance). As such, they run counter to the development of social and community cohesion in an era of urban change and diversity.

Notes

[1] In what follows we refer to the tolerance of 'conduct' as a convenient shorthand for all objects of tolerance.

[2] In this case, juvenile delinquency.

References

Atkinson, R. and Flint, J. (2005) 'Fortress UK? Gated communities, the spatial revolt of the elites and time-space trajectories of segregation', *Housing Studies*, 19(6), 875–92.

Bannister, J., Fyfe, N. and Kearns, A. (2006) 'Respectable or respectful? (In)civility and the city', *Urban Studies*, 43(5/6), 919–37.

Berman, M. (1982) *All That Is Solid Melts into Air: The Experience of Modernity*, New York, NY: Simon and Schuster.

Blair, T. (2005) 'Blair pledges new "yob" crackdown'. Available at: http://news.bbc.co.uk/1/hi/uk_politics/4538599.stm.

Boyd, R. (2006) 'The value of civility?', *Urban Studies*, 43(5), 863–78.

Bunting, M. (2008) 'From buses to blogs, a pathological individualism is poisoning public life'. Available at: http://guardian.co.uk/commentisfree/2008/jan/28/comment.society.

Burns, T.R. (1992) *Erving Goffman*, London: Routledge.

Calder, A. (1991) *The Myth of the Blitz*, London: Pimlico.

Cavan, R.S. (1961) 'The concepts of tolerance and contraculture as applied to delinquency', *The Sociological Quarterly*, 2(4), 243–58.

Daily Telegraph (2007) 'Manners make a nation', Comment, 2 June, p 27.

Ellickson, R.C. (2001) 'Controlling chronic misconduct in city spaces: of panhandlers, skid row and public-space zoning', in N. Blomley, D. Delaney and R. Ford (eds) *The Legal Geographies Reader: Law, Power and Space*, Oxford: Blackwell, pp 19–30.

Fyfe, N., Bannister, J. and Kearns, A. (2006) '(In)civility and the city', *Urban Studies*, 43(5/6), 853–61.

Graham, S. and Marvin, S. (2001) *Splintering Urbanism: Networked Infrastructures, Technological Mobilities and the Urban Condition*, London: Routledge.

The Guardian (2007) 'Ministers scrap Blair's Respect taskforce', 24 March, p 4.

Hancock, L. and Matthews, R. (2001) 'Crime, community safety and toleration', in R. Matthews and J. Pitts (eds) *Crime, Disorder and Community Safety*, London: Routledge, pp 99–119.

The Herald (2007) 'Huge rise in Scots with racist prejudices: study shows anti-Muslim feeling', 12 December, p 1.

Home Office (2003) *Respect and Responsibility: Taking a Stand against Anti-social Behaviour*, London: Home Office.

Home Office (2004) *Confident Communities in a Secure Britain: The Home Office Strategic Plan 2004–08*, London: Home Office.

Horton, J. and Nicholson, P. (1992) 'Philosophy and the practice of toleration', in J. Horton and P. Nicholson (eds) *Toleration: Philosophy and Practice*, Aldershot: Avebury.

Hunter, A. (1985), 'Private, parochial and public social orders: the problem of crime and incivility in urban communities', in G. Suttles and M. Zald (eds) *The Challenge of Social Control: Citizenship and Institution Building in Modern Society*, Norwood, NJ: Ablex. (Reprinted in Kasinitz, P. (ed) *Metropolis: Centre and Symbol of Our Times*, London: Macmillan), pp 209–25.

Jenkins, R. (1996) *Social Identity*, London: Routledge.

Karstedt, S. (2007) 'Tolerance', in G. Ritzer (ed) *Blackwell Encyclopedia of Sociology*, Blackwell Reference Online. Accessible at: www.sociologyencyclopedia.com/public/book.

Keun, O. (1934) *I Discover the English*, London: John Lane, The Bodley Head.

Knowles, D. (2001) *Political Philosophy*, London: UCL Press.

Mendus, S. (1989) *Tolerance and the Limits of Liberalism*, Hampshire: Macmillan Education Ltd.

Newey, G. (1999) 'Tolerance as a virtue', in S. Mendus and J. Horton (eds) *Toleration: Identity and Difference*, London: Macmillan, pp 38–64.

Nicholas, S., Kershaw, C. and Walker, A. (eds) (2007) *Crime in England and Wales 2006/07, 4th Edition*, Home Office Statistical Bulletin 11/07, London: Home Office.

Parekh, B. (2000) *Rethinking Multiculturalism: Cultural Diversity and Political Theory*, Basingstoke: Palgrave.

Paxman, J. (1999) *The English: A Portrait of a People*, Harmondsworth: Penguin.

Respect Task Force (2006) *Respect Action Plan*, London: Home Office.

Scottish Executive (2003) *Putting Our Communities First: A Strategy for Tackling Anti-social Behaviour*, Edinburgh: Scottish Executive.

Seligman, A.B. (1999) 'Toleration and religious tradition', *Society*, 36(5), 47–53.

Sennett, R. (1996) *The Uses of Disorder: Personal Identity and City Life*, London: Faber and Faber.

Sennett, R. (2003) *Respect: The Formation of Character in an Age of Inequality*, London: Penguin.

Sullivan, J.L. and Transue, J.E. (1999) 'The psychological underpinnings of democracy: a selective review of research on political tolerance, interpersonal trust, and social capital', *Annual Review of Psychology*, 50, 625–50.

Sylvester, R. and Thomson, A. (2007) 'Good manners "can triumph over Britain's yob culture"', *The Daily Telegraph*, 2 June, p 1.

Watson, S. (2006) *City Publics: The (Dis)enchanments of Urban Encounters*, London: Routledge.

Watts, B. (2008) *What are Today's Social Evils? The Results of a Web Consultation*, York: The Joseph Rowntree Foundation.

Wood, M. (2004) *Perceptions and Experience of Antisocial Behaviour: Findings from the 2003/2004 British Crime Survey*, Online Report 49/04, London: Home Office.

Young, J. (2007) *The Vertigo of Late Modernity*, London: Sage.

EIGHT

Respect and city living: contest or cosmopolitanism?

Andrew Millie

The contemporary western city attracts people with different cultures, values, backgrounds, beliefs, languages and traditions. Of course, I am stating the obvious and, in fact, this has been true for most cities, for most of the time. However, understanding how these differences can work together as a cosmopolitan whole, or whether they work in contest to cause suspicion, strife and resentment, is key to the promotion of respectful city living, to promoting urban cultures of respect for the 'other'. For instance, different groups can have contested understandings of what is acceptable or unacceptable behaviour, with those seen as unacceptable being labelled as anti-social or disrespectful 'others'. In urban spaces young people, particularly when in groups, are often seen as fitting this 'disrespectful' category and are regarded as a source of nuisance and incivility; similarly, street sex workers, the homeless, street people, those with mental health problems, or other problematic or challenging categories of 'them'. In this chapter city living is considered as a contest of behavioural expectations, with different groups being more or less willing to have their expectations challenged. In anticipation of the conclusions, it is suggested that urban living should test our beliefs and expectations, that there needs to be an element of risk because this is what urban living is all about. It is argued that, rather than leading to contest and fear of the other, urban encounters can in fact help to nurture mutual respect; as Richard Sennett (1970: 108) suggested nearly 40 years ago, a more *mature* urban living is

> a life with other people in which men [sic] learn to tolerate painful ambiguity and uncertainty. To counter the desire for slavery ... [and] grow to need the unknown, to feel incomplete without a certain anarchy in their lives, to learn ... to love the 'otherness' around them.

A similar claim was made by Kevin Robins (1995: 48), that fear and anxiety are worth encountering as they are 'the other side of the stimulation and challenge associated with cosmopolitanism' (see also Bannister and Fyfe, 2001). Admittedly, there are numerous events that are painful, fearful or anxiety inducing and that are certainly *not* worth encountering; and such a 'mature' or 'cosmopolitan' perspective leans towards the utopian. However, in this chapter it is argued that mutuality of respect is possible and that this might require 'a certain anarchy'. This is, of course, something quite different from the type of respect sought by the British government. The view from New Labour has been that 'the values the majority hold dear are not shared by a selfish minority' (Respect Task Force, 2006: 3). It is this 'selfish minority' that is targeted by a huge armoury of anti-social behaviour enforcement measures; as Hazel Blears MP has similarly stated, 'the decent people [need] to be able to take control of their neighbourhoods and communities' (Respect Task Force 2006: 37). However, in what follows I argue that the division between 'decent people' and a selfish or disrespectful minority is not so clear cut.

The chapter considers the relationships between respect and plurality, consumerism and urban aesthetics and performance. The discussion is framed by the notion of 'cosmopolitanism'. Like its close relations 'multiculturalism' and 'globalisation' (and, for that matter, 'respect') it is a concept that has proved problematic; but as Appiah (2006: xii) notes, it is also a term that 'can be rescued'.

Context

But first it is worth providing some context. In political discourse anti-social behaviour is frequently regarded as a problem of predation by a disrespectful minority on a law-abiding majority. As noted, it is a simple divide between decent people (us) and bad people (them). It is a perspective that Tony Blair noted in the Foreword to the *Respect Action Plan* (Respect Task Force, 2006: 1):

> We will take tough action so that the majority of law-abiding, decent people no longer have to tolerate the behaviour of the few individuals and families that think they do not have to show respect to others.

It is highly questionable that a lack of respect is restricted to the few. The claim that a majority is law-abiding is also dubious. The vast majority will have broken the law at some point, be it motorway speeding, 'dodgy' tax returns, or perhaps minor fraud to get a child into a good school (Millie, 2008a). Even if people have been entirely law abiding, in line with Durkheim's (2003) society of saints, they will almost certainly have breached some generally accepted norm of behaviour. (And their behaviour may also have been regarded as disrespectful.) But a dichotomised view between a good 'us' and a bad 'them' makes for expedient – albeit lazy – politics. For instance, in announcing 40 'Respect Zones'[1] across England in January 2007, Blair is reported as having said, 'We are not demonising them. We are simply asking that the local community can get to have the power to make these people conform or face the consequences' (*BBC News Online*, 2007). Blair may have thought he was not demonising 'these people', but his view of 'conform or face the consequences' was a little bit chilling. It is a view of respect on the majority's (or perhaps the government's?) terms. Does this mean anyone who holds a different perspective of what is acceptable behaviour is disrespectful of this majority? Of course not; but it is a view that has shaped the government's agenda on respect. Further, in the *Respect Action Plan* Blair states that, 'Everyone can change – [but] if people who need help will not take it, we will make them' (Respect Task Force, 2006: 1). His replacement as Prime Minister, Gordon Brown, continued in a similar vein, stating that 'we want to see young people who get into trouble made to take the help they need to mend their ways' (Youth Taskforce, 2008: 34). Clearly, those who step over the respect/disrespect line will be made to 'conform', 'mend their ways', *or* 'face the consequences'.

Of course, it is true that some people are anti-social and disrespectful, that they can cause great misery to others, and their behaviour will certainly need attention. But anti-social behaviour can be misidentified and overestimated (Millie, 2007; 2008b). Where the line between respect and disrespect sits, and how serious or repetitive misbehaviour has to become before it is deemed to be anti-social, is not easy to determine. In an urban situation, determining behavioural acceptability may be doubly problematic, as there are going to be plural norms, all competing for a dominant position. It is this plurality that is considered next.

Respect and plurality

Plurality is central to a postmodern take on society (eg Milovanovic, 1997); however, as outlined in the Introduction to this volume, as a concept it clearly predates postmodernism (or, for that matter, late modernity), with writing on pluralism, for example, going back to Kant (see Hill, 2000). During the twentieth century much was made of the notion of liberal or consensual pluralism. For instance, John Horton (1973) considered how societies consisting of different or plural social and cultural norms could be governed. He cited the earlier work of Furnivall (1948: 304) on colonialism in Asia, where there was thought to be a 'medley of peoples ... [who] mix but do not combine'. According to Horton (1973: 17), in such circumstances order was reliant on 'political force and economic expediency', a situation clearly at odds with liberalism *and* consensus. Others were equally pessimistic about a broader application of liberal pluralism; for instance, Horton quotes Norman Podhoretz, writing in the *Washington Post* (1964):

> The vision of a world in which many different groups live together on a footing of legal and social equality, each partaking of a broad general culture and yet maintaining its own distinctive identity: this is one of the noble dreams of the liberal tradition. Yet the hard truth is that little evidence exists to suggest that such a pluralistic order is possible. Most societies throughout history have simply been unable to suffer the presence of distinctive minority groups among them ...

This type of pluralism (or lack thereof) relates largely to issues of governance and state power (see also Berlin, 1969; Galston, 2005) and is relevant to attempts at multiculturalism (more of which later). Writing from an American perspective, David Matza (1964; 1969) more specifically related what he termed cultural pluralism to deviancy in stating that 'In a pluralistic society, one man's deviation may be another's custom' (1969: 11). Essentially, the same behaviour or action could be differently interpreted by groups or individuals as normal or deviant, as acceptable or unacceptable. Such a situation may seem ungovernable; as Downes and Rock (1982: 4) have noted: 'If "pluralism" and "shifting standards" work on deviant behaviour to render it ambiguous and fluid, no coherent and definitive argument can ever completely capture it.' This may be true, but it does not mean a single moral, cultural or behavioural perspective should dominate.

Matza (1964: 62) also warned of the dangers of 'confusing a richly pluralistic ... normative system with a simple puritanism' (see also Hill, 2000). However, with the neoliberalism promoted from 1979 onwards by the Conservatives under Thatcher in the UK (and by Reagan in the US, as well as elsewhere), came a distinctly puritanical political and policy discourse. According to Anthony Giddens (1994: 9), this is a central contradiction within neoliberal politics:

On the one hand neoliberalism is hostile to tradition – and is indeed one of the main forces sweeping away tradition everywhere, as a result of the promotion of market forces and an aggressive individualism. On the other, it *depends upon* the persistence of tradition for its legitimacy and its attachment to conservatism – in the areas of the nation, religion, gender and the family. Having no proper theoretical rationale, its defence of tradition in these areas normally takes the form of fundamentalism.

Clear examples would be the 1979–97 Conservative government's agendas on 'family values' and 'back-to-basics'. And despite claims for a new, third way agenda (Blair, 1998), a great deal of New Labour's approach followed a similar course, both in terms of neoliberal economics and in moralising discourse. Drawing on the communitarian writing of Etzioni (eg 1996), Blair followed a moralising path aimed at individual and collective obligations and responsibilities, alongside inclusion and opportunity (Lister, 1998). Policies to tackle anti-social behaviour, and New Labour's focus on respect *and* responsibility clearly fitted in with this moral and political positioning (as explored in Chapter One by Elizabeth Burney).

In translating the ideas of neoliberalism and pluralism to behaviour in urban spaces there is clearly scope for conflict. On the one hand, there is the government's neoliberal stance that individual enterprise is 'good'; but individualism that leads to behaviour that does not fit in with (the government's) moral position is 'bad' or 'disrespectful'. Yet there is the liberal and pluralist position centred on a multiplicity of norms and that – particularly in an urban environment – difference should be *at least* tolerated, if not actively embraced. How tolerance can be negotiated in an urban environment was explored by Jon Bannister and Ade Kearns in the preceding chapter. In what follows I focus on the position of respect within the neoliberal consumerist city. The scope for a true cosmopolitanism is considered, that allows for plurality of behavioural norms and expectations, and where mutual respect between city dwellers becomes more of a possibility.

Respect in the consumerist city

According to Keith Hayward (2004: 3): 'The vast majority of people in the industrialised West now live in a world in which their everyday existence is, to a greater or lesser degree, dominated by the pervasive triad of advertising/marketing, the stylisation of social life, and mass consumption.' He is certainly not alone in this observation (eg Sibley, 1995; MacLeod and Ward, 2002; Clarke, 2003), and there would be little argument that the dominant culture within the neoliberal city *is* consumption. For decades the active promotion of this consumption has been integral to the regeneration and viability of urban centres in the UK. For instance, in the early 1980s many city centres were in decline. There was increasing economic competition from emerging out-of-town retail and leisure developments, economic uncertainty accompanying recession, plus rioting within major cities, including London, Bristol, Liverpool and Birmingham. Following the 1981 Brixton riots in London, Lord Scarman called for an 'effective co-ordinated approach to tackling inner city problems' (see Scarman, 1984: 260). The Conservative government responded via Michael Heseltine's (1983) inner city revival plans, which later evolved into policies for 'vital and viable' urban living (URBED/DoE, 1994). When New Labour came to power in 1997 one of the main policy agendas was for 'urban renaissance', as promoted by Lord Rogers' Urban Task Force (1999). For all of these policy developments a healthy urban centre was deemed to equate with a place were retail consumption could flourish. And, for consumers to be attracted back to these centres, they needed to be safe places (or at least perceived to be safe places). For instance, a stated aim for the Safer Cities programme that ran from 1988 to 1995 was to reduce crime and fear in order to 'create safer cities where economic enterprise and community life can flourish' (Home Office, 1984). Much more recently, the Labour government has called for 'cleaner, safer, greener' urban living. As part of this policy agenda, the link between consumption and perceived safety is made clear by Phil Hope, MP (ODPM, 2005), who claimed:

> Our success in revitalising town centres should be celebrated
> – we have a new vibrancy and vitality at the heart of our
> major cities throughout the day and night which would
> have been unthinkable twenty years ago. We are committed
> to continued growth and development of our town centre
> as the heart of our communities. But this success has also
> concentrated our minds on the need to respond to the
> challenges it brings, including alcohol harm and anti-social
> behaviour. We know that it is possible to take a stand and
> combat poor behaviour to build the respect and pride
> people have in their town and city centres.

According to Phil Hope, there needs to be respect for our town and city centres. But it seems that this respect is tied to the promotion of consumption, be it the retail that dominates the day, or the alcohol that characterises the night-time economy, despite claims that 'alcohol harm' needs to be tackled. On the surface, there may not be a great deal wrong with the promotion of consumption. During the day, like most other people, I can enjoy (or at least tolerate) shopping in an attractive urban centre. But the cost of such a consumerist – or neoliberal – approach can be the exclusion of those seen as a threat to this consumption; what some writers regard as a blurring between *urban renaissance* objectives and *revanchism* aimed at reclaiming public spaces from 'undesirables' (eg Smith, 1996; MacLeod, 2002; Holden and Iveson, 2003). As Bannister et al (2006) have commented, it is an attempt to reclaim public spaces for a 'consuming majority'. Don Mitchell (2001:71) has explained the situation rather well:

> In the punitive city, the post modern city, the revanchist city, diversity is no longer maintained by protecting and struggling to expand the rights of the most disadvantaged, but by pushing the disadvantaged out, making it clear that, as broken windows rather than people, they simply have *no* right to the city.

In line with Wilson and Kelling's (1982) 'broken windows' thesis, the homeless and other 'undesirables' are seen merely as incivilities that mark the decline of a neighbourhood (as broken windows) rather than as people who have equal rights to public space. They need to be removed as part of consumption-oriented urban regeneration. Here the work of Tim Cresswell (1996) is relevant in what he sees as behaviour or people who are either 'in place' or 'out of place'. Clearly, shoppers are 'in place' within urban centres. The question is whether there is also a place in the city for alternative cultural expressions, behavioural expectations and uses of public space. To bring the discussion back to respect, it is whether someone will be respected in the city centre *only* if there to consume. As Jones and Foust (2008:2) have recently written about experiences in the US: 'As the downtown's diversity cedes to a more homogenous class of affluence, people who are "out of place" in gentrified space become increasingly unwelcome.' This situation is equally applicable to the UK. For instance, writing about the out-of-town MetroCentre retail development in Gateshead, Adam Crawford has noted: 'Their enticement to "good customers" is mirrored by their interdiction of "failed customers"' (Crawford, 2006: 126). Further, Crawford has claimed:

> Those who are 'not good for the image' of the centre are 'asked to leave' as a type of pre-emptive exclusion of those who have no commercial value or who are not seen to 'belong'. (2006: 127)

Writing over a decade earlier, Jon Goss (1993: 35) observed that the North American mall user 'cannot escape the imperative to consume: she or he cannot loiter in the mall unless implicitly invited to do so'. More recently, also writing from an American perspective, Staeheli and Mitchell (2008: 87) have similarly noted:

> the publicly private spaces of the mall are cleansed of those people whom 'legitimate' members of the public find offensive or worrying, or more specifically, the mall is cleansed of those people who may challenge social norms and expectations related to civility (and perhaps consumption).

Those who were 'not good for the image', or 'challenge social norms and expectations' for these semi-public spaces are, according to Goss (1993: 35), '[loiterers] without shopping bags and other suspicious individuals (teenagers, single men, the unkempt, and social science researchers) [who] will draw the attention of security, who use the charge of loitering as grounds for eviction'.

A high-profile example in Britain was the exclusion in 2005 of young people wearing 'hoodies' from the Bluewater retail centre in Kent. In my own experience, trying to take photos in a British city centre as part of my research, I have had security guards tell me not to use a camera in a privately owned shopping mall, and similarly in a local authority owned bus station. My experience was one of inconvenience, but for many young people in groups (and other 'loiterers') such intervention from 'security' has more serious exclusionary consequences. Young people have for decades chosen the mall as a place to hang out (Matthews et al, 2000; Manzo, 2004), yet they are regarded as 'out of place' if they are there to congregate and not to consume. The relevance to the Respect Agenda is that the views of the 'consuming majority', who may perceive groups of youths as potentially troubling, are catered for. In fact, in a recent national survey (Millie et al, 2005), groups of young people 'hanging about' was thought to be the biggest anti-social behaviour problem in places where people live. It seems these concerns are also present within the urban centre. Yet the views of the young people – who may not be doing anything wrong by 'hanging about' – are not always heard or respected. The same could apply to other supposedly 'problematic' users of public space who are seen as 'out of place', including street drinkers or homeless people. In the neoliberal British city their presence is frequently relabelled as anti-social behaviour.

The 2003 Anti-Social Behaviour Act (section 30) took the idea of problematic presence a step further with the introduction of Dispersal Order powers (Crawford and Lister, 2007; Millie, 2008b; 2009). Under a Dispersal Order, within a designated area a police officer or community support officer can disperse groups if he or she 'has reasonable grounds for believing that the presence or behaviour of a group of two or more persons ... has resulted, or is likely to result, in any members of the public being intimidated, harassed, alarmed or distressed'. The key phrase is 'presence or behaviour'. In effect, if an officer believes that a group *may* be anti-social, just by being present, then that group can be moved on. There are parallel measures in some American states, including various anti-homeless laws (Mitchell, 1997) and gang loitering ordinances introduced for 'apparent' gang members (Levi, 2008).

Things get a little more complicated in the evening and night, with urban centres taking on a very different character. The consuming majority still dominates, but this majority is invariably highly fuelled on alcohol and includes some who may commit anti-social behaviour and violence – to the extent that the reputation of the city centre in the evening is often exclusionary to people seeking alternative entertainments (Bromley et al, 2000). It may not be the case that drunken anti-social behaviour and violence are tolerated in the night-time economy because people are spending money; but a lot of 'rowdy' behaviour or 'high spirits' that is acceptable at night would not be tolerated in the daytime city. Within this different context it would be deemed as inappropriate drunken behaviour and would deter others from consuming, from shopping.

There is a clear contest between the provision of urban public spaces appropriate for maximising consumption, both during the day and in the night-time economy (a neoliberal approach), and the creation of cities that respect and embrace difference (a liberal pluralist approach). Invariably, the consuming majority wins, either the shopping majority during the day, or the drinking majority at night.

Respect and cosmopolitanism

As stated at the start of this chapter, cities are attractors for people with different beliefs and backgrounds. These may be derived from, for instance, national or regional identity, class, language, ethnicity, religion, sexuality, resident or asylum status, mainstream or alternative cultures, youth, middle or old age, and so on. The question is whether mutual respect is possible in the midst of this diversity. Multiculturalism is one option but, despite its recognition of plural cultural experiences and perspectives, it is criticised for being 'past-oriented' and for being an idea where 'community, culture, tradition and identity are privileged and respected above all else' (McGhee, 2005: 168) (see also Parekh, 2000).[2] With suitable journalistic hyperbole, Alibhai-Brown (2001: 47) claims this 'old' multiculturalism 'has come to the end of its useful life'. A possible alternative is suggested by Leonie Sandercock (2006: 46), that:

> The concept of multiculturalism needs to be transformed in response to critiques of its fatal flaws, rather than abandoned. This leads me to define an *intercultural perspective* (or cosmopolitan urbanism) as a political and philosophical basis for thinking about how to deal with the challenge of difference in the mongrel cities of the twenty-first century.

Interculturalism accepts that people have multiple or plural identities, but also looks to bridge divides. According to Wood and Landry (2008: 16) interculturalism emphasises a spectrum of 'acceptance of difference', from 'coexistence, tolerance, to active interaction, cooperation and … co-creation', rather than the alternatives of 'active hatred, passing through aversion … to sufferance [and] benign indifference' (see also Bloomfield and Bianchini, 2004; Wood, 2004). In simple terms, we are presented with a choice; whether to embrace difference – or otherness – or to retreat into our particular sociocultural-ethno-religious (or other) silos. As Wood and Landry (2008: 24) have suggested:

> Many people believe they have more important duties to family members, friends, compatriots and their ethnicity rather than to strangers, foreigners or the planet. The 'intercultural city' notion challenges us to re-engage with the strange and the different and the planet. Indeed,

welcoming the stranger is part of the tradition of most cultures.

Without such re-engagement, the views of the (consuming) majority will dominate. As Sandercock (2006: 40) has noted: 'In the absence of a practice of intercultural dialogue, conflicts are insolvable except by the imposition of one culture's views on another.' To return to the British Respect Agenda, there is the Hazel Blears view, as already noted, that 'the decent people [need] to be able to take control of their neighbourhoods and communities' (Respect Task Force 2006: 37). Rather than all groups retreating into their particular silos, the only retreating – and with some encouragement – is by minorities labelled as disrespectful, or as 'not decent people'.

In order to understand better this relationship between respectable majority and disrespectful minority, as played out in the neoliberal consumerist city, I use the concept of 'urban cosmopolitanism', a perspective closely allied to interculturalism (eg Binnie et al, 2006; Sandercock, 2006). The cosmopolitan city is one that, at least, has the potential to accommodate diversity – or plurality – of experience and expectation; similarly, it is where mutual respect within and between different groups is possible, as much as the alternative scenario, contest. But first, it is worth considering what is meant by cosmopolitanism.

As noted, like 'respect', cosmopolitanism can be a contested concept. It is a notion that dates back to the Cynics of the fourth century BC, was taken up by the Stoics a century later, and then proved attractive to early Christianity with an emphasis on 'the oneness of humanity' (Appiah, 2006: xii). As a concept, cosmopolitanism was elaborated by Kant (1957 [1795]), who used it in relation to international political relations. For others, it equated to a desire for global citizenship, for moving beyond the nation state (eg Bohman and Lutz-Bachmann, 1997; Fine and Boon, 2007). The narrower concept of urban cosmopolitanism translates into 'an openness to, desire for, and appreciation of, social and cultural difference' (Binnie et al, 2006: 7). Rather than being a 'philosophy of world citizenship' (Binnie et al, 2006: 13), it is locally based, focusing on the 'skills and attitudes' required for the formation of relationships, communities, neighbourhoods and cities that embrace difference. The writing of Leonie Sandercock (1998; 2003; 2006) is important here, especially her work on a utopian cosmopolitan city she called 'Cosmopolis', where there is 'genuine acceptance of, connection with, and respect and space for the cultural other, and … the possibility of a togetherness in difference' (2003: 2).

Ulrich Beck has expressed scepticism as to whether such a state is possible, instead recognising a conflict between 'cosmopolitanization *and its enemies*' (Beck, 2002: 29). The enemies were identified as nationalism, globalism and democratic authoritarianism. These may be also the enemies of mutual respect. For instance, nationalism is a resurgent feature of many UK cities – especially post-devolution in Scotland, Wales and Northern Ireland[3] – and can be powerfully allied to notions of respect and disrespect (as explored in relation to sectarianism in Scotland by Flint and Powell in Chapter Nine). Beck's concepts of globalism and democratic authoritarianism are also relevant to respect in the neoliberal city. According to Beck (2002: 40):

> Global capitalism *threatens* the culture of democratic freedom in that it radicalizes social inequalities and revokes the principles of fundamental social justice and security. In this sense, globalism is a powerful opponent of cosmopolitan societies.

If a true reading of *mutual* respect is related to cosmopolitan living (and I think it is), then, if Beck is right, the capitalist system itself is a brake on the creation of respectful city living. Urban individualism and the urge to consume certainly make 'respect and space for the cultural other' (Sandercock, 2003: 2) a lot less likely. Further, the state's puritanism or moralising discourse (what Beck terms 'democratic authoritarianism'[4]) can also hinder the development of respect. As already noted, it becomes respect on the majority's, or the government's, terms.

Cosmopolitanism, respect and urban aesthetics

According to Ulf Hannerz (1990:239): 'A more genuine cosmopolitanism is first of all an orientation, a willingness to engage with the Other. It entails an intellectual and aesthetic stance toward divergent cultural experiences, a search for contrast rather than uniformity.' He goes on to state: 'To become acquainted with more cultures is to turn into an *aficionado*, to view them as art works' (1990: 239). Despite the danger that some cultures may be viewed as *bad* works of art, Hannerz's emphasis on aesthetics is significant. In terms of the current discussion, aesthetics also may be important in determining what (or who) is a respectable presence in the city; however, this will be determined by an aesthetic of neoliberal consumption rather than of the discerning cosmopolitan.

With consumption being the dominant activity in the neoliberal city, it is possible that the dominant aesthetic is also one of consumption. Correspondingly, any activity or presence that does not fit this model may be viewed as having a disrespectful or anti-social aesthetic (Millie, 2008b; 2008c), and can be excluded from urban streets or malls. Writing about North American experiences, Sharon Zukin (1995: 7) has a similar perspective:

> The look and feel of cities reflect decisions about what – and who – should be visible and what should not, on concepts of order and disorder, and on uses of aesthetic power.

Mitchell (1997: 324) has also observed in America that: 'Anti-homeless laws are ... an intervention in urban aesthetics, in debates over the look and form of the city.' Again, Tim Cresswell's (1996) idea of being 'in place' or 'out of place' is of relevance. For instance, Wright (1997) has written about the contested landscapes of urban America where homeless people are routinely seen as 'out of place'. The same would be true in the UK, where encounters with street people do not fit in with a city centre shopping aesthetic. Similarly in Australia, Nolan (2003) has written about skateboarding in urban spaces as being a transgressive act that is either 'in place' or 'out of place'. However, Nolan claims that skateboarding can be both in place and out of place at the same time, depending on whether it is perceived as being 'good' skateboarding (for transport) or 'bad' skateboarding (damaging property) (2003: 323). Accordingly, Nolan claims that total bans become a nonsense. I want to extend this analogy to consider the *aesthetic* of skateboarding. For instance, an area under the Queen Elizabeth Hall on London's South Bank has been a site for skateboarding for at least 30 years (Ward, 1978; Millie, 2009). It is a site ideal for skaters, with various ramps and rails used for jumps or tricks. Initially this activity was merely tolerated. But over this period the act of skating shifted from transgressive, disrespectful or 'out of place', to accepted and 'in place', and having an entertaining aesthetic that now draws tourists to the area. The site is now also a draw for BMX riders, graffiti writers and free runners, as well as for numerous tourists who enjoy the spectacle, the performance.

I shall return to this idea of urban performance, but first I want to consider further the links between an acceptable aesthetic and consumption, and how certain forms of behaviour become respected and celebrated in one situation, but are differently interpreted in another space as disrespectful and anti-social. A simple example is the acceptability or otherwise of graffiti. I've mentioned that graffiti writing has become acceptable at the Queen Elizabeth Hall site. This is the more traditional forms of Hip Hop and tag graffiti that originated in 1960s New York and Philadelphia (eg Ferrell, 1993). At this location the artistry and skill of the graffiti writers are tolerated and have become respected and celebrated. But this is unusual; the same activity conducted elsewhere in the city is seen as anti-social, disrespectful, and frequently also criminal damage. In extreme cases it has resulted in the writer going to prison. In this example, location is the determining factor for acceptability and respectability; yet, *style* can similarly be key. For instance, writers who follow a post-graffiti (Dickens, 2008a; 2008b), more European aesthetic, using stencils, stickers, as well as spray paint (for example, Banksy, D*Face, and Jef Aérosol[5]) can find their work more often tolerated and, in certain instances, celebrated. A case in point is the work of Banksy, which has gained celebrity status to the extent that in his home town of Bristol – and elsewhere – it is seen as a tourist attraction (Millie, 2008b). To illustrate this point, according to a report in London's *Evening Standard* (Lefley, 2007), council workers in Islington have been seen 'touching up' a Banksy piece, while at the same time painting over tag graffiti at the same site. A representative of the local authority defended this action thus:

> 'We take a very hard line on graffiti and remove it within 24 hours when it is reported to us. However, residents have been telling us Banksy is in a class of his own, his art sells for thousands, and they don't want us to remove the work. Because of the quality and renown of Banksy's work in Islington many people want to see it preserved.'

There is clear respect from the local authority for Banksy's work. Yet, the same action by another graffiti writer would have quite a different response. Aesthetics and style clearly have a part to play in determining respectability. But, as the above quote demonstrates, the perceived *value* of the work is also important, as 'his work sells for thousands'. This brings me back to the importance of consumption. For both Banksy's work, and the Hip Hop graffiti at Queen Elizabeth Hall, the tourist potential (and therefore money-earning potential[6]) is important in determining the graffiti as 'in place', and as being respectable. If a graffiti writer's work does not fit a certain aesthetic, or is not seen as a draw to the area, then it is disrespected (and similarly seen as disrespectful). Basing acceptability and respect on an aesthetic of consumption is a peculiar way of working and is something quite different from the ideals of cosmopolitanism.

It is possible that most users of public spaces do not want a city covered in graffiti (whatever the style). Similarly, when people go shopping they could find the sight of street people upsetting, or might be intimidated by groups of young people congregating. Skateboarders may distract from spending money on shopping, or be seen as a threat to public safety (see also Chapter Four by Helen Woolley). But if such different interpretations of urban living are excluded, the risk is that we are left with a sanitised, or 'Disneyfied' (Sorkin, 1992; Amster, 2003) version of urbanity. In such a city difference is only allowed in strictly controlled circumstances; as Lyn Lofland commented over 35 years ago about American urban planning: 'Having set aside certain public areas for certain activities, city fathers and populace alike look askance at any spill-over' (1973: 69).

It may be that for a true urban cosmopolitanism, and the creation of cities that respect diversity, that respect difference, we need to leave room for disorganised public spaces – not in some out-of-the-way location, but central to the urban experience. True, there will be more scope for contest and conflict; but following the principles of mutuality, these problems can be negotiated. The result will be cities characterised by vitality and conviviality – in short, they will be more cosmopolitan. According to Nigel Thrift (2005: 140):

> There is … a misanthropic thread that runs through the modern city, a distrust and avoidance of precisely the others that many writers feel we ought to be welcoming in a world increasingly premised on the mixing which the city first brought into existence.

It is such 'mixing' that is at the very heart of cosmopolitanism and of the creation of cities of mutual respect.

Respect as urban performance

As already noted, much of what goes on in urban public spaces can be regarded as a performance. This is not a new idea with, for instance, Lefebvre (1996) writing about the rhythm of the city. Jane Jacobs (1961: 50) was more specific, comparing a successful city sidewalk to a dance:

> not to a simple-minded precision dance with everyone kicking up at the same time, twirling in unison and bowing off en masse, but to an intricate ballet in which the

individual dancers and ensembles all have distinctive parts which miraculously reinforce each other and compose an orderly whole.

For the ballet to work, each performer has to mutually respect the other dancers. Richard Sennett (2003) similarly compared the formation of mutual respect to a musical performance, where each player is dependent on the other. Just as Jacob's sidewalk dancers are not 'twirling in unison', the rhythm of mutuality (and of a successful city) is not meant to be regimented. In fact, there is plenty of room for improvisation, for new interpretations of how urban spaces can be used. For these improvisations to work they need to be performed with respect to other players; it is what the journalist Lynne Truss (2005: 12) has stated in her book on 'the utter bloody rudeness of everyday life': 'remember you are with other people; show some consideration'.

But this is where things become problematical for the contemporary city, where consideration – and respect – is shown *only* to those who consume. The neoliberal city clearly does not welcome improvisation. For instance, according to Jones and Foust (2008: 10):

> Non-consumers do not perform 'properly' the consumer quest for unique identities; instead their performances offer varying degrees of interruption or transgression to the neoliberal order of The Mall. Some teens, for instance, may appear to seek public identifications, while simultaneously resisting a mass-produced consumer aesthetic (eg looking 'Goth' rather than *Gap*).

Jones and Foust refer to the lack of a place for non-consumers in the mall; however, this view is equally applicable to the city centre's streets. An urban performance based upon consumption *can* work in creating a 'safe' environment; however, it will only be 'safe' for the consumer and will not be as dynamic or inclusionary as the full cosmopolitan experience.

Conclusions

So are cities characterised by mutual respect possible, a truly cosmopolitan urbanity based on liberal pluralism? Despite the exclusionary nature of neoliberal consumerism, I believe there are reasons to be hopeful; as Thrift (2005: 135) has observed, 'Cities may have … a large reservoir of enmity but they also have a surplus of hope, an unconscious hunger for the future as well as the past.' It is a question of whether 'contest' becomes the defining quality of urbanism, or 'cosmopolitanism'.

The emphasis of the government's Respect Agenda has been that it is on the side of 'decent people', on the side of 'the law-abiding majority'. Unfortunately this simplistic dichotomising instantly creates a situation of contest and is likely to lead to less respect, rather than more. Further, what this chapter has demonstrated is that the defining quality of acceptability and respectability within an urban environment has *not* been simply whether someone is law-abiding; rather, acceptance has been determined by consumption, with the people seen to offend the sensibilities or aesthetics of a consuming majority becoming pathologised, being labelled as an anti-social and disrespectful other – and thereby excluded. This may create urban centres that are appealing to the majority of shoppers (or businesses), but at great cost.

Urban living should test our beliefs and expectations. As noted, there needs to be an element of risk, as this is what urban living is all about. Rather than leading to contest and fear of the other, urban encounters can in fact help to nurture mutual respect. This may seem idealistic, and perceptions of urban insecurity have certainly had an exclusionary effect on particular groups – notably women (Pain, 1997; Valentine, 1989) and, more broadly at night, those who do not fit a youthful demographic (Bromley et al, 2000). But if risk is minimised to the extent that encounters with others unlike ourselves disappear, then the urban experience will be sanitised, and be the lesser for it. Moreover, our preconceived ideas of how to live in the city will not be challenged. True, some disrespectful or anti-social behaviour should always be intolerable; but there is a lot below this that is simply 'different'. It is encounters with this difference that can encourage an urban culture of mutual respect.

How mutuality is encouraged is not an easy question to answer, but I do not believe it is the government's job always to step in and dictate what is respectable and what is not. The government should not get involved in the neoliberal moralising game, especially if it cannot lead by example. According to Bagnoli (2007: 117), 'respect requires that we do not impose our views on others, but it also requires that we engage in a frank dialogue with them ... The conclusion of this dialogue may be informed disagreement.' This is the heart of mutual respect and cosmopolitanism, that there is room for other expressions of urban living outside our individual and group expectations. In line with Jacobs (1961) and Sennett (2003), the result is urban living as performance, with each of us having a part to play in that performance. But fundamental to the success of this performance is that each player respects the others' part in the (cosmopolitan) whole. As with any performance there will be individual and group mistakes or unusual improvisations; but the key will be forgiveness, tolerance and even empathy for the others' perspective.

Notes

[1] These 'Respect Zones' were all located in urban areas, reportedly chosen on the basis of high levels of deprivation, crime, truancy and school exclusion.

[2] A response from government to bring different cultures together under one 'Britishness' has been the promotion of citizenship, with, for example, new UK citizens asked to attend Citizenship Ceremonies and having citizenship classes in schools (see also Chapter Three by France and Meredith, and Chapter Seven by Bannister and Kearns).

[3] Of course, nationalism has been an issue for far longer than this, especially in Northern Ireland.

[4] Beck defines democratic authoritarianism as a modernisation and increase in 'the State's capacity to enforce decisions' at a time when 'potential for achieving consensus in a democratic manner is diminishing' (2002: 41).

[5] An example of Jef Aérosol's work is used for the front cover of this book.

[6] Some graffiti and post-graffiti writers are quite happy to embrace consumption, accepting commissions from companies to spread a brand image or message through their art – both legally and illegally (Fuller et al, 2003).

References

Alibhai-Brown, Y. (2001) 'After multiculturalism', *Political Quarterly*, 72(1), 47–56.

Amster, R. (2003) 'Patterns of exclusion: sanitizing space, criminalizing homelessness', *Social Justice*, 30(1), 195–221.

Appiah, K.A. (2006) *Cosmopolitanism: Ethics in a World of Strangers*, London: Penguin Books.

Bagnoli, C. (2007) 'Respect and membership in the moral community', *Ethical Theory and Moral Practice*, 10(2), 113–28.

Bannister, J. and Fyfe, N. (2001) 'Introduction: fear and the city', *Urban Studies*, 38(5), 807–13.

Bannister, J., Fyfe, N. and Kearns, A. (2006) 'Respectable or respectful? (In)civility and the city', *Urban Studies*, 43(5/6), 919–37.

BBC News Online (2007) 'Ministers reveal "respect zones"', *BBC News Online*, 22 January. Available at: http://news.bbc.co.uk/1/hi/uk_politics/6285679.stm.

Beck, U. (2002) 'The cosmopolitan society and its enemies', *Theory, Culture & Society*, 19(1/2), 17–44.

Berlin, I. (1969) *Four Essays on Liberty*, Oxford: Oxford University Press.

Binnie, J., Holloway, J., Millington, S. and Young, C. (2006) *Cosmopolitan Urbanism*, London: Routledge.

Blair, T. (1998) *The Third Way: New Politics for the New Century*, London: Fabian Society.

Bloomfield, J. and Bianchini, F. (2004) *Planning for the Intercultural City*, Bournes Green: Comedia.

Bohman, J. and Lutz-Bachmann, M. (1997) *Perpetual Peace: Essays on Kant's Cosmopolitan Ideal*, Cambridge, MA: MIT Press.

Bromley, R., Thomas, C. and Millie, A. (2000) 'Exploring safety concerns in the night-time city: revitalising the evening economy', *Town Planning Review*, 71(1), 71–96.

Clarke, D.B. (2003) *The Consumer Society and the Postmodern City*, London: Routledge.

Crawford, A. (2006) 'Policing and security as "good clubs": The new enclosures?' in J. Wood and B. Dupont (eds) *Democracy, Society and the Governance of Security*, Cambridge: Cambridge University Press, pp 111–38.

Crawford, A. and Lister, S. (2007) *The Use and Impact of Dispersal Orders: Sticking Plasters and Wake-up Calls*, Bristol: The Policy Press.

Cresswell, T. (1996) *In Place/Out of Place: Geography, Ideology and Transgression*, Minneapolis, MN: University of Minnesota Press.

Dickens, L. (2008a) '"Finders keepers": performing the street, the gallery and the spaces in-between', *Liminalities: A Journal of Performance Studies*, 4(1), 1–30.

Dickens, L. (2008b) 'Placing post-graffiti: the journey of the Peckham Rock', *Cultural Geographies*, 15(4), 471–96.

Downes, D. and Rock, P. (1982) *Understanding Deviance: A Guide to the Sociology of Crime and Rule Breaking*, Oxford: Oxford University Press.

Durkheim, E. (2003) 'The normal and the pathological', in E. McLaughlin, J. Muncie and G. Hughes (eds) *Criminological Perspectives: Essential Readings*, 2nd edn, London: Sage, pp 65–8.

Etzioni, A. (1996) 'Erasing our moral deficit', *Philanthropy*, 10(2), 8–9. Available at: www.gwu.edu/~ccps/etzioni/B280.html.

Ferrell, J. (1993) *Crimes of Style: Urban Graffiti and the Politics of Criminality*, New York and London: Garland Publishing.

Fine, R. and Boon, V. (2007) 'Cosmopolitanism: between past and future', *European Journal of Social Theory*, 10(1), 5–16.

Fuller, D., O'Brien, K. and Hope, R. (2003) *Exploring Solutions to 'Graffiti' in Newcastle upon Tyne*, Newcastle: Northumbria University.

Furnivall, J.S. (1948) *Colonial Policy and Practice: A Comparative Study of Burma and Netherlands India*, Cambridge: Cambridge University Press.

Galston, W.A. (2005) *The Practice of Liberal Pluralism*, Cambridge: Cambridge University Press.

Giddens, A. (1994) *Beyond Left and Right: The Future of Radical Politics*, Cambridge: Polity Press.

Goss, J. (1993) 'The "magic of the mall": an analysis of form, function, and meaning in the contemporary retail built environment', *Annals of the Association of American Geographers*, 83(1), 18–47.

Hannerz, U. (1990) 'Cosmopolitans and locals in world culture', in M. Featherstone (ed) *Global Culture: Nationalism, Globalization and Modernity*, London: Sage, pp 237–52.

Hayward, K.J. (2004) *City Limits: Crime, Consumer Culture and the Urban Experience*, London: Glasshouse Press.

Heseltine, M. (1983) *Reviving the Inner Cities*, London: Conservative Political Centre.

Hill, T.E. (2000) *Respect, Pluralism, and Justice: Kantian Perspectives*, Oxford: Oxford University Press.

Holden, A. and Iveson, K. (2003) 'Designs on the urban: New Labour's urban renaissance and the spaces of citizenship', *City*, 7(1), 57–72.

Home Office (1984) *Joint Circular on Crime Prevention*, London: HMSO.

Horton, J. (1973) 'Order and conflict theories of social problems as competing ideologies', in R.S. Denisoff and C.H. McCaghy (eds) *Deviance, Conflict, and Criminality*, Chicago, IL: Rand McNally & Company, pp 6–24. (Originally published in *The American Journal of Sociology*, 71(6) (1966), 701–13.)

Jacobs, J. (1961) *The Death and Life of Great American Cities*, New York, NY: Vintage Books.

Jones, R.G. and Foust, C.R. (2008) 'Staging and enforcing consumerism in the city: the performance of othering on the 16th Street Mall', *Liminalities: A Journal of Performance Studies*, 4(1), 1–28.

Kant, I. (1957 [1795]) *Perpetual Peace*, trans L.W. Beck, Indianapolis, IN: Bobbs-Merrill.

Lefebvre, H. (1996) *Writings on Cities*, trans and ed E. Kofman and E. Lebas, Oxford: Blackwell.

Lefley, J. (2007) 'Council adds its own touch to a Banksy', *Evening Standard* (London), November 7. Available at: www.thisislondon. co.uk/standard and www.banksy.co.uk.

Levi, R. (2008) 'Loitering in the city that works: on circulation, activity and police in governing urban space', in M.D. Dubber and M.Valverde (eds) *Police and the Liberal State*, Stanford, CA: Stanford University Press, pp 178–202.

Lister, R. (1998) 'From equality to social inclusion: New Labour and the welfare state', *Critical Social Policy*, 18(55), 215–25.

Lofland, L.H. (1973) *A World of Strangers: Order and Action in Urban Public Space*, Prospect Heights, IL: Waveland Press.

McGhee, D. (2005) *Intolerant Britain: Hate, Citizenship and Difference*, Maidenhead: Open University Press.

MacLeod, G. (2002) 'From urban entrepreneurialism to a "revanchist city"? On the spatial injustices of Glasgow's renaissance', *Antipode*, 34(3), 602–24.

MacLeod, G. and Ward, K. (2002) 'Spaces of Utopia and Dystopia: landscaping the contemporary city', *Geografiska Annaler: Series B, Human Geography*, 84(3/4) 153–70.

Manzo, J. (2004) 'The folk devil happens to be our best customer: security officers' orientation to "youth" in three Canadian shopping malls', *International Journal of the Sociology of Law*, 32(3), 243–61.

Matthews, H., Taylor, M., Percy-Smith, B. and Limb, M. (2000) 'The unacceptable flaneur: the shopping mall as a teenage hangout', *Childhood*, 7(3), 279–94.

Matza, D. (1964) *Delinquency and Drift*, New York, NY: John Wiley & Sons.

Matza, D. (1969) *Becoming Deviant*, Englewood Cliffs, NJ: Prentice-Hall.

Millie, A. (2007) 'Looking for anti-social behaviour', *Policy & Politics*, 35(4), 611–27.

Millie, A. (2008a) 'Crime as an issue during the 2005 UK general election', *Crime, Media, Culture*, 4(1), 101–11.

Millie, A. (2008b) 'Anti-social behaviour, behavioural expectations and an urban aesthetic', *British Journal of Criminology*, 48(3), 379–94.

Millie, A. (2008c) 'Anti-social behaviour in British cities', *Geography Compass*, 2(5), 1681–96.

Millie, A. (2009) *Anti-social Behaviour*, Maidenhead: Open University Press.

Millie, A., Jacobson, J., McDonald, E. and Hough, M. (2005) *Anti-Social Behaviour Strategies: Finding a Balance*, Bristol: The Policy Press.

Milovanovic, D. (1997) *Postmodern Criminology*, New York, NY: Garland.

Mitchell, D. (1997) 'The annihilation of space by law: the roots and implications of anti-homeless laws in the United States', *Antipode*, 29(3), 303–35.

Mitchell, D. (2001) 'Postmodern geographical praxis? Postmodern impulse and the war against homeless people in the "Post-Justice" city', in C. Minca (ed) *Postmodern Geography: Theory and Praxis*, Oxford: Blackwell, pp 57–92.

Nolan, N. (2003) 'The ins and outs of skateboarding and transgression in public space in Newcastle, Australia', *Australian Geographer*, 34(3), 311–27.

ODPM (2005) *How to Manage Town Centres*, London: Office of the Deputy Prime Minister.

Pain, R. (1997) 'Social geographies of women's fear of crime', *Transactions of the Institute of British Geographers*, 22(2), 231–44.

Parekh, B.C. (2000) *Rethinking Multiculturalism: Cultural Diversity and Political Theory*, Basingstoke: Macmillan.

Podhoretz, N. (1964) 'The melting-pot blues', *Washington Post*, 25 October.

Respect Task Force (2006) *Respect Action Plan*, London: Home Office.

Robins, K. (1995) 'Collective emotion and urban culture', in P. Healey, S. Cameron, S. Davoudi, S. Graham and A. Madani-Pour (eds) *Managing Cities: The New Urban Context*, Chichester: John Wiley & Sons, pp 45–62.

Sandercock, L. (1998) *Towards Cosmopolis: Planning for Multicultural Cities*, Chichester: John Wiley & Sons.

Sandercock, L. (2003) *Cosmopolis II: Mongrel Cities of the 21st Century*, London: Continuum.

Sandercock, L. (2006) 'Cosmopolitan urbanism: a love song to our mongrel cities', in J. Binnie, J. Holloway, S. Millington and C. Young (eds) *Cosmopolitan Urbanism*, London: Routledge, pp 37–52.

Scarman, Lord (1984) 'An epilogue', in J. Benyon (ed) *Scarman and After: Essays Reflecting on Lord Scarman's Report, the Riots and their Aftermath*, Oxford: Pergamon Press, pp 259–61.

Sennett, R. (1970) *The Uses of Disorder: Personal Identity and City Life*, New York, NY: W.W. Norton.

Sennett, R. (2003) *Respect: The Formation of Character in an Age of Inequality*, London: Penguin.

Sibley, D. (1995) *Geographies of Exclusion*, London: Routledge.

Smith, N. (1996) *The New Urban Frontier: Gentrification and the Revanchist City*, London: Routledge.

Sorkin, M. (1992) *Variations on a Theme Park: The New American City and the End of Public Space*, New York, NY: Hill & Wang.

Staeheli, L.A. and Mitchell, D. (2008) *The People's Property? Power, Politics, and the Public*, New York, NY: Routledge.

Thrift, N. (2005) 'But malice aforethought: cities and the natural history of hatred', *Transactions, Institute of British Geographers*, 30(2), 133–50.

Truss, L. (2005) *Talk to the Hand: The Utter Bloody Rudeness of Everyday Life (or Six Good Reasons to Stay Home and Bolt the Door)*, London: Profile Books.

Urban Task Force (1999) *Towards an Urban Renaissance*, London: DETR.

URBED/DoE (Urban and Economic Development Group and the Department of the Environment) (1994) *Vital and Viable Town Centres: Meeting the Challenge*, London: HMSO.

Valentine, G. (1989) 'The geography of women's fear', *Area*, 21(4), 385–90.

Ward, C. (1978) *The Child in the City*, London: Architectural Press.

Wilson, J.Q. and Kelling, G.L. (1982) 'Broken windows: The police and neighbourhood safety', *The Atlantic Monthly*, March, 249(3), 29–38.

Wood, P. (2004) *The Intercultural City: A Reader*, Bournes Green: Comedia.

Wood, P. and Landry, C. (2008) *The Intercultural City: Planning for Diversity Advantage*, London: Earthscan.

Wright, T. (1997) *Out of Place: Homeless Mobilizations, Subcities, and Contested Landscapes*, New York, NY: State University of New York Press.

Youth Taskforce (2008) *Youth Taskforce Action Plan: Give Respect, Get Respect – Youth Matters*, London: Department for Children, Schools and Families.

Zukin, S. (1995) *The Culture of Cities*, Oxford: Blackwell.

Part Five
Respect, identities and values

Civilising offensives: education, football and 'eradicating' sectarianism in Scotland

John Flint and Ryan Powell

Introduction

In 2006 the Scottish Executive published an *Action Plan on Tackling Sectarianism in Scotland* (Scottish Executive, 2006a). The action plan was the culmination of a growing governmental focus upon acknowledging and addressing inter-Christian sectarianism[1] within Scottish society. This chapter applies the work of Norbert Elias on the *Civilising Process* (Elias, 2000 [1939]) and *The Established and the Outsiders* (Elias and Scotson, 1994 [1965]) to explore how norms, values and habits become inculcated and reformed within populations. We argue that the unprecedented contemporary policy crusade to address sectarianism in Scotland represents an example of a civilising offensive, a concept developed from the work of Elias to describe governmental attempts to reform the orientations, manners and conduct of citizens.

The chapter begins with an account of the key concepts within Elias's social theory of the civilising process and continues by describing how both the anti-sectarianism and Respect agendas may be characterised as civilising offensives. The chapter then provides an account of key elements of the governance of sectarianism in Scotland, focusing on the arenas of education and football. We argue that the anti-sectarianism agenda symbolises an ambitious attempt to reframe the values and traditions of sections of the Scottish population within a 'respect' paradigm and to build an ever-wider apparatus of governmental (including non-state) mechanisms for reshaping the conduct of citizens. We attempt to identify common rationales and techniques shared by both the anti-sectarianism and Respect agendas, and suggest that Elias's theories provide an important conceptual framework for understanding and critiquing social processes and government attempts to realign these processes.

The civilising process and established-outsider relations

The work of Elias is concerned with the relationship between the individual and society and can be seen as a critique of the *homo clausus* (the closed person). Elias argued that the concept of an isolated individual person, unaffected by group processes beyond those of early childhood and socialisation,[2] is an intellectual aberration, as society cannot be separated from the units from which it is made (Elias, 1978). This is illustrated to great effect in *The Civilizing Process*, in which Elias shows how long-term[3] changes in human behaviour, power and habitus are inextricably linked to the wider development of society. Drawing on historical documentation, and in particular the development of etiquette books from the medieval period onwards, Elias shows how the long-term trend towards a seemingly more refined standard of social conduct in Western Europe went hand in hand with the development of society in terms of its increasing differentiation and integration, resulting in more dense and numerous 'webs of interdependence' (Elias, 2000). As different classes, groups and nations became more interdependent there was a corresponding shift in manners towards a 'more refined' standard and a related increase in *mutual identification*.

Taking the medieval period as his starting point, Elias showed how, over centuries, state formation and the resultant monopolisation of violence led to the internal pacification of society and the gradual occlusion of violence from the public realm. Society was therefore less dangerous and violence was more calculable, as individuals, through foresight and reflection, were able to restrain their behaviour in accordance with the social situation. Developments such as urbanisation and industrialisation placed ever greater demands of self-restraint and self-management on individuals in order for them to function adequately as members of society (van Krieken, 2005). Social processes that impact on the psychological make-up of individuals as social constraints (for example, the threat of violence from the state) are gradually converted to self-constraints and internalised within the individual through the continuous process of socialisation. Individuals are therefore more able to attune their conduct to the actions of others, and behaviour which was once admissible in social settings (for example, bodily functions) is 'removed behind the scenes of social life' (Elias, 2000) as the threshold of shame and repugnance advances.

Over the course of the long-term development of Western European society 'more people are forced more often to pay more attention to more other people' (Goudsblom, 1989: 11) and the result is a stricter code of behaviour and a greater degree of consideration expected of others (Elias, 2000: 69). Such accounts resonate with the contemporary discourses on the governance of respect and sectarianism.

Shame and embarrassment are important mechanisms of self- and social control, but their functions and effects are also evident on the macro scale (see Scheff, 2004). It has been argued that the civilising of punishment in western societies is closely related to the sense of shame and repugnance derived from a punitive penal regime, and that a more ameliorative penal policy – a marker of civilisation – involves the removal of prisons 'behind the scenes', from urban to rural locations (Pratt, 1998). Shame is a powerful individual process, but it also operates at collective levels, including those of nations. This was evidenced most recently in February 2008, with the Australian government's apology to the 'stolen generation' of indigenous Australians, separated from their parents in the name of civilisation (see van Krieken, 1999). In official discourses, sectarianism in Scotland has similarly been viewed as the nation's 'shame' (Devine, 2000).

The civilising process denotes the *overall* trend of Western European societies and is only discernible from a long-term perspective, countered as it is by 'decivilising spurts' that occur over shorter time frames (see Mennell, 1990; Fletcher, 1997; Wacquant, 2004). It would be wrong to interpret *The Civilizing Process* as an optimistic theory of human progress, and the concept of *civilising offensives* developed by Eliasian scholars provides a complement to Elias's account of blind, unplanned processes by drawing attention to 'the active, conscious and deliberate civilizing projects of powerful groups' (van Krieken, 1999: 303). Scholars have argued that civilisation should be seen as an inherently *ambivalent* process, citing the contradictions of the colonial project which sought to spread 'civilisation' often through barbaric and violent means (Burkitt, 1996; van Krieken, 1999).

Elias argued that by the end of the eighteenth century civilisation as a concept had come to express 'the self-consciousness of the West' (2000: 5) and was deemed a 'firm possession' of the middle classes. The goal then became the dissemination of civilisation: 'people only wanted to accomplish this process for other nations and ... for the lower classes of their own society' (2000: 88). Thus, the concept of the civilising offensive resonates with a form of governance characterised by the explicit goal of 'improving' or 'correcting' the social conduct of certain sections of the population deemed to be unacceptable to the rest of the society (see Powell and Flint, 2009). Contemporary attempts to govern sectarianism in Scotland represent a manifestation of such a civilising offensive targeted at certain populations in particular social settings.

The civilising process charts developments across the whole of society, and while Elias goes into great detail about the dissemination of conduct across classes and groups, the diminishing contrasts in standards of behaviour between them, and the power struggles therein, it is useful to turn to the theory of established–outsider relations for an appreciation of group relations in particular sites and settings (Elias and Scotson, 1994). The theory is important in illustrating the centrality of power and interdependencies as key determinants of group conflict and related processes of disidentification and stigmatisation (see Powell, 2008).

Elias's theory of established–outsider was developed through his 1950s study with Scotson of community relations on a suburban housing estate in Leicester (given the fictitious name of Winston Parva). The estate was characterised by conflict between two distinct groups: the 'established', who had resided there for several generations; and the 'outsiders', who were relative newcomers. Elias observed the systematic stigmatisation of the outsider group, who were thought to lack the superior human virtues which the established group attributed to itself (Elias and Scotson, 1994). The two groups were similar in most other respects, such as social class, ethnicity, nationality and religion, with the only discernible difference relating to the internal cohesion of the two groups and the access to power and resources – both of which favoured the established. The result was a strong group orientation:

> In Winston Parva, as elsewhere, one found members of one group casting a slur on those of another, not because of their qualities as individual people, but because they were members of a group which they considered collectively as different from, and as inferior to, their own group. (Elias and Scotson, 1994: xx)

A key theme in established–outsider relations is the notion of group charisma (relating to one's own group) and group disgrace (the outsider group). A common group charisma is derived from what Elias terms the 'we-image' of individuals, which enables a collective sense of higher human value from the sense of belonging to a group and adhering to internal norms. This impacts upon the control of behaviour, as the 'self-regulation of members of a closely knit group is linked to the internal opinion of that group' (Elias and Scotson, 1994: xli). Group members deviating from the expected behaviour are likely to see their 'internal group opinion' diminish and this threat serves to keep them in check.

The integration and mutual identification outlined above in the civilising process were clearly lacking and, as Rodger notes, 'in those circumstances where marginality, social exclusion or sectarianism emerges, the sense of empathy for the other and the mutual restraint on behaviour which are built by frequent social interaction are absent' (Rodger, 2006: 129). An appreciation of the specificity of locational and social contexts and the internal group dynamics highlighted by Elias therefore offers insights into the expressions (and legitimisation) of sectarian views in certain settings (for example, football grounds and religious parades).

De Swaan (1995) uses the examples of Serb–Bosnian and Hutu–Tutsi conflicts to illustrate how the power of the internal group opinion that Elias identifies may be so strong, binding and long lasting as to resist the civilising offensives of elite governance processes, as conduction (face-to-face relations) outweighs the radiation of more socially distant mechanisms for shaping required conduct. This is also very evident in the embedded forms of sectarianism in Scottish society and the active resistance among some groups to the realignment of their group identities.

In the case of Winston Parva, the established 'had undergone a group process – from the past via the present towards the future – which provided them with a stock of common memories, attachments and dislikes' (Elias and Scotson, 1994: xxxviii). Building on this, Elias and Scotson give the example of 'declining nations' to show how past victories or glories are called upon by political establishments in order to invoke and maintain identifications (and, by extension, disidentifications): the group's special charisma is kept alive through the teaching of history (Elias and Scotson, 1994: xliv). This applies just as readily to other groups and identifications as it does to nations, and there are arenas where this is manifested with regard to sectarianism in Scotland. Also of particular relevance for the discussion that follows is the interplay of multiple identifications. Elias and Scotson argued that in an earlier period religious establishments were significant, but now 'group charisma' is formed from 'a common social belief in a unique national virtue and grace' (Elias and Scotson, 1994: xli). This appears to be too simplistic in the case of Scottish sectarianism and, as we shall see, the groups involved call upon both national and religious identifications and refer to these in the context of past battles and victories.

This indicative discussion of Elias points to a substantial theoretical work, grounded in empirical investigation, which can illuminate contemporary processes and rationales of governance related to group dynamics and the changing concept and construction of 'civility' and 'respect' (for a fuller application of Elias's work to the Respect Agenda see Powell and Flint, 2009).

Governing sectarianism in Scotland

Given Elias's focus on the mechanism of shaming within the civilising process, it is noteworthy that the phenomenon of sectarianism within Scottish society has been explicitly defined within a paradigm of national shame. The speech in 1999 by the composer James Macmillan that reignited contemporary civic society and governmental interest in the subject was entitled 'Scotland's Shame', a title shared by a prominent contemporary academic work on the issue (Devine, 2000), while the Scottish Executive has described sectarianism as 'a shameful fact of Scottish life for generations' (Scottish Executive, 2006a: 1) which '*humiliates* everyone involved' (Scottish Executive, 2006b: 3, our emphasis). The extent to which sectarianism is a 'national' problem has been subject to considerable controversy. Some research suggests that the manifestations of sectarianism are concentrated in the central belt, and particularly west central Scotland – a pattern that reflects the industrial heritage of, and impact of Irish immigration upon, these areas (see Bruce et al, 2004 and Flint, 2008 for further discussion).

Since 1999 there has been increasing governmental activity acknowledging and attempting to address inter-Christian sectarianism in contemporary Scottish society. (For overviews of the historical and contemporary causes, definitions and manifestations of sectarianism in Scottish society and sources of further reading, see Devine, 2000 and Bruce et al, 2004.) The Scottish Executive, charities and local authorities have conducted evidence reviews (Nicolson, 2002; NFO Research, 2003; Scottish Executive, 2003; McAspurren, 2005; O'Loan et al, 2005) and the Scottish Executive has commissioned a review of religious parades (Orr, 2005). The Scottish Parliament has passed legislation introducing new categories of religiously aggravated offences. The Scottish first minister convened a National Summit on Sectarianism in 2005 and the Scottish Executive launched the national *Anti-Social Behaviour Action on Tackling Sectarianism in Scotland* in January 2006 (Scottish Executive, 2006a).

The anti-sectarianism campaign in Scotland shares a number of similarities with the Respect Agenda south of the border (see Flint, 2008 for a fuller account of these parallels). Indeed, tackling sectarianism is explicitly framed within a need to 'respect' different cultural traditions (Scottish Executive, 2005: 2) or the fostering of mutual identification that Elias (2000) described. Sectarianism has also been conceptualised by some commentators as essentially a problem of 'urban incivility' (Bruce et al, 2004: 173). Much of the emerging governance of sectarianism in Scotland is framed within an anti-social behaviour paradigm focused on reducing its visible manifestations as displayed through verbal and physical violence, noise and drunkenness in urban public spaces, particularly in football grounds and on the routes of religious parades. Both the anti-sectarianism and Respect agendas may be classified as contemporary civilising offensives through which new mechanisms of governance are used to inculcate perceived decivilising elements within society. Both agendas represent a 'broadening, deepening and furthering' (Respect Task Force, 2006) of attempts to regulate and challenge particular forms of 'shameful' social conduct and to inculcate 'a certain discipline and rigour in how [citizens] comport themselves' (Blair, 2007).

We now focus upon two social arenas that have been inherently linked to the conceptualisation of sectarianism in Scottish society: first, schools and education, and second, football (see also Chapter Ten by Peter Squires). We argue that these arenas reveal key parallels with the Respect Agenda in their mechanisms of governance, including the incorporation of new institutions and actors into governing processes, a focus upon responsibilisation, self-policing and active citizenship, the new regulation of wider forms of behaviour, the use of contract and the explicit codification of acceptable and unacceptable behaviour and new forms of authority and legal techniques.

Emerging arenas for the governance of sectarianism

Education

Most of the etiquette books that Elias (2000) studied were aimed at inculcating forms of desired behaviour in young people. Both the Respect and anti-sectarianism agendas' focus on achieving the 'cultural shifts' (Home Office, 2003: 6) that characterise a civilising offensive conceptualise young people as a key population whose future habits and orientations may be more easily moulded towards desired norms: 'It is important that this process [tackling prejudice and bigotry] begins in pre-school when a child's view of the world is formed' (Scottish Executive, 2006a: 2). Both the anti-sectarianism and Respect action plans therefore identify schools and education as key sites and mechanisms for ensuring that 'young people have the necessary values and attitudes' (Scottish Executive, 2006b: 2).

The Scottish Executive launched the *Sectarianism: Don't Give It, Don't Take It* web-based educational resource,[4] produced a training DVD for teachers and youth workers and funded anti-sectarianism project work in schools (Scottish Executive, 2006a; 2006c). Roles in the governance of sectarianism in Scottish society are thereby created for teachers, youth workers and young people themselves in the same way that the Respect Agenda has increasingly implicated a range of actors, including housing officers, teachers, private landlords and publicans in governing anti-social behaviour. The Scottish Executive also introduced a *One Scotland – Anti-Sectarianism Award* category within the Scottish Education Awards. This award is 'about eradicating religious divides in communities' (Scottish Executive, 2006c: 4). The establishment of this award symbolises the onus upon active citizenship and the responsibilisation of new actors in the governance of sectarianism, similarly to how the 'Taking a Stand' (in England and Wales) and 'Standing Up to Anti-Social Behaviour' (in Scotland) awards operate within the Respect Agenda.

Higher and further education establishments are also included in this widening governmental apparatus, with the National Union of Students Scotland launching a 'Stamp Out Sectarianism: Give it the Boot' campaign (NUS Scotland website). This campaign defines a new population (students) and new sites (college and university campuses) where sectarianism is acknowledged to exist and required to be regulated. One component of the 'Stamp Out Sectarianism' campaign is the use of a 'pledge' mechanism. Students are asked to pledge: 'To challenge sectarianism when I see it among my friends' and 'not to take part in sectarian behaviour or use sectarian language' (NUS Scotland website). This mechanism symbolises key motifs of the new governance of social conduct, including the formalised and symbolic acts of engagement required through signing a pledge (just as in the signing of Acceptable Behaviour Contracts) and the emphasis on the proactive governance and challenging of others as well as the self.

The anti-sectarianism campaign in Scotland has also focused on 'building friendships and strengthening communities' between denominational (Roman Catholic) and non-denominational schools (Scottish Executive, 2006c). The presence of Roman Catholic schools in Scotland, with no parallel Church of Scotland schools structure, has long been a key site of contestation in definitions of sectarianism in Scottish society (see Devine, 2000; Bruce et al, 2004; Flint, 2007).

What is important in the context of a civilising offensive is that, while the Scottish Executive and its Scottish government successor continues to defend the state funding of Roman Catholic schools, it has increasingly sought to mitigate the perceived social and symbolic segregation arising from them. Its two principal mechanisms for doing so have been a programme of shared campus construction, where two schools share the same site, and twinning initiatives through which pupils and staff from denominational and non-denominational schools are brought together in a range of educational, sporting and leisure activities (Scottish Executive, 2006c).

These initiatives highlight three important elements of contemporary civilising offensives. First, the construction of shared campuses, for example in North Lanarkshire, has been fiercely contested by the Catholic Church and many parents, illustrating how top-down 'civilising' initiatives can be met with resistance by their intended subjects and demonstrates the limitations of central state power. Second, the shared campus at Dalkeith in Midlothian received considerable media attention for alleged disorder and conflict between pupils and staff, indicating how state-facilitated new sites for interaction can generate as well as mitigate localised social conflicts. Third, the complexity of governing state-sponsored institutional diversity in the school system demonstrates the strengths of historical, cultural and social identities and the constraints that governments face in attempting to reconfigure or realign the manifestations of these identities. As Elias (2000) argued, contemporary exhortations to populations to realign their identities or social practices do not, in the short term, bring about fundamental shifts in individuals' orientations or values. This is particularly the case when what actually constitutes 'legitimate' expressions of cultural identity as opposed to 'obvious' sectarian disrespect is subject to so much contestation (religious icons in schools, Union or Tricolour flags, or Orange parades as examples). In these instances a narrative of traditional behaviour being 'uncivilised' becomes much more difficult to sustain.

Football

Football in Scotland, and particularly the Old Firm institutions of Glasgow Celtic and Glasgow Rangers and the matches between them are inherently defined within the sectarianism problem in Scottish society (see for example, Burdsey and Chappel, 2003; Bradley, 2004), mirroring the connection between urban disorder and largely white working-class populations that characterises the discourse around the Respect and anti-social behaviour agendas. In 2006 the Scottish Executive published its *Calling Full Time on Sectarianism* strategy, arguing that 'tackling sectarianism in football is central to creating [a] truly multi-cultural and multi-faith Scotland' based on 'mutual respect', and suggesting that 'it is time to eradicate it [sectarianism] from Scottish football' (Scottish Executive, 2006b: 2–3). This central government strategy had been preceded by a range of initiatives aimed at addressing sectarianism in the sport, including those of Celtic and Rangers football clubs' 'Pride Over Prejudice' and 'Bhoys Against Bigotry' campaigns and their joint 'Old Firm Alliance' initiative;[5] Glasgow City Council's 'Sense Over Sectarianism' funding programme; and anti-sectarianism charities such as Nil By Mouth.

The evolving regime for governing sectarianism in Scottish football illustrates many of the key techniques that characterise the wider civilising offensive against the problem, and the linked phenomenon of anti-social behaviour, in Scottish society. The first of these is the incorporation of a wider range of institutions into the attempts to enhance civility, and an attempt to require these institutions to focus on sectarianism. For example, the Scottish Football Association introduced a National Club Licensing Scheme which required professional Scottish football clubs to demonstrate clear policies against sectarianism. This mirrors the new licensing schemes for private landlords in England and Wales, which require them to tackle anti-social behaviour. These licensing schemes embed non-state organisations within governmental regimes and formally enshrine their responsibilities to regulate certain forms of problematic conduct that previously they were not required to.

The embedding of football clubs within the anti-sectarianism agenda has been further facilitated through the establishment of the 'Kick Out Bigotry' campaign, coordinated by the Football for All charity. The campaign aims to 'tackle religious bigotry and sectarian attitudes and behaviour, in, and associated with, Scottish football' (Kick Out Bigotry website). In common with the Respect Agenda on anti-social behaviour, a key component of the campaign is to 'Assist and empower football supporters' organisations to tackle religious bigotry' (Kick Out Bigotry website). This mirrors the attempts to 'empower' individuals to tackle anti-social behaviour, and in both cases the empowerment of individuals is located within a contractual framework which emphasises their responsibilities and appeals to acts of citizenship to facilitate the self-policing of social conduct (Home Office, 2003). Such techniques involve the creation of non-state 'surrogate regulators' within a widening of the governmental capacity for addressing 'unacceptable' behaviour (Crawford, 2006).

Two mechanisms are used to enact these forms of active citizenship among football supporters. First, as with the National Union of Students Scotland campaign, supporters are encouraged to sign an online pledge committing them to 'use all available means to advise fans attending football matches that bigoted behaviour will not be tolerated' and to 'work in partnership to identify and deal with individuals whose behaviour is bigoted and unacceptable' (Kick Out Bigotry website). These techniques require an engagement by individuals into a contractual arrangement whereby they will be active in the education and governance of themselves and others, in much the same way as tenancy agreements in social housing, Acceptable Behaviour Contracts, Good Neighbour Agreements and Parenting Contracts, necessitate a voluntary and proactive engagement by individuals in order not only to police themselves but also to become implicated in the regulation of the conduct of others, including family members and neighbours. Second, as with anti-social behaviour policy, this organic self-policing is complemented by attempts to strengthen the interaction of individuals with traditional forms of 'official' policing, with the Kick Out Bigotry website providing a 'sectarian incident notification' from where incidents may be reported to the authorities, similar to the plethora of anti-social behaviour telephone hotlines, incident report forms, witness diaries and other new bureaucracies for reporting and tackling unacceptable conduct.

An examination of how Rangers Football Club attempts to govern sectarianism illuminates many of these techniques and dilemmas of governance. We focus on Rangers here, due to space constraints, but it should be noted that Celtic Football Club has been equally involved in anti-sectarianism campaigns, such as Bhoys Against Bigotry, and adopts similar governance mechanisms (see Celtic website), as do other Scottish football clubs. Rangers' 'Follow with Pride' campaign 'recognises the rights and responsibilities of being a Rangers fan' (Rangers Football Club website) and thereby frames supporters' conduct in the same contractual paradigm of wider anti-social behaviour policy (eg Home Office, 2003). The campaign is also based on a 'continued self-policing drive by supporters groups to tackle inappropriate behaviour' (Rangers Football Club website).

The formal codification of conduct and a written articulation of acceptable and unacceptable behaviour that Elias (2000) describes as central to civilising processes are also evident. Within the wider framework of the Scottish Football Association and the Scottish Premier

League issuing detailed definitions of 'unacceptable' conduct, Rangers has issued 'The Blue Guide' (Rangers Football Club, undated) which sets out 'what is expected' of supporters and has also produced 'The Wee Blue Book' (Rangers Football Club, undated) which prescribes authorised songs that may be sung within the Ibrox Stadium, in an attempt to prevent the articulation of sectarian sentiments. Both of these documents represent modern variants of the books of etiquette Elias studied and correspond to the expansion in the use, within the Respect Agenda, of Acceptable Behaviour Contracts and Good Neighbour Agreements, which aim to prescribe required forms of daily conduct within residential neighbourhoods.

The emerging governance of sectarianism in Scottish football results in an extension of new mechanisms of governance to wider forms of behaviour and new populations. These include the use of undercover stewards to eject supporters engaging in sectarian abuse in football grounds, the use of Football Banning Orders (which have similarities to Anti-Social Behaviour Orders) against those engaged in sectarian behaviour, and licensing enforcement action against street traders selling sectarian and paramilitary materials outside football stadia (Scottish Executive, 2006a). This new regime of governance epitomises a state-sponsored civilising offensive through which traditionally tolerated, if not officially condoned, forms of conduct are deemed unacceptable and become the subject of governmental intervention.

There is also evidence that, as Elias identified, civilising processes evolve and change their focus. It is clear that some campaigns that began with a focus on sectarianism have broadened into wider attempts to inculcate wider forms of civility. For example, Rangers' 'Pride over Prejudice' initiative, with its overt focus on tackling sectarianism, has been succeeded by the 'Follow with Pride' campaign, aimed at promoting 'family, friendship and sportsmanship' (Rangers Football Club website), with Rangers supporters expected to be 'ready to show respect and courtesy to the general public in the street, on public transport and in the community at large' (Rangers Football Club, 2003a). The arenas in which supporters are expected to conduct themselves in certain ways and to be regulated are therefore extended well beyond the immediate locality of a football ground, in the same way that the regulation of social housing tenants in relation to anti-social behaviour has been extended from their home to the 'immediate locality' of home, and subsequently to the wider neighbourhood (Hunter, 2006). Similarly, the 'True Hearts Against Bigotry' campaign states that Heart of Midlothian Football Club[6] 'have recognised that the *boorish* behaviour of some elements among football fans is hindering them from creating the family atmosphere where everyone can enjoy an afternoon's sporting entertainment that they aspire to' (True Hearts Against Bigotry website, our emphasis). The governance of sectarianism is thereby extended to other incivilities such as swearing and drunkenness. These processes mirror the evolution of the Respect Agenda towards the 'deeper, broader and wider' regulation of social conduct, from prohibiting criminal offences to the promotion of 'civility and good manners' (Respect Task Force, 2006: 5) through, for example, the use of Good Neighbour Agreements that extend to prohibiting some non-criminal forms of conduct and advocate neighbourliness and volunteering in the community.

The governance of sectarianism in Scottish football, as with anti-social behaviour policy, is an ambitious project aimed at changing cultural values and identities, as well as the manifestation of these identities in public space. However, Elias's argument that such changes in cultural orientations and conduct actually occur over very much longer historical processes is relevant here. As one example, although Rangers' 'Pride over Prejudice Policy Statement' defines the club as a 'multi-cultural, multi-denominational and non-political organisation' (Rangers Football Club, 2003a) the Blue Guide defines supporting Rangers as being about 'pride, history and tradition'. This history and tradition is partly built upon an overt sectarian expression of identity. While Rangers supporters are encouraged to sing 'traditional songs which glorify the history of the Club', at the same time 'rejecting obscene or bigoted words which cause offence', many of these 'traditional' songs are inherently about the historical political and religious conflict in Ireland. Similarly, while the 'Pride Over Prejudice External 10-Point Plan' (Rangers Football Club, 2003c) requires Rangers supporters to 'carry only legitimate flags, ideally Saltires and Union Jacks, reflecting we are a Scottish Club that's proud to be British', this connection with British identity is one dimension of the sectarian conflict, in the same way that Celtic's dual Scottish/Irish identity is. What these examples illustrate is that, while civilising offensives attempt to accelerate a process of cultural and behavioural change, Elias argues that such processes actually occur over more protracted historical periods. This explains a common view that changing sectarianism in Scotland will 'take at least a generation' (McLaughlin, 2007).

Governing sectarianism and respect as civilising offensives

Both the anti-sectarianism and Respect agendas are examples of civilising offensives characterised by a renewed governmental focus on the 'automatic behaviour and values' of individuals and the 'habits of everyday life' (Respect Task Force, 2006: 5). They exemplify key characteristics that Elias identified in civilising processes, including the problematisation and shaming of some existent forms of behaviour, the gradual expansion in the range of actors and institutions involved in the regulation of habits, the importance of the written and formal codification of acceptable and unacceptable behaviour and the attempts to facilitate the internalisation of self-policing mechanisms among individuals.

There is, however, one fundamental difference between the anti-sectarianism and Respect agendas. While the Respect Agenda attempts to re-establish social norms and habits that are perceived to have previously existed in society, and is aimed at '*bringing back* a proper sense of respect' (Blair, 2005, our emphasis), the anti-sectarianism agenda aims to challenge habits and values that 'have been a shameful fact of Scottish life *for generations*' (Scottish Executive, 2005: 1, our emphasis) and 'are *still* prevalent ... and have *long* poisoned the lives of people in many parts of Scottish Society' (NUS Scotland website, our emphasis). In this sense, the anti-sectarianism agenda is closer to Elias's account of a civilising process gradually requiring new standards of conduct and a rejection of behaviours that were traditionally unremarkable or tolerated, rather than the attempt to return to historical forms of etiquette within the Respect Agenda.

Although the discourse underpinning both agendas locates problematic behaviour in the minority of the population and, as Elias illustrates, thereby makes distinctions and classifications between sections of society, there is an acknowledgement that 'Sectarianism is still deeply engrained in many areas of Scottish society' (Scottish Executive, 2006b: 3) and 'firmly entrenched in Scottish life' (Scottish Executive, 2006a: 1). It is this 'engraining' and 'entrenching' of sectarianism that makes Elias's work so relevant in rethinking our analysis of the governance of problematic social conduct. For, despite the ambitious rhetoric in the anti-sectarianism and Respect agendas about achieving 'cultural shifts' in populations (Home Office, 2003), 'putting sectarianism in the dustbin of history' (Scottish Executive, 2006a: 1), or 'eradicating' the problem (Scottish Executive, 2006c: 5), the focus of these civilising offensives has primarily been on habits and conduct rather than values.

As one example, in relation to sectarian singing at football matches the Scottish Executive (2006a: 6) argues that 'fans sometimes go along with [sectarian singing and chanting] without really considering the effects of what they are saying'. Like Rangers Football Club's regulation of flags, this negates the fact that conduct is also a manifestation of historical and still strongly held social and cultural identities. There is therefore a need to combine the analysis of government documentation and techniques presented in this chapter with an understanding of the complex processes through which certain values and forms of conduct, including sectarian acts, become embodied within individuals (see, for example, Charlesworth, 2000; Leonard, 2006).

Although Elias focused his studies on court societies – and thinkers influenced by him have defined civilising offensives as essentially elite and often state-sponsored projects of social reform – both the anti-sectarianism and Respect agendas are characterised by an attempt to implicate problematised (white working-class) populations in the governance of their own and others' behaviour. However, far more research is required to understand to what extent individuals actually modify either their values or their behaviour in response to these civilising offensives (see, for example, a recent evaluation suggesting the limited impact of anti-social behaviour publicity campaigns in Scotland, mruk Research, 2007). There is a further need to identify new sites and processes which may emerge for sectarian behaviour to be enacted as the governance of 'traditional' arenas such as football grounds intensifies. A very good example of this is the growing prevalence of sectarian interfaces on the Internet (see Leonard, 2006; Ó Dochartaigh, 2007).

Elias also identifies how civilising processes are inherently characterised by attempts to magnify distinctions between social classes. This is apparent in the gaze of the governance of sectarianism in Scotland, which to date has emphasised visible urban disorder involving largely working-class populations in particular public arenas. Hence the focus has been on verbal and physical violence, damage to property and disturbance to local communities. This focus on episodic manifestations of sectarianism such as football matches and religious parades negates more mundane forms of urban sectarian disturbance, for example the continual vandalism of green traffic lights in some Lanarkshire towns (McLaughlin, 2007). Additionally, although there is a focus on verbalised forms of sectarianism (hence, for example, the anti-sectarianism charity being named Nil By Mouth), the emphasis on public disorder also diverts governance attention from other forms of sectarianism that may be present in Scottish society, for example in the middle-class professions. As with anti-social behaviour, sectarianism becomes equated with particular populations, in specific locations at certain times.

Conclusions

This chapter has illustrated how a 'respect' paradigm of addressing incivility and urban disorder is apparent in the governance of a range of social phenomena in the UK, including sectarianism in Scotland. We have sought to show how the Respect and anti-sectarianism agendas share commonalities in governance rationales and the techniques deployed to change the habits of particular sections of the population in targeted social arenas.

We have also sought to illustrate that the social theory of Norbert Elias provides an important analytical framework for examining civilising offensives such as the Respect and anti-sectarianism projects of government. In particular, Elias requires us to focus on the historical and social contexts within which civilising offensives are constructed and enacted, and the complexity of the internal and external individual and group processes through which sectarianism and anti-social behaviour come to be manifested in urban societies. In identifying the breadth of ambition evident in government attempts to bring about cultural shifts in the habits of populations in order to 'eradicate' sectarianism and other forms of incivility, we have also sought to illustrate the complex interplay between techniques of governance, shaming processes, social identities and behaviour which characterised Elias's work. The future research agenda on respect should, as Elias teaches us, focus equally on the social dynamics underpinning sectarianism and anti-social behaviour as well as on the civilising offensives of governance regimes being erected to tackle these problems.

Notes
[1] Sectarianism, like respect, is a vaguely defined and contested term. The Scottish Executive (2006b: 5) states that 'Sectarianism is easy to recognise but can be difficult to define,' while the Respect Task Force (2006: 5) states that 'almost everyone of any age or from any community understands what it [respect] is and thinks this is right'. However, governance understandings of sectarianism have primarily focused upon verbal and physical conflict and associated urban disorders such as drunkenness.

[2] For Elias, socialisation is a continuous, ever-present process throughout the life course.

[3] It should be noted that long-term in the Eliasian sense refers to several generations and, in the case of *The Civilizing Process*, considers the development of manners from the medieval period through to the twentieth century.

[4] Available at: www.Itscotland.org.uk/antisectarian

[5] The Old Firm Alliance is an educational programme for children in Glasgow aimed at improving health and fitness and tackling sectarianism and anti-social behaviour. This initiative illustrates how football clubs, as well as schools, are involved in mechanisms of education as a means of tackling sectarianism.

[6] The True Hearts Against Bigotry campaign was launched in the aftermath of the disruption and abandonment of a minute's silence to commemorate the death of Pope John Paul II before the Scottish Cup semi-final at Hampden between Hearts and Celtic in April 2005. This illustrates the extent to which sectarian articulations are not limited to the Old Firm. The debate following the incident was framed within the parameters of 'respecting' diversity and religious affiliation.

References

Blair, T. (2005) Speech in Downing Street, London, 6 May.

Blair, T. (2007) Jim Callaghan Memorial Speech, Cardiff, 11 April.

Bradley, J. (2004) 'Orangeism in Scotland: unionism, politics, identity and football', *Eire-Ireland*, 39(1/2) 237–161.

Bruce, S., Glendinning, T., Paterson, I. and Rosie, M. (2004) *Sectarianism in Scotland*, Edinburgh: Edinburgh University Press.

Burdsey, D. and Chappell, R. (2003) 'Soldiers, sashes and shamrocks: football and social identity in Scotland and Northern Ireland', *Sociology of Sport Online*, 6(1). Available at: http://physed.otago.ac.nz/sosol/v6i1/v6i1_1.html.

Burkitt, I. (1996) 'Civilization and ambivalence', *British Journal of Sociology*, 47(1), 135–50.

Celtic Football Club website. Accessible at: www.celticfc.net/home.aspx.

Charlesworth, S. (2000) *A Phenomenology of Working Class Experience*, Cambridge: Cambridge University Press.

Crawford, A. (2006). 'Networked governance and the post-regulatory state? Steering, rowing and anchoring the provision of policing and security', *Theoretical Criminology*, 10(4), 449–79.

de Swaan, A. (1995) 'Widening circles of identification: emotional concerns in sociogenetic perspective', *Theory, Culture and Society*, 12(2), 25–39.

Devine, T. (ed) (2000) *Scotland's Shame? Bigotry and Sectarianism in Modern Scotland*, Edinburgh: Mainstream.

Elias, N. (1978) *What is Sociology?* London: Hutchinson.

Elias, N. (2000) [1939] *The Civilizing Process*, Oxford: Blackwell.

Elias, N. and Scotson, J.L. (1994) [1965] *The Established and the Outsiders*, London: Sage.

Fletcher, J. (1997) *Violence and Civilization*, Cambridge: Polity Press.

Flint, J. (2007) 'Faith schools, multiculturalism and community cohesion: Muslim and Roman Catholic state schools in England and Scotland', *Policy & Politics*, 35(2), 251–68.

Flint, J. (2008) 'Governing sectarianism in Scotland', *Scottish Affairs*, 63(Spring), 107–24.

Goudsblom, J. (1989) 'Stijlen en beschavingen' ('Styles and civilisation'), *De Gids*, 152, 720–2.

Home Office (2003) *Respect and Responsibility: Taking a Stand against Anti-social Behaviour*, London: Home Office.

Hunter, C. (2006) 'The changing legal framework: from landlords to agents of social control', in J. Flint (ed) *Housing, Urban Governance and Anti-social Behaviour: Perspectives, Policy and Practice*, Bristol: The Policy Press, pp 137–54.

Kick Out Bigotry website. Accessible at: www.kickoutbigotry.org.

Leonard, M. (2006) 'Teenagers telling sectarian stories', *Sociology*, 40(6), 1117–33.

McAspurren, L. (2005) *Religious Discrimination and Sectarianism in Scotland: A Brief Review of the Evidence 2002–2004*, Edinburgh: Scottish Executive.

McLaughlin, M. (2007) 'Green light spells danger for traffic signals as bigots hit out at their least favourite colour', *The Scotsman*, 10 August, p 3.

Mennell, S. (1990) 'Decivilizing processes: theoretical significance and some lines of research', *International Sociology*, 5(2), 205–23.

mruk Research (2007) *Anti-social Behaviour (ASB) 2006 Campaign Evaluation*, Edinburgh: Scottish Executive.

NFO Research (2003) *Sectarianism in Glasgow*, Glasgow: Glasgow City Council.

Nicolson, L. (2002) *Identification of Research on Sectarianism, Religious Hatred and Discrimination within a Scottish Context: Briefing Paper*, Edinburgh, Scottish Executive.

NUS Scotland (undated) 'Stamp Out Sectarianism'. Available at: www. stampoutsectarianism.co.uk

Ó Dochartaigh, N. (2007) 'Conflict, territory and new technologies: online interaction at a Belfast interface', *Political Geography*, 26(4), 474–91.

O'Loan, S. Poulter, A. and McMenemy, D. (2005) *The Extent of Sectarianism On-line*, Glasgow: Nil By Mouth.

Orr, J. (2005) *Review of Marches and Parades*, Edinburgh: Scottish Executive.

Powell, R. (2008) 'Understanding the stigmatization of Gypsies: power and the dialectics of disidentification', *Housing, Theory and Society*, 25(2), 87–109

Powell, R. and Flint, J. (2009, forthcoming) '(In)formalisation and the civilising process: applying the work of Norbert Elias to housing-based anti-social behaviour interventions in the UK', *Housing, Theory and Society*, 26(1).

Pratt, J. (1998) 'Towards the "decivilizing" of punishment', *Social and Legal Studies*, 7, 487–515.

Rangers Football Club (2003a) *The Blue Guide*, Glasgow: Rangers Football Club.

Rangers Football Club (2003b) *Pride Over Prejudice Policy Statement*, Glasgow: Rangers Football Club.

Rangers Football Club (2003c) *Pride Over Prejudice Internal and External 10-Point Plans*, Glasgow: Rangers Football Club.

Rangers Football Club website. Accessible at: www.rangers.premiumtv. co.uk/page/Home/0,,5,00.html.

Respect Task Force (2006) *Respect Action Plan*, London: Home Office.

Rodger, J.J. (2006) 'Antisocial families and withholding welfare support', *Critical Social Policy*, 26(1), 121–43.

Scheff, T. (2004) 'Elias, Freud and Goffman: shame as the master emotion', in S. Quilley and S. Loyal (eds) *The Sociology of Norbert Elias*, Cambridge: Cambridge University Press, pp 229–42.

Scottish Executive (2003) *Tackling Religious Hatred: Report of Cross-Party Working Group on Religious Hatred*, Edinburgh: Scottish Executive.

Scottish Executive (2005) *Record of the Summit on Sectarianism 14 February 2005*, Edinburgh: Scottish Executive.

Scottish Executive (2006a) *Action Plan on Tackling Sectarianism in Scotland*, Edinburgh: Scottish Executive.

Scottish Executive (2006b) *Calling Full Time on Sectarianism*, Edinburgh: Scottish Executive.

Scottish Executive (2006c) *Building Friendships and Strengthening Communities: A Guide to Twinning between Denominational and Non-Denominational Schools*, Edinburgh: Scottish Executive

True Hearts Against Bigotry website. Accessible at: www.godward. co.uk/THAB/Home%20Page.html.

van Krieken, R. (1999) 'The barbarism of civilization: cultural genocide and the "stolen generations"', *British Journal of Sociology*, 50(2), 297–315.

van Krieken, R. (2005) 'The "best interests of the child" and parental separation: on the "civilizing of parents"', *Modern Law Review*, 68(1), 25–48.

Wacquant, L. (2004) 'Decivilizing and demonizing: the remaking of the black American ghetto', in S. Loyal and S. Quilley (eds) *The Sociology of Norbert Elias*, Cambridge: Cambridge University Press, pp 95–121.

TEN

'You lookin' at me?' Discourses of respect and disrespect, identity and violence

Peter Squires

Introduction

This chapter attempts to develop an argument about the awkward parallels and contrasts between the use of a discourse of 'respect' as a policy tool – the Respect Agenda – and notions of 'street respect'. There seems some irony in the fact that the issue of 'respect governance' surfaced, as a continuation of the government's anti-social behaviour (ASB) agenda, at a time when a street discourse of 'respect' was coming to be increasingly associated with urban youth violence in a number of cities. At a time when the government was insisting on a new culture of respect as a purported solution to many of our crime and disorder problems it has been instructive, to say the least, to reflect upon the ways in which some of the 'least respected' appeared to negotiate this scarce commodity among themselves. As well as comparing and contrasting these different discourses, the chapter also reflects upon some of the issues which may, arguably, underpin both.

An international language of respect?

The aim of this discussion is to ask some questions about the language of 'respect' and the ways in which it has been deployed in recent years. There may even be a case for saying that the notion of 'respect' has been rather overplayed of late; even as the government was subtly de-emphasising the Blairite Respect Agenda, with Louise Casey, the former 'Respect Tsar', reassigned to exploring how to more effectively 'engage the public' in 'fighting crime' (Casey, 2008).[1] Yet just as this happened, the notion underwent a brief European renaissance as a

'Respect' logo decorated the shirtsleeves of the players and officials in the 2008 European football championships.

At the beginning of the EURO 2008 football championships UEFA President Michel Platini unveiled a campaign entitled 'Respect', which featured prominently throughout the event in Austria and Switzerland.[2] According to Platini, 'respect', was part of an international language which could 'be used as an umbrella term for lots of different initiatives'. UEFA was supporting social projects, each dedicated to a specific target group – schoolchildren, fans or disabled people. But the international language of 'respect' was also 'a strong social, civic and humanitarian message', highlighting 'a concept which epitomizes all of our work at the level of social responsibility'. This involved respect for opponents – in the cities, in the stands and on the pitch – while also embracing 'the difference and diversity that enriches our continent', said Mr Platini. 'In concrete terms,' he continued, 'this means strengthening the fight against social ills such as racism, violence, xenophobia and homophobia.'

It is a message that has clear parallels with the anti-sectarian work in Scottish football, as examined in Chapter Nine by John Flint and Ryan Powell. Platini's message was also thoroughly Blairite in its broad-based appeal to a currency of cultural values running, apparently seamlessly, from feted multimillionaire superstars to the lowliest fan. For UEFA, the veneer of mutual respect embraced both diversity and difference but, arguably, the equivalence ends when the 90 minutes are up and the carnival is over, and inequality, opportunities and rights re-enter the equation. With this in mind, we need to ask, what is it all about, what are the issues for which this conspicuous display of 'respect' is contrived as a response? Are these strived-for measures of respect meaningful, achievable and sustainable? And do the various uses of 'respect' with which we are confronted mean the same things? Do they speak the same language?

Central to the argument being developed here is an attempt to disentangle different conceptions or dimensions of respect; there is even the suggestion that, as presently conceived, they may be incompatible. None of this, however, necessarily implies that we give up on 'respect', even though it demands that we are a little more careful in handling such complex psychosocial notions. There is rather more to 'respect' than a simple measure of less or more, rooted in utilitarian thinking (the conventional measure of distributional justice), might encapsulate. As Sennett has argued, the meaning of respect 'is both socially and psychologically complex' (2003: 59). That said, it is probably most appropriate to begin this discussion with the governmental project of 'respect', inaugurated by Tony Blair in 2003 (Home Office, 2003) as a further rolling-out of the ASB agenda.

The domestic governance of respect

As noted elsewhere in this volume, the Respect Agenda was effectively introduced with the 2003 *Respect and Responsibility* White Paper. The issues this sought to address had a much wider social and cultural resonance, involving specific concerns about crime, disorder and ASB, as well as the wider 'broken society' commentary which, under David Cameron's leadership, the Conservative Party began to articulate also, in 2007 (Squires, 2008). Addressing this theme in 2007, John Carvel, writing in *The Guardian* newspaper, reported on the latest Office of National Statistics Social Trends analysis. He remarked that, according to the evidence, 'Britain ha[d] become a more anti-social and less tolerant society' (Carvel, 2007). Such a comment stood at the very epicentre of the political terrain aspired to by both of the main political parties, even though these conceptions of tolerance and of anti-social attitudes and behaviour were but two sides of the same coin (Waiton, 2008). Further, they raise a number of issues, in part concerning cause and context, and also regarding what it is, precisely, that ASB amounts to and what we are being intolerant of.

A further characteristic of these ideas, perhaps best outlined by Rodger (2008), concerns the disconnectedness of these ideas – or complaints – from the material realities of which they form a part. We have come to focus on the behaviour as self-evidently troublesome and allegedly anti-social, without a situated understanding of the circumstances which produced it or the norms it is perceived to threaten. In fact, as has been argued before, 'anti-social behaviour' has been subject to a marked process of redefinition over recent decades (Squires and Stephen, 2005). What is now regarded as 'anti-social youth' was, in a former time, the very normal street socialisation of young people (Corrigan, 1978; Measor and Squires, 2000). In a second sense, while public complaints about youths 'hanging about on the street' and in other public areas continue to top the list of ASB indicators reported in the British Crime Survey (Bottoms, 2006; Moley, 2008: 124), this needs to be set alongside the well-recognised dearth of other social activities open to teenagers in the 14- to 15-plus age group. The substantial decline of youth service provision in many areas is sufficiently well known not to require too much elaboration (Hallsworth, 2002).

But if the understanding of allegedly 'anti-social' behaviour lacked context and understanding, the same could also be true of our notions of tolerance and intolerance (see also Chapter Seven by Bannister and Kearns). Tolerance, understood as a component of what is sometimes termed 'social capital', requires careful accounting for. We need to appreciate the factors that can tend to either diminish or erode it. Jock Young is surely correct to refute any supposed long-term erosion of tolerance in late modernity; as he puts it:

> the modern urban dweller has a tolerance far in excess of the average pre-industrial society ... the city spins with a kaleidoscope of subcultures while the electronic media delivers daily a menu of extensive cultural variety ... Difference and diversity are the staples of lifestyle, consumerism of late modernity ... Late modern societies *consume* diversity. (Young, 1999: 59, emphasis in original)

Yet he points to a particular shift with the coming of late modernity whereby, although diversity is increasingly tolerated and even consumed, what he calls *difficulty* (risks, threats, challenges, or any perceived hindrances to the smooth satisfaction of our interests and desires) comes to be resented as the target of our intolerance. The notion is undoubtedly embedded in a culture of increasingly competitive individualism which has eroded, in Putnam's terms, the 'bridging social capital' of relations of mutuality between strangers (Putnam, 2000). And while, in one sense, the values of this culture establish the residues of social capital out of which contemporary notions of 'respect' are fabricated, the veneer of formally rule-governed late modern civility is both thin and brittle, and over-reliant on external sources of surveillance or control – for example, situational guardians or deterrents such as CCTV, wardens, or neighbourhood policing systems (Rodger, 2008: 167).[3]

Deep mutual respect is a scarce resource and it evaporates quickly in the heat of competitive exchange, even among supposed equals. According to Young, where unequals are concerned, or where the 'difficult groups' come already stigmatised – as dangerous, immoral or burdensome – then deep mutual respect is a scarce commodity indeed. Risk-averse societies tend to cultivate what Putnam terms 'bonding capital', comprising associations which are essentially inward looking and homogenous in nature (Putnam, 2000: 22). Arguably, we have a surfeit of this insular, self-regarding 'social capital' which, as Rodger (2008: 166–7) notes,

> encourages the anticipatory social reaction to people and groups *thought* to pose a threat rather than reacting only

to those that *are* posing a threat. We live in a risk society and communities are being mobilised to anticipate threats and label and classify those that do not conform to what is typical, routine and predictable. (Emphasis in original)

Indeed, as Young concludes, what the late modern world 'cannot abide is difficult people and dangerous classes [against] which it seeks to build the most elaborate defences, not just in terms of insiders and outsiders, but throughout the population' (Young 1999: 59).[4]

Further, ASB and intolerance – both understood as values and practices orchestrated through populist discourses – are also mutually reinforcing and largely interchangeable (although disconnected from the material conditions in which they were formed and typically in denial about the political interests they may be said to represent). Perhaps this was where the politics of social exclusion (disconnecting the problems of poverty and deprivation from a politics of class, inequality and power) have led us. In some ways it was anticipated by Giddens (1998: 103), who recognised exclusionary social processes operating at both ends of the social spectrum. At the upper end it is marked by a kind of withdrawal into exclusivity. An exit from society based upon a 'fortress community' of choice, excluding all those without the required entry fee. Or, as Turner (2007) has put it, acknowledging the pejorative turn taken by the language of 'community' in the hands of the modern risk management professionals, 'community' 'is what you leave once you have enough money to buy your own place'.

At the other end of the social spectrum different forms of expulsion and containment dominate the treatment of those labelled 'difficult' or 'dangerous'. Whether Giddens' Blairite disciples fully appreciated the implications of these processes remains an open question. That the Respect Agenda was introduced as a response to this condition of late modernity suggests not. It has largely served to accelerate the very processes (distinctions, intolerances, exclusions) to which it purported to offer a solution. A vicious circle of expulsion – Young's conception of 'social bulimia' (1999: 81–2) – and withdrawal has characterised contemporary culture, leaving us with anti-social symptomatic expressions, whether these are articulated as intolerance, contempt, distrust, punitiveness, aggression, harassment, nihilistic excess or merely a persistent lack of consideration for others.

Other accounts of the late modern condition describe a process of crimogenic decline into distrust, disrespect and intolerance. Halpern (2001), for instance, argues that both crime and ASB are strongly influenced by social values, social capital deficits and levels of trust and mutual respect. Where social capital is in short supply or where levels of trust and respect are diminished, crime, ASB *and* intolerance appear more prevalent. This is not to claim that one *causes* the other; rather, that they are connected in a dynamic fashion, that each further mobilises the other. It follows that ASB legislation and 'respect' agendas are not solutions for the cultural crisis but, rather, symptoms of it.

Nevertheless, the Respect Agenda was conceived as a broad-based 'cultural' response for this social crisis. We can discern these grand ambitions in the White Paper *Respect and Responsibility* itself. The government was intent on engineering

> a cultural shift ... to a society where we respect each other ... a society where we have an understanding that the rights we all enjoy are based in turn on the respect and responsibilities we have to other people and to our community. (Home Office, 2003: 6)

The point is an important reminder of the extent to which ASB policy was firmly rooted in a cultural politics. It was an attempt to implement a model of active social democratic citizenship, where rights, as Tony Blair frequently argued, were closely tied to duties in a 'something for something' society. More than this, ASB had acquired something of a symbolic quality, it was important for what it signalled.

Even more specifically, as far as the government was concerned, ASB, impinging upon our fellow citizens' quality of life and 'ontological securities', was interfering with the plausibility of the message about falling crime levels. Consequently, New Labour sought to achieve a dramatic sea change in public attitudes, behaviour and perceptions, by exhortation, moral and community rearmament and the selective use of new sanctions and enforcement powers (Squires, 2008). This much is apparent in the *Respect Action Plan* launched in January 2006 (Respect Task Force, 2006). This document consisted of a series of appealing, homespun, motivational slogans, including:

> '*The only person who can start the cycle of respect is you*'; and

> '*Respect cannot be learned, purchased or acquired it can only be earned.*'

Implicit within such snippets of folk wisdom lay the assumption that questions of respect and disrespect, and the behaviour to which they referred, were understandable entirely as questions of choice and personal motivation. Perhaps we ought not to be surprised that the 'solutions' for ASB were presumed to be addressed through behaviourism. Extracted from its context, 'denatured' and viewed in the abstract, behaviour was only ever regarded as that – behaviour. Perpetrators simply needed to recognise their problem, take responsibility and grasp the solution (or face the consequences). Problematic behaviour, irrespective of how this was constructed, caused or contextualised, could apparently be banished by a concerted application of will-power. 'Gaining respect' was thereby reframed as a kind of twelve-step motivational challenge which the virtuous or committed might choose to attempt. Self-respect was apparently within everyone's grasp, although there remained a degree of ambiguity about how the broader community might acknowledge those restored to a new-found respectability.

In this sense respect was not unlike the 'American dream' (or even Platini's European football dream), and as soon as we acknowledge this some further flaws become apparent, as Young has observed. Culturally dominant aspirations of self-improvement certainly 'carry notions of reward [and] also measures of merit: success is open to all, your success depends on how hard you try' (Young, 1999: 82). In reality, despite the attractiveness of the dream, the commitment to the values or the sheer hard work undertaken, the limits of meritocratic individualism as a vehicle for widespread social inclusion have probably been reached in our late modern, post-deferential societies. We seem much less content to embrace the sermons which R.H.Tawney (1931) characterised as a 'tadpole philosophy', preached by successful frogs over 70 years ago.[5] As Mike Davis has noted, the 'American dream' probably has more prisoners (many of them actually incarcerated in the world's largest criminal justice industrial complex) than rags-to-riches successes (Davis, 1999).

Notwithstanding the powerful cultural message of this 'dream', and the rather more parochial concerns of the British Respect Agenda, I will argue in the later sections of this chapter that it is in the risky capitalism of 'violent street cultures' (Hallsworth, 2008) that some of the most embedded and committed representations of 'respect' might still be found. For the moment, there are further difficulties with the governmental ambition to reconstruct respectful social relations across society that we need to address. Questions of psychology and redemption are important here.

Psychology and redemption

Reinforcing unpalatable conceptions of the excluded and difficult, ASB discourses also seemed a little short on redemption, even despite some 'restorative' packaging. In part this can be accounted for by the fact that, as noted already, no real attempt was ever made to understand the behaviour attracting the complaint, still less to understand reactions to it. Intolerance was simply seen as a legitimate response to 'intolerable' behaviour: end of story. As Christie (2004) has argued, this was where explanation and understanding stopped: 'Evil people are their own explanation. The discussion comes to a stop, the phenomenon is understood, there is no further need for intellectual efforts' (p 49). Anti-social behaviour was of a similar order – precisely 'the behaviour we might expect from "them" … and part of their very "anti-social" otherness … the labels stick serving as shortcuts to an entire worldview of crime and punishment' (Squires and Stephen, 2005: 23).

However, without some understanding of the production of tolerance and the social relations of *in*tolerance, the question of redemption – or inclusion – remains unresolved. However diligently those deemed 'anti-social' might strive to alter their behaviour they may never quite make it in the eyes of those sitting in judgement. Perhaps the diminished faith in rehabilitation also translates into a more generic scepticism about the reintegration of 'outsiders'; although, perhaps, some people may always seem outsiders, it is at least arguable that a discourse of the 'anti-social' will foster this exclusion more profoundly than any other. Its purpose, after all, is not to redeem but to exclude. David Downes' insightful book, *Contrasts in Tolerance* (1988), based on a comparison of the British and Dutch criminal justice systems during the period from the end of the Second World War to the mid 1970s, makes an important point about tolerance and the social and political relations upon which it rests. Political and administrative systems are embedded *within* sociopolitical cultures, they reflect and embody them rather than offering antidotes to them. We delude ourselves to think that 'respect' can be grafted onto a criminal justice culture which largely points in another direction entirely.

So we are not required to understand 'intolerance', it speaks for itself (loudly and quite often), invoking rules of civilised community that some (allegedly, apparently) seem to ignore. But within our presumptively shared interest in an individualised, bourgeois, consumerist life-style lurks a more sectarian interest that responds with mistrust and suspicion to those suggesting risks, threats or difficulties to us. It may not be their fault, they may not be aware of the impact they are having or the rules they are breaking; or they may indeed be actively resisting or just plain irresponsible. These differences hardly matter; from the point of view of tolerance, motives are irrelevant. It is the fact of the behaviour itself, causing hindrance to our own interests – or maybe just symbolising that potential – which counts. Even so, inclusion and exclusion are not fixed and immovable thresholds. Like the turnstiles of Michel Platini's EURO 2008 football stadia, they are flexible, relative and rooted in judgements over which their subjects may have little control. It is conceivable that the once 'anti-social' underclass might press endlessly upon the metaphorically gated communities of contemporary society but never gain admission, except, perhaps, as cheap, dispensable, manual service labour; they are de facto second-class citizens, permanently. The issue here is not just a question of personal effort, social circumstance or even the need to create opportunities for people to earn respect and acquire and demonstrate responsibility, it is also about other people's perceptions and judgements. This was always something of a blindspot in the Respect Agenda; it lacked a proper understanding of these issues of respect, redemption and mutuality. How, indeed, are we to cultivate respect for those whose legal rights we restrict, whose motivations we question, whose integrity we doubt, whose behaviour we condemn and whose mug shots we reproduce on 'name and shame' leaflets distributed throughout their communities? When we add to this the routine scapegoating by tabloid media and politicians alike, it becomes difficult to reconcile real 'respect' with the ASB and Respect agendas. Sennett (2003) argues, in particular, that the attempt to legislate for respect shares many of social policy's more familiar shortcomings.

In his 2003 book *Respect: The Formation of Character in an Age of Inequality*, Richard Sennett, develops a conception of 'mutual respect' as a positive-sum relationship. This is not unlike Titmuss's concept of altruistic blood donorship in *The Gift Relationship* (Titmuss, 1970), where constructive social interactions can progressively build social capital. All this is very positive, for, as the government and some academics appear to agree, respect seems in short supply; we have, apparently, as a society become more disrespectful, intolerant and anti-social (Office of National Statistics, Social Trends, 2007). The question is how we reverse these trends. As previously noted in this volume (for example, in Chapter One by Burney), the official Respect Agenda is substantially rooted in a broadly communitarian discourse, stressing mutuality, obligations and self-discipline in return for rights and considerations. Yet, as I argued, many of the *Respect Action Plan's* supposedly inspirational slogans are formulated in largely individual terms, and devoid of context.

In the same book, Sennett also argues that politicians and policy makers are often poor psychologists, making the point that the measures we may adopt to address social problems or influence behaviour often have adverse, unforeseen consequences. Means testing might be one familiar example, seeking to target resources onto the 'truly needy', but doing so in a fashion which demeans and stigmatises the recipients of public welfare. Likewise, the propensity of early-intervention youth crime measures to label young offenders and to reinforce rather than remove their delinquent self-images, might be another. In these terms the Respect Agenda may represent part of a problem rather than part of a solution: social context may be a key. In developing this argument, the chapter will later consider findings from some research on gangs and gun crime, drawing upon social contexts where respect is vital yet violently contested, and 'social capital' a rather mixed blessing. In this 'underworld', awash with respect (and disrespect) issues, lie important questions about respect and power, competitive individualism, identity and social exclusion, which could have a major bearing on contemporary policy initiatives.

The lack of a real opportunity to gain respect was at the heart of a basic weakness in the Respect Agenda. To be fair, it was always more to do with requiring respect *from* anti-social subjects rather than conferring it upon them. The anti-social had to earn their quota of respect rather than obtain it unconditionally: 'give respect, get respect', as both the *Respect Action Plan* (Respect Task Force, 2006) and the recent *Youth Taskforce Action Plan* (Youth Taskforce, 2008) put it. In this sense, in Titmuss's terms, respect acquisition became more of a bilateral transfer, respect was conditional upon being earned. The question remained as to how the excluded were to obtain this scarce social capital.

This can be especially difficult, given the social and psychological exclusions operating here. A first difficulty involves the impact of stigmatising social processes (labelling, criminalisation, blame and demonisation) on one's own sense of self-respect. As McCarthy and Walker have noted (2006: 27), it is hard to imagine that a culture of respect can be cultivated by increasing social controls. The opposite seems more plausible, the cultivation of resistance: 'challenges to the legitimacy of the authority being exercised, and disrespect towards those attempting to exercise it'. A second difficulty concerns the relations of inequality (power, opportunity and rights) and whether the 'disrespected' possess the desire or the means to positively influence their interactions with agents capable of conferring respect. And finally, a third issue concerns the variety of dimensions to contemporary respect and social capital. Conferring respect upon those generally considered by one's peers to be 'undeserving' (or allowing them access to scarce social capital resources) may negatively influence the regard in which one is held. McCarthy and Walker (2006) cite Bell's (1995) point about the difficulties associated with cultivating self-respect in a culture dominated by 'adultism', 'the essence of which is "disrespect for the young"' (McCarthy and Walker, 2006: 19). Further, subtle distinctions between class and caste (wealth and income, accent, dress, mannerisms) may be vigorously policed to maintain the exclusivity of one's own position, the respect which is due to it and the social capital it embodies. The point is further illustrated in work by Hayward and Yar (2006) discussing the so-called 'chav' phenomenon in British working-class culture. Here, certain traits of youthful, affluent, conspicuous consumption of once-expensive and exclusive 'designer' labels came to be condemned as a form of tasteless excess. Respect clearly could not be bought. Even in a consumer culture it had to be earned in other ways. And yet respect *among* 'chavs' was precisely dependent on adopting the appropriate styles, logos, jewellery and behaviour. Respect could be a very slippery concept.

Respect and street credibility

The moment we begin to consider 'respect' in other contexts, however, what we might call 'non-governmental' forms of respect intrinsic to peer-group relationships and contexts (or even respect among 'chavs'), then different respect relations become apparent. Sandberg's discussion of what he terms 'street capital' (Sandberg, 2008) provides us with a useful opening into this issue.[6] Sandberg writes in an ethnographic tradition that owes much to the street ethnographies and cultural theorisation of Anderson (1999), Bourdieu (1991) and Bourdieu and Wacquant (1992), and a long tradition of (mainly) American gang studies. Two key insights form the core of Sandberg's approach: first, the idea 'that street culture should be analysed as a social system with its own rules and regulations', and second, that the street subculture can be understood as 'marginalised groups' response to socio-economic suppression' (Sandberg, 2008: 155). He cites Anderson's (1999) conception of being 'street wise' as the basis for a negotiated self-respect that is the cornerstone of a person's 'street credibility'. As Anderson argued:

> Once mastered the *savoir faire* of the street world – knowing
> how to deal coolly with people, how to move, look, act, dress
> – is a form of capital, not a form that middle-class people
> would respect, but capital that can, nonetheless, be cashed
> in. (Anderson, 1999: 134, cited in Sandberg, 2008: 155)

Other writers, in particular Philippe Bourgois in his work on street
crack dealing, draw attention to the 'street culture of resistance',
which he describes as 'not a coherent, conscious universe of political
opposition but rather a spontaneous set of rebellious practices that in
the long term have emerged as an oppositional style' (Bourgois, 2003:
8). It is of especial interest to Bourgois that:

> through fashion, music, film and television … mainstream
> society eventually recuperates and commercialises many
> of these oppositional street styles, recycling them as pop
> culture. In fact some of the most basic linguistic expressions
> for self-esteem in middle-class America, such as being 'cool,'
> 'square,' or 'hip,' were coined on inner city streets. (p 8)

As already noted, according to Young, mainstream society typically
consumes difference voraciously.

The important issue for our conceptions of 'street capital' and
'respect' is that these components of street credibility are not stripped
of meaning and context, nor imposed from without. Rather, they
arise in the context of daily interactions, but they are far from benign.
Short (1997) and Anderson (1990; 1999) go some way to explain the
importance of violence as a component of 'respect' in street culture.
'The seemingly inordinate concern with "respect" – resulting in a
low threshold for being "dissed" (disrespected) can be traced to the
profound alienation from mainstream American society felt by many
inner city blacks, particularly the poorest' (Anderson, cited in Short,
1997: 65). And, as Short concludes,

> out of concern for being disrespected, respect is easily
> violated. Because status problems are mixed with extreme
> resource limitations, people – especially young people
> – exaggerate the importance of symbols, often with life-
> threatening consequences. (1997: 65)

In case there might be some tendency to 'romanticise' this street culture
(perhaps through the lens of popular media), it is worth noting that

Bourgois, in particular, has little regard for the violent street culture, seeing it essentially as a form of negative social capital which is as destructive of communities as of individual lives. Illegal street cultures, he notes, embroil most participants

> in lifestyles of violence, substance abuse and internalised rage. Contradictorily therefore, the street culture of resistance is predicated on the destruction of its participants and the community harboring them. In other words, although street culture emerges out of a personal search for dignity and a rejection of racism and subjugation, it ultimately becomes an active agent in personal degradation and community ruin. (Bourgois, 2003: 9)

As violent and destructive as this street 'respect' capital is, it has something that a governmental Respect Agenda clearly lacks – an authenticity and a rootedness in a given social context. But it is not that we are being called upon to *choose* between these contrasting conceptions of governmental and street 'respect', simply that each shows up in stark relief some of the inadequacies of the other.

The governmental conception of respect, premised on the 'bonding social capital' of an exclusive controlling culture whose interests it broadly endeavours to sustain, operates in the face of (and to the detriment of) those its seeks to bring to order. It is imposed on, and is perceived as alien to, the social relations it seeks to manage. Not surprisingly, it engenders a resistance rooted in the culture, context and social relations of the subordinate culture. For instance, the significance with which the breach of ASBOs is treated in the media in part reflects these relations of resistance to social control; likewise the cultural subversion of ASBOs by youth as 'street diplomas', signs of street credibility quite contrary to the intentions of the ASB managers. In other words, the governmental conception of respect lacks a reflexive conception of the unforeseen psychological consequences of disciplining. What you do is not necessarily what you get. Imposing 'respect' or an ASBO – applying discipline – is not like applying a fresh coat of varnish; it does not do 'exactly as it says on the tin'. Rather, what we might term New Labour's 'Ronseal'[7] approach to public policy making merely camouflages the cracks. One commentator has suggested that contemporary ASB management effects the 'reduction of public policy to pest control' (Davies, 2006). Here I would simply add that the policy also has the added, largely cosmetic (or ideological) character of window dressing.

By contrast, the social capital rooted in the street culture of competitive respect does contain a complex reflexive psychological dimension, concerned with perceiving how you are perceived and responding accordingly. Yet it comes at a high price. In the longer term it is, as we have seen, destructive of both self and community. It is predicated on a strategy for survival in a world of adversaries armed and dangerous to one another – literally a 'hair-trigger' culture without a safety catch. Collins' study on the 'micro-sociology of violence' (Collins, 2008) may help us to illuminate some of the foreground dynamics of this violent street culture and its links with notions of 'respect'. He develops a concept of 'forward panic' to account for the emotional rush to violence brought on by the tensions and fears of a conflict situation. Collins articulates his theory in the context of a number of military encounters, to account for the kind of frenzied killing rampage that results when an incident is triggered, although his contexts are not exclusively military.[8] On the contrary, it seems reasonable to extend the analysis to the dangerous context of the inner city, where a careful presentation of self and a subtle appreciation of the signals given and received concerning mutual respect and recognition are essential to survival. Alternatively, fine-tuning the attitudes and skills of a lethal pre-emptive violence (or 'getting your retaliation in first', or 'shooting first and asking questions later') may be the best way to survive, at least in the short term.[9] For example, the hard-core street villains who provided Mullins (2006) with their testimonies of what it took to survive on the 'mean streets' of St Louis, Missouri, all claimed that it was unmanly (and thereby disreputable) to launch an unprecedented attack on an unsuspecting victim (to do so was to be a 'punk', and 'on the streets, reputation is everything' (2006: 2)). However, virtually without exception, they all admitted to having done so as and when the need arose. Such contradictions negotiated within the discourse of street masculinity point to the kind of perceptual and psychological reflexivity in the situated notions of respect at street level. Here, in marked distinction to 'governmental projects of respect', street respect was a flexible currency emphasising 'variety, ambivalence and agency' (Sandberg, 2008: 157) rooted in a context and endlessly negotiated in daily interactions. It was also, as Sandberg notes, something of a dead end, a trap.

As Sandberg argues, following Bourdieu, the very notion of 'street capital' reflects

> a tension between economical and cultural analysis ... Street capital is based upon having little to lose in mainstream

> society … a form of power the structurally oppressed can utilize. At the same time, when accumulating street capital they uphold and develop a violent street culture. (2008: 158)

We might go further: it is less a question of this violent culture being simply chosen or freely embraced, it is part of a context that young people must carefully negotiate on a daily basis. In this sense, as with Katz's (1988) discussion of the role of a violent reputation, and the necessary performance of tough masculinity reported by Mullins (2006), Sandberg's interviewees affirmed that when they were confronted in a hostile fashion 'a response indicating lack of fear of physical confrontation was seen as necessary' (Sandberg, 2008: 161). And when the stakes were further raised, 'when challenged or harassed, it was important to retaliate, "otherwise it would only be more and more pressure"' (p 161). In short, 'building a violent reputation or building street capital, not only commands respect but also serves to deter future assaults' (p 161).

However, this currency of respect has only a limited shelf life – it is only as good as the last confrontation, where it can be quickly won or lost; it travels badly, having relatively little import in wider, mainstream, society;[10] and the flimsy bridges it establishes do not extend beyond the street culture itself. Finally, it socially disables its exponents, whose 'ghetto skills' are censured or sanctioned by society at large. In Sandberg's research, the confining character of these social relations of street culture are exacerbated by a marked symbolic association between respect and street credibility, and the membership of certain ethnic minority groups. As Sandberg notes, racist discrimination is undoubtedly a disadvantage,

> but [racist] stereotypes can be used strategically. For boys on the street, [such stereotyping] may serve as a resource when posing as gangsters, and creating a dangerous appearance … in this way, racism is turned on its head and black becomes a symbol of strength. (Sandberg, 2008: 163)

Even so, affecting the style (dress, mannerisms, language and associates) of a street hard man can also be guaranteed to draw additional police attention. 'Thugging up' (Hallsworth, 2005) may solve certain street problems but it certainly has its disadvantages outside the immediate relationships of street culture.

Bringing it all back home?

Moving beyond the more international discussion of respect and street capital, we can bring the discussion full circle by reference to an all-too-familiar example of 'respect gone wrong' in a British context, and then conclude by drawing out some 'respect' issues arising from a piece of research on the seeming gang-and-gun 'scene' in a British city.

The first illustration arises in the context of the revenge drama behind a murder trial in a British city. The trial itself gave us a glimpse of a British nightmare played out in the full glare of the media. It is something that, of late, we have had to deal with on a seemingly more regular basis. Guns, shootings and murderous gang feuds belong somewhere else: the ghetto cities of America, and perhaps further back, the Jamaican slums, or even Hollywood. They belong *anywhere* else, the Third World, where poverty, drugs and desperate young men come together (Gunst, 1995). Even a growing recognition of gun crime occurring in a few places in a handful of British cities (South London, Manchester's Moss Side, Birmingham, Nottingham) fails to erase the sense that it was still confined, part of another world.

Much the same thing has been said about British teenage gangs. For a long time they were thought to be a pale, even timid, shadow of their American counterparts. Over the past decade things may have appeared to change in Britain, although the scale of young people's involvement in 'gangs' still seems relatively low – less than 6% of the 10 to 19 age group appeared to be involved in 'delinquent youth groups' (Sharp et al, 2006), while the very definition of 'gangs' in the British context is undoubtedly contested (Bennett and Holloway, 2004). As gangs – or, 'violent youth subcultures' (Hallsworth, 2008) – have become influential in certain communities they have apparently attracted 'wannabe gangsters', impetuous, unstable or even deluded young men keen to acquire the successful trappings of their peers. There are also those whose 'gang' involvements are rather more ambiguously motivated, or those who may be more ambivalent, or even reluctant (Pitts, 2007).

Violent, perhaps 'gang-associated' youth activity is often highly localised around certain residential neighbourhoods, reinforcing control over local drug dealing, prostitution, protection rackets or markets in stolen goods: just protecting their 'turf'. Many in the local community live in fear, no one talks to the police or wants to be labelled a 'grass'. Young people often find it safer to join in, looking the part, walking the walk; however reluctantly, safety lies in numbers. What the Home Office now distinguishes as 'gang association', rather than membership, is sometimes thrust upon you by where you grew up, the school you attended, or your postcode.

So when the self-styled S4 'gang' members went looking for JM, a member of S3, a rival group, with the intention of seeking revenge for what they thought was the serious insult he had perpetrated against them – firing his gun into a family member's home – they were enacting what impetuous, reckless and violent young men have probably done for generations (Newburn and Stanko, 1994; Nisbet and Cohen, 1996; Spierenberg, 1998). Not to act in the way they did would be to lose face, to suggest they did not have the 'bottle' (or, in a longer masculine tradition, the 'honour') to protect their 'turf'. Weakness or retreat would only invite further violence. Research from many countries suggests a reputation for violence to be a necessary component of successful participation in street culture (Katz, 1988; Anderson, 1999; Bourgois, 2003; Mullins, 2006; Sandberg, 2008). Typically, you cannot call the police if a drug deal goes bad or a customer refuses to pay for contraband or illegal services. A capacity for violence is your credibility, your 'capital' – the respect you are due. Respect has to be won, both earned and protected, your reputation is what prevents others from trying to 'mess' with you, what makes them take you seriously. Despite the common media rhetoric of 'mindless violence', such violence is seldom 'meaningless' – it means precisely the same as the warning notices to shoplifters in high street shops: 'we always prosecute'. It means 'I always retaliate – you know I've done it before, and that I will do it to you.' For example, one of Hales et al's (2006) interviewees put it this way: 'You have to deal with certain people in a certain way. So the word gets round so that no-one else tries robbing you or tries and pulls a fast one' (2006: 37). A propensity to carry and use weapons is a notable feature of this reputation making.

The fact that violent feuds are now periodically reported in Britain, perpetrated by young men who seem to feel they have nothing much to lose and who have stronger obligations to their fellow gang/peer-group members or friends than to the wider community, is perhaps symptomatic of an erosion of mutual and collective social capital in poor communities (an erosion that violent behaviour seems likely to accelerate (Currie, 1997). In other words, it marks the displacement of one form of organic social capital (mutual respect) by another more chaotic, fluid and negotiated street capital (street respect, due to violence) and the absence (or failure) of an effective, state-orchestrated, top-down imposition of 'respect governance'.

Evidence on the precise role of gang cultures as incubators of tensions over 'street respect' may remain contested in Brtiain, but there seems little shortage of empirical evidence of 'violent street cultures' fomenting conflicts about respect in British cities. Hales et al (2006) cite a comment by one of their imprisoned gun-offender interviewees which establishes the value of respect in street networks and relationships:

> '... from when I was young [XX has] been my top number one guy. Only because, he was on top, he had respect, the police couldn't chat shit to him. The police didn't even stop him. The police couldn't stop him. He was my ideal guy like. He got respect off everyone. And like, I wanted to be him for a while.' (Hales et al, 2006: 63)

Illegal economies (drug dealing, markets in stolen goods, door security work, prostitution) provided an economic basis for many of the violent street networks, not to mention some of the underlying causes of ongoing disputes (turf wars, debts and grudges). As Hales et al put it, violence could be 'particularly related to drug dealing activity, including turf wars, but [was] more generally related to long-standing conflicts and tit-for-tat violence ... conflict [formed] a significant dimension of their social relations, especially disputes related to status and respect' (2006: 32, xiv).

Developing these themes, a recent research initiative led by the author explored police perceptions of gang- and gun-related offending in Manchester and attempted to explore the motivations ascribed by the police officers to the perpetrators of the armed street violence they had to deal with (Squires, 2007). In keeping with other police 'gang intelligence' assessments (eg BBC News website, 21 February 2007: 'Police Identify 169 Gangs in London'), the Greater Manchester Police officers[11] surveyed were generally accepting of the role of gangs as key factors in Manchester's street crime problems. But while gangs were seen to play a part in accelerating and facilitating (although not mediating or restraining) street violence, gang activity or disputes were certainly not seen as responsible for all of the violence that took place. Nevertheless, by virtue of the conflicts about 'respect' occurring between supposed 'gang' members (members of either the same 'gang' or different 'gangs'[12]) or between people 'associated' with 'gangs' and their 'members', incidents still tended to be lumped together by both police intelligence reports and the media as 'gang-related'. In this sense, as Hallsworth (2008) has argued, there is a significantly self-fulfilling quality to discussions of youth violence as being 'gang-related'. That said, in the Manchester study the issue of 'respect and disrespect' certainly dominated the police officers' remarks about the factors triggering violent conflicts in the city. The following remarks are fairly typical:

> 'A lot of it is to do with "disrespect". Gangs and their members seem to have a heightened sensitivity to incidents they perceive as insulting or challenging them. The culture of most gangs is violent and leaders are expected to fight to attain the top positions and then "see off" any challenges. Loss of "face" can have serious, even fatal consequences.... In a violent sub-culture like this it is often a case of "get them before they get you".' (Squires, 2007: 42)

> 'It can be a range of things but at the bottom it is about earning "respect" by showing you are willing to be the most ruthless.' (Squires, 2007: 43)

> 'The "street cred" factor is probably central, joining a gang and being part of a group who are seen as the group to be with. Trying to earn more respect from others, and self preservation (not being isolated from these groups) are reasons for sticking with this life.' (Squires, 2007: 31)

'Respect' formed a central element of the currency of street credibility, part of a moral economy which motivated behaviour and allegiances and underpinned, in the eyes of the police officers, the role, place and significance of 'gangs' in a community:

> 'Status is one key, gang members and especially the leaders, are often seen as having the respect of the community, or at least a kind of power over it. Lifestyle is also a factor, gang members and armed criminals often have a lifestyle that is the envy of elements in their community. The disposable income and access to cars and women is very attractive to young males who are unlikely to ever attain this from legitimate work.' (Squires, 2007: 31)

> '... many factors are involved, however the main factors appear to initially evolve around "Street Cred", "Image" and "Respect". With regard to gang culture it can vary from wanting to control areas and neighbourhoods, "turf",

using ... intimidation by numbers, to self preservation at the street and local level.' (Squires, 2007: 29)

Yet 'respect' was also seen as the 'spark' which caused underlying tensions to burst into violence:

> 'Minor incidents at parties/events between rival factions where disrespect is perceived are a main trigger in my experience. Any retaliation usually involves a wholly disproportionate response to the original minor slight and usually involves guns. This can then trigger a series of tit for tat shootings as each gang responds to the slight to their status.' (Squires, 2007: 42)

Some officers saw the respect issue as enabling some distinction to be drawn between the newer 'gang-related' offending of younger groups and the more instrumentally motivated offending of older groups:

> '... gang culture appears to involve disaffected youth looking for an identity and purpose in life. I see this as being distinct from organised crime groups whose aim is to further a criminal enterprise rather than being the purpose of the "gang".' (Squires, 2007: 18)

While these comments – and many more like them – may be criticised as evidence of a police 'cultural criminology' (Cope, 2004; Innes et al, 2005), furthering the interests of a particular style of enforcement culture with respect to violent street cultures, it is a different matter entirely to suggest that the insights they reveal are unfounded, incorrect or irrelevant. And as has been demonstrated, police perceptions of the drivers of street violence are replete with accounts of the significance of 'respect' and 'disrespect'. Further, as we have seen, the police accounts correspond closely to the qualitative and ethnographic findings produced by other researchers.[13]

Conclusion

This chapter has tried to engage with a number of different, but arguably related, discourses of respect: a supposedly 'international language' of respect articulated in conjunction with the European Football Championships of 2008; the attempt to bring 'governance' to respect through the UK government's attempts to add a so-called

Respect Agenda to its ASB management strategy; finally, I have explored the contours and workings of a discourse of 'street respect' associated with 'gangs' or 'violent street cultures'. There has truly been a proliferation of 'respect' talk of late. As McCarthy and Walker (2006) have noted, using the example of Otis Redding and Aretha Franklin's song, the concept has a proud musical and cultural pedigree associated with the advancement of African-American civil rights. In the UK, 'Respect' became the name of an anti-war political party, while comedy even tried to poke some fun at the concept of 'street respect'. In the 2002 film *Ali G in da House*, Ali's suped-up yellow Renault 5 displayed the licence plate number RE58ECT.[14]

But what do these contrasting discourses of respect tell us, what do they have in common and what can we learn from juxtaposing them, as this chapter has attempted to do? In one sense it is clear that they do point to a particular late modern preoccupation with 'reputation' in social relations. As a broad social phenomenon, this was particularly evident in the cultural politics which, fairly explicitly (Squires, 2008), lay behind the government's Respect Agenda. A lack of respect, no doubt with many historical antecedents (see Pearson, 1983, as well as Chapter Two, this volume), was deemed to have reached crisis proportions in the 1990s and appeared to explain (to some degree) the perceived tidal wave of youth crime and disorder that many appeared to feel the decade was experiencing. At the same time, disrespect in 'sink' estates and socially excluded communities was seen as a driver of further neighbourhood decline. In fact, when the issue is flipped around, as suggested in the first part of this chapter, notions of 'anti-social behaviour' become increasingly interchangeable with notions of intolerance. And both are connected to profound social and economic changes, on which the language and politics of respect are unlikely to impact. In fact, as a growing range of commentators have come to suggest, the essentially authoritarian, top-down premise which the Respect Agenda's dispersal of discipline (Brown, 2004; Squires and Stephen, 2005) conveys is an essentially self-defeating and 'disempowering premise ... For example, who accords the status of being respected, who deems respect to have been earned, and by what criteria? What opportunities do we have to gain respect, and how are these opportunities distributed through society? ... Respect is not experienced equally' (Harris, 2006: 6).

And yet, as we have seen, there is another discourse of respect widely acknowledged and in play 'on the street'. It is, contrary to the heavy-handed discourse of respect governance, psychologically nuanced, subtle, flexible and negotiated – and also potentially lethal, it is important not to forget. What both these discourses appear to have in common is certainly a profound preoccupation with the 'worth' of individuals at a time when some individuals appear to be 'worth' less than others. As Katz (1988) has noted, it is no doubt true that, where 'respect' is most scarce, it is treated most carefully. The central issue connecting *both* discourses of respect is perhaps about opportunities. Respect governance needs to prioritise (as Harris (2006) has noted) the importance of equal opportunities to gain respect. 'Street respect' likewise needs an opportunity to grow and develop beyond the street and into the wider community without the seeming necessity of violence and intimidation.

Notes

[1] Louise Casey's new role was not dissimilar to the one she held with the Respect Task Force, having at its heart issues of safety, confidence and, in particular, the clarification of responsibilities and expectations concerning community crime and disorder management.

[2] UEFA European Championships 2008 website: http://en.euro2008. uefa.com/news/kind=1/newsid=671250.html.

[3] The mores of queuing, driving and even, to prolong the football-related metaphor with which we began, watching live football games, expose these fault lines in late modern sociability. Road rage and even 'trolley rage' illustrate the way resentments can rapidly spring to the fore when people engaged in formally rule-governed behaviour perceive that others are gaining an advantage or passing on a disadvantage by their non-observance of widely understood 'rules' of conduct. In football grounds such tensions arise concerning standing in seated areas. Despite the health and safety agenda which brought us all-seater stadia for most top-flight games, some die-hard fans prefer to stand, thereby unilaterally forcing all those behind them to do likewise. The exchanges which result are indicative of a dearth of respect even between supporters of the same team. The insults hurled at an opposing team's fans are rather irrelevant to the mutual contempt between groups of fans who are simply using the same space in different ways.

[4] Young's point is well made, while the illustrations in note 3 above support the point about mutual disrespect within groups of 'insiders'. In this sense, competitive interactions within rule-governed contexts seem destined to make 'Wayward Puritans' (Erickson, 1966) of us all. This is a useful corrective to a notion of disrespect centred exclusively upon supposed 'outsiders'. Most of our 'enemies' certainly seem to start from 'within'. The sociologically interesting question, as Rodger (2008)

has noted, is why, at various times and places, given societies embark upon a process of 'defining deviancy up', expelling, stigmatising and criminalising more vehemently than usual.

[5] R.H. Tawney states in *Equality* (1931: 142): 'It is possible that intelligent tadpoles reconcile themselves to the inconvenience of their position that, though most of them will live and die as tadpoles and nothing more, the more fortunate of the species will one day shed their tails, distend their mouths and stomachs, hop nimbly onto dry land and croak addresses to their former friends on the virtues by means of which tadpoles of character and capacity can rise to be frogs…. This conception of society may be described perhaps as the tadpole philosophy since the consolation which it offers for social evils consists in the statement that exceptional individuals can succeed in evading them.'

[6] Sandberg's (2008) research was based upon interviews and fieldwork largely with ethnic minority youth in Oslo, Norway.

[7] The paints and wood preserver company Ronseal has for many years had the no-nonsense slogan that it 'does exactly what it says on the tin'.

[8] Collins also discusses, in this context, the beating of Rodney King by Los Angeles Police Department officers in 1991 and the 1999 killing of Amadou Diallo in New York City by four undercover New York Police Department officers. The four officers together fired 41 shots from a range of less than seven feet, 19 bullets striking and killing the unfortunate Mr Diallo.

[9] Among their discussion of 'gangs' as potential facilitators and accelerators of violence, Hales et al (2006) also comment on the role of weapons, specifically firearms, as drivers of violent conflict. Thus, 'in the context of [illegal] firearm ownership, even quite trivial disputes may result in shootings as the presence of guns elevates threat levels and the so-called "shoot or be shot" scenario precipitates pre-emptive violence. Gang structures serve to escalate and perpetuate violence, and violent conflict may transcend individual incidents and become generalised' (p 91). At the same time, the point being made here is that mutually recognised signals of 'street respect' can also help avoid or prevent conflict escalation. 'Gangs' – or whatever concept we might employ – do not simply promote violence; they may also mediate and restrain it. Rather less attention is paid to this aspect of 'violent street cultures'.

¹⁰ One has to say 'relatively' little import in wider society, given the immense significance of 'gangster reputations' in the popular music culture of Hip Hop and Rap artists such as NWA, Tupac, Fifty Cent, Puff Daddy and Snoop Dogg. For such artists, narrations of violence are fused together in both street and musical reputations (Armstrong, 2001). In Young's (1999) terms this is but a further illustration of the commodification of deviance in consumer culture.

¹¹ All the officers contacted were part of the Greater Manchester Police specialist firearms team or specialist intelligence officers.

¹² See Hallsworth's (2005) point about the fluid nature of youth subculture groups, which lack the structure and defined membership traditionally associated with 'gangs'.

¹³ It has to be acknowledged that some of the police respondents (perhaps not surprisingly) added a very pejorative spin to their accounts of 'respect relations' and their role in street violence. This aside, the accounts of respect that they articulated remained essentially very similar to those reproduced in this chapter.

¹⁴ I am grateful to my son, Matthew, for pointing this out to me.

References

Anderson E. (1990) *Streetwise: Race Class and Change in an Urban Community*, Chicago, IL: University of Chicago Press.

Anderson, E. (1999) *Code of the Street: Decency, Violence and the Moral Life of the Inner City*, New York, NY: Norton & Co.

Armstrong, E.G. (2001) 'Gangsta misogyny: a content analysis of the portrayals of violence against women in rap music 1987–1993', *Journal of Criminal Justice and Popular Culture*, 8(2), 96–126.

Bell, J. (1995) 'Understanding adultism: a key to developing positive youth–adult relationships'. Available at: www.freechild.org/bell. htm.

Bennett, T. and Holloway, K. (2004) 'Gang membership, drugs and crime in the UK', *British Journal of Criminology*, 44(3), 305–23.

Bottoms, A.E. (2006) 'Incivilities, offence and social order in residential communities', in A. von Hirsch and A.P. Simester (eds) *Incivilities: Regulating Offensive Behaviour*, Oxford: Hart Publishing, pp 239–80.

Bourdieu, P. (1991) *Language and Symbolic Power*, Cambridge: Polity Press.

Bourdieu, P. and Wacquant, L. (1992) *An Invitation to Reflexive Sociology*, Cambridge: Polity Press.

Bourgois, P. (2003) *In Search of Respect: Selling Crack in El Barrio*, 2nd edn, Cambridge: Cambridge University Press.

Brown, A.P. (2004) 'Anti-social behaviour: crime control and social control', *Howard Journal*, 43(2), 203–11.

Carvel, J. (2007) 'Fivefold rise in rows over noise marks less tolerant society', *The Guardian*, 11 April.

Casey, L. (2008) *Engaging Communities in Fighting Crime*, Crime and Communities Review, London: Cabinet Office.

Christie, N. (2004) *A Suitable Amount of Crime*, London: Routledge.

Collins, R. (2008) *Violence: A Micro-sociological Theory*, Princeton, NJ, and Oxford: Princeton University Press.

Cope, N. (2004) 'Intelligence led policing or policing led intelligence: integrating volume crime analysis into policing', *British Journal of Criminology*, 44(2), 188–203.

Corrigan, P. (1978) *Schooling the Smash Street Kids*, Basingstoke: Macmillan.

Currie, E. (1997) 'Market, crime and community: towards a theory of post-industrial violence', *Theoretical Criminology*, 1(2), 147–72.

Davis, M. (1999) *Prisoners of the American Dream*, London: Verso.

Davies, W. (2006) 'Potlach weblog', http://potlach.typepad.com 5 July 2006, cited in K. Harris (ed) *Respect in the Neighbourhood*, Lyme Regis: Russell House Publishing, p xiii.

Downes, D. (1988) *Contrasts in Tolerance: Post-war Penal Policy in the Netherlands and England and Wales*, Oxford: Clarendon Press.

Erickson, K.T. (1996) *Wayward Puritans: A Study in the Sociology of Deviance*, New York, NY: John Wiley.

Giddens, A. (1998) *The Third Way: The Renewal of Social Democracy*, Cambridge: Polity Press.

Gunst, L. (1995) *Born Fi'Dead: A Journey through the Jamaican Posse Underworld*, New York, NY: Henry Holt & Co.

Hales, G., Lewis, C. and Silverstone, D. (2006) *Gun Crime: The Market in and Use of Illegal Firearms*, Home Office Research Study 298, London: Home Office.

Hallsworth, S. (2002) 'Representations and realities in local crime prevention', in G. Hughes and A. Edwards (eds) *Crime, Control and Community: The New Politics of Public Safety*, Cullompton: Willan Publishing, pp 197–215.

Hallsworth, S. (2005) *Street Crime*, Cullompton, Willan Publishing.

Hallsworth, S. (2008) 'Interpreting violent street worlds', inaugural lecture, Department of Applied Social Sciences, London Metropolitan University, 27 February.

Halpern, D. (2001) 'Moral values, social trust and inequality: can values explain crime?' *British Journal of Criminology*, 41(2), 236–51.

Harris, K. (2006) 'To doff my cap: talking about respect', in K. Harris (ed) *Respect in the Neighbourhood*, Lyme Regis: Russell House Publishing, pp 1–18.

Hayward, K.J., and Yar, M. (2006) 'The "chav" phenomenon: consumption, media and the construction of a new underclass', *Crime, Media, Culture*, 2(1), 9–28.

Home Office (2003) *Respect and Responsibility: Taking a Stand against Anti-social Behaviour*, London: Home Office.

Innes, M., Fielding, N. and Cope C. (2005) '"The appliance of science?" The theory and practice of crime intelligence analysis', *British Journal of Criminology*, 45(1), 39–57

Katz, J. (1988) *Seductions of Crime*, New York, NY: Basic Books.

McCarthy, P and Walker, J. (2006) 'R–E–S–P–E–C–T, find out what it means to me: the connection between respect and youth crime', *Crime Prevention and Community Safety: An International Journal*, 8(1), 17–29.

Measor, L. and Squires, P. (2000) *Young People and Community Safety: Inclusion, Risk, Tolerance and Disorder*, Aldershot: Ashgate.

Moley, S. (2008) 'Public perceptions', in C. Kershaw, S. Nicholas and A. Walker (eds) *Crime in England and Wales 2007/08: Findings from the British Crime Survey and Police Recorded Crime*, London: Home Office.

Mullins, C.W. (2006) *Holding Your Square: Masculinities, Streetlife and Violence*, Cullompton: Willan Publishing.

Newburn, T. and Stanko, E. (eds) (1994) *Just Boys Doing Business: Men, Masculinities and Crime*, London: Routledge.

Nisbet, R.E. and Cohen, D. (1996) *Culture of Honour: The Psychology of Violence in the South*, Boulder, CO: Westview Press.

Pearson, G. (1983) *Hooligan: A History of Respectable Fears*, Basingstoke: Macmillan.

Pitts, J. (2007) *Reluctant Gangsters: Youth Gangs in Waltham Forest*, Luton: University of Luton.

Putnam, R. (2000) *Bowling Alone: The Collapse and Revival of American Community*, New York, NY: Simon & Schuster.

Respect Task Force (2006) *Respect Action Plan*, London: Home Office.

Rodger, J.J. (2008) *Criminalising Social Policy: Anti-social Behaviour and Welfare in a De-civilised Society*, Cullompton: Willan Publishing.

Sandberg, S. (2008) 'Street capital: ethnicity and violence on the streets of Oslo', *Theoretical Criminology*, 12(2), 153–71.

Sennett, R. (2003) *Respect: The Formation of Character in an Age of Inequality*, London: Penguin/Allen Lane.

Sharp, C., Aldridge, J. and Medina, J. (2006) *Delinquent Youth Groups and Offending Behaviour: Findings from the 2004 Offending, Crime and Justice Survey*, Home Office Online Report 14/06, London: Home Office.

Short, J.R.F. (1997) *Poverty, Ethnicity and Violent Crime*, Boulder, CO: Westview Press/HarperCollins.

Spierenberg, P. (ed) (1998) *Men and Violence: Gender Honour and Rituals in Modern Europe and America*, Columbus, OH: Ohio State University Press.

Squires, P. (2007) 'Police perceptions of gang and gun related offending: A key informant survey', Magnet Project, Greater Manchester Police. Available at: https://www.york.ac.uk/management/magnet/.

Squires, P. (2008) 'Introduction: why anti-social behaviour? Debating ASBOs', in P. Squires (ed) *ASBO Nation: The Criminalisation of Nuisance*, Bristol: The Policy Press, pp 1–33.

Squires, P. and Stephen, D.E. (2005) *Rougher Justice: Anti-social Behaviour and Young People*, Cullompton: Willan Publishing.

Tawney, R.H. (1931) *Equality*, London: Allen and Unwin.

Titmuss, R.M. (1970) *The Gift Relationship: From Human Blood to Social Policy*, London: Allen and Unwin.

Turner, P. (2007) ''Nuff respect? Questioning the Respect Agenda', *Battle of Ideas*. Available at: www.battleofideas.co.uk/C2B/document_tree/ViewAdocument.asp?ID=295&CatID=42&Search=true.

Waiton, S. (2008) 'Asocial not anti-social: the "Respect Agenda" and the "therapeutic me"', in P. Squires (ed) *ASBO Nation: The Criminalisation of Nuisance*, Bristol: The Policy Press, pp 337–58.

Young, J. (1999) *The Exclusive Society*, London: Sage.

Youth Taskforce (2008) *Youth Taskforce Action Plan: Give Respect, Get Respect – Youth Matters*, London: Department for Children, Schools and Families.

ELEVEN

Conclusions: promoting mutual respect and empathy

Andrew Millie

In historical (and philosophical) terms, as noted in the Introduction, the search for 'respect' is nothing new. So why in the first decade of the twenty-first century is 'respect' seen to be such an important issue in the UK? As Geoffrey Pearson notes in Chapter Two, there is an assumed decline in standards of behaviour – that 'young people *no longer* respect the law, *no longer* respect their parents and neighbours, they *no longer* show any obedience to authority'. But Pearson's evidence makes a nonsense of such claims and, in fact, people have been behaving in what would be regarded as an anti-social or disrespectful manner for a very long time. There have been broader changes in how we view each other in the contemporary UK, including a decline in deference that occurred during the second half of the twentieth century (although, as noted, this certainly is not all bad). The individualism that has accompanied late modernity also contributed, with behaviour (or even presence) that interferes with neoliberal consumption being seen as anti-social or disrespectful (see Chapter Eight). Late modernity has also brought with it greater expectations and demands of our children and young people, and correspondingly lower tolerances of difference (see France and Meredith's Chapter Three, and Helen Woolley's Chapter Four). Children and young people may not be any more disrespectful than a century ago, but perhaps we have higher expectations of them.

All these factors will have had an effect; however, the main reason why 'respect' has become such a talking point and a focus for policy is political. It's hard to imagine now, but before New Labour's victory in 1997 very few people were talking about anti-social behaviour, and ASBOs did not exist until the 1998 Crime and Disorder Act. The media was quick to pick up on this agenda and, in the 10 years that followed the introduction of ASBOs, it has been hard to miss TV and other media reports of anti-social youth. On TV there is a proliferation of cheap-to-make reality cop shows which regularly bring the misbehaviour of the few into our living rooms. And when the behaviour of our youth is questioned in news bulletins, editors have tended to go for the easy option and have reused the same images time and again of children jumping on car roofs, or pushing a brick through a car window. The result has perpetuated the discourse of decline and contributed to a politics- and media-led 'moral panic'. Again, this is nothing new (see Cohen, 1972); but from the media's perspective, at least, we have become an 'ASBO Nation' (eg Squires, 2008). The apparent solution offered by the state is a demand for respect.

While 'respect' as a concept has had a life of its own, quite separate from government policy (as explored by Peter Squires in Chapter Ten), it was not a policy issue until New Labour made it one. True, the previous Conservative government talked about 'family values' and 'back-to-basics', but New Labour took such moralising discourses a step further. In fact, New Labour talked in terms of 'respect' long before the formation of a Respect Agenda, and before coming to power in 1997. As Elizabeth Burney noted in Chapter One, Tony Blair was concerned about 'rights', 'responsibilities', 'self respect' and 'respect for others' back in 1993. Blair was always good at absorbing the language (if not the precise ideas) of key social thinkers of the time, be they the Third Way ideas of Giddens (1998), the communitarianism of Etzioni (1993) and others, or the call for 'respect' by Sennett (2003). Add to these the particular brand of Christian Socialism that Blair brought to the mix (and more recently that of Gordon Brown), then the result has been what Flint and Powell in Chapter Nine have called a 'contemporary civilising offensive'.

Flint and Powell are right to call it an offensive, with calls for respect being backed by a full armoury of anti-social behaviour enforcement measures. And where support is offered, then this is with the threat of censure. The view is that we will make you more respectful, we will make you more civilised. But definitions of respectful or civilised behaviour have been based on governmental assumptions of what the majority of (so-called) law-abiding citizens want. There is little room for difference or plural expressions and expectations. Rather than aiming to foster *mutual* respect and tolerance of difference, the Respect Agenda has focused on the moral and behavioural improvement of a minority deemed to be 'anti-social' or 'disrespectful'. This is neatly encapsulated in the Foreword to the *Respect Action Plan* (Respect Task Force, 2006: 1), where Tony Blair set out his position:

> Everyone can change [but] if people who need help will not take it, we will make them. If we are to achieve the vision of the Britain that we all want, then there is no room for

cynicism. We need to take responsibility for ourselves, our children and our families, support those who want to do the same – and challenge those who do not.

In this one quotation there are some key phrases that reveal a lot about the New Labour approach. First, if people do not take the help on offer, 'we will make them'. As highlighted in this volume, such an authoritarian or paternalistic perspective implies the state knows best. If you turn down the help the government is offering, then there must be something wrong (and of course this must be corrected, and enforced). This paternalism was recognised by Judy Nixon and Caroline Hunter in Chapter Five in identifying families – and in particular mothers – as the focus of much anti-social behaviour policy. Returning to the quote from Blair, his emphasis on family values – 'taking responsibility for ourselves, our children and our families' – is clear. Blair also shows a low tolerance for those who might question such a perspective, assuming that everyone is in agreement with the government's plan, 'the vision of Britain *that we all* want' (emphasis added). This shows some degree of arrogance, that if you question this vision you are a cynic, and 'there is no room for cynicism'.

I do not believe any of the authors who contributed to this volume has written from a cynical standpoint. Instead, all have intelligently questioned the approach to securing respect that has been promoted by the New Labour government. But over recent years Labour has become suspicious of those who question policy – for instance, that we all know what anti-social behaviour is, so why ask what it means? (Millie, 2009). Similarly, it has been assumed that we all know when someone is being disrespectful, so where is the mileage in considering the origins, contemporary meanings and possible futures for respect? What I hope this book has achieved is to ask questions about the behavioural and moral politics of this agenda, and its close alliance with an anti-social behaviour enforcement drive. The authors have considered the targets of this enforcement, as well as links to other (civilising) agendas, such as efforts to tackle sectarianism (Flint and Powell, Chapter Nine). Other wider policy and philosophical debates have also been considered. In these conclusions the possible future for 'securing respect' is considered.

What has happened to the Respect Agenda?

At the time of writing in 2008, the *Youth Taskforce Action Plan* had overtaken the *Respect Action Plan*. And in the recently published *Youth Crime Action Plan* (HM Government, 2008) there was no mention of 'respect'. It seems that, with Gordon Brown having been Prime Minister for over a year, it was time for him to ditch some of the language associated with his predecessor. Perhaps he had bigger issues to deal with, such as the economy (and keeping his backbenchers in check).

However, as noted previously, it would be premature to mark the demise of 'respect' as a policy issue. Much of the Respect Agenda *has continued* and has simply been re-badged under the work of the Youth Taskforce in the Department for Children, Schools and Families. And, as noted, the Youth Taskforce (2008) still talks in terms of 'giving respect' in order to 'get respect'. The *Youth Crime Action Plan* similarly talks of 'dealing with unacceptable behaviour' (and there is plenty of talk of anti-social behaviour in this document!). The same triple-track approach that the Youth Taskforce has promoted is emphasised, based on 'enforcement, [non-negotiable] support and challenge and prevention' (HM Government, 2008: 17). And the message of behaviour on the majority's (or the government's) terms remains the same, and that if you do not conform you will be dealt with:

> We are ... sending a clear message that the behaviour of the minority will not be tolerated at the expense of the majority. All young people should play by the rules and will be dealt with appropriately when they do not. (HM Government, 2008: 17)

While the word 'respect' may have been dropped from this particular document, the behavioural and moral politics remains the same. Clearly, there is always some anti-social and disrespectful behaviour that is going to be intolerable; and I do not want to belittle the cumulative impact that this can have on victims. But narratives of respect and disrespect, or this more recent demand for young people to 'play by the rules', can lead to the pathologising or criminalising of youthful (mis)adventure. There is a lot of youthful activity that is simply 'different' or 'challenging' as young people make – as France and Meredith put it in Chapter Three – their transitions towards citizenship. If this 'will not be tolerated at the expense of the majority', then policy is clearly *disrespectful* of the young.

What the government's broader push for respect has highlighted is an increasing emphasis on moral and behavioural improvement in UK politics, and that this improvement is on the government's terms, or what it believes the majority wants. This has relevance to agendas and political thinking beyond 'respect'. For instance, the anti-sectarian work in Scotland has already been highlighted. Other examples of this wider 'civilising offensive' might include the ban on smoking in public places, anti-foxhunting legislation, or even recent government rhetoric on reducing plastic bag use (Number 10 website, 2008). Thus, the civilised UK citizen *respectfully* plays by the rules, would never smoke in public, or kill a fox, and always carries a 'bag-for-life'! OK, so I may be being flippant here, but the message is an important one. All these civilising agendas aim to 'remoralise the immoral minority' (see France and Meredith, Chapter Three), and they come with the threat of censure from the state if you do not conform (with the exclusion of using plastic bags, but time will tell).

But what happens to the Respect Agenda, should New Labour lose power? Well, the Opposition under David Cameron has also talked in terms of respect, and of making the country a 'civilised place'. But the Conservatives have a slightly different perspective from the government's, with less emphasis on state involvement and more of a focus on improvements in individual civility that come from individual 'social responsibility':

> So, before we can offer real hope of changing the culture of our country – to make it a more civil and civilised place to live we must first change the culture of our politics, to end the state's perceived monopoly over social progress ... the idea that there is such a thing as society, it's just not the same thing as the state. That, put simply, we all have a role to play. (Cameron, 2007)

Of course, should the Tories gain power, they may be tempted to go down a similar path to New Labour, with the state dictating (and enforcing) standards of behaviour; that if you do not agree with them you are clearly being disrespectful. With their record it is entirely possible – we shall wait and see. But, like New Labour's Respect Agenda, Cameron has emphasised the centrality of the family, that the country needs to be 'more family-friendly so we can turn around the social breakdown, turn around the crime and anti-social behaviour ...' (Cameron, 2008). It seems that calls from the centre for more respect and civility are not going to disappear in a hurry, and that families – or, more particularly, families that do not conform to a political ideal – are continually going to be blamed for young people's poor behaviour.

Both New Labour and the Conservatives have emphasised a drive for civilisation. And 'respect' may have been the right answer to their question, 'How can we create a more civilised or civil society?'. The evidence presented in this book has highlighted that 'respect' can be an important idea, and something that should be encouraged. But in reaching this answer the wrong equation has been used. For New Labour in particular (but maybe the Tories in the future?), it has been assumed that respect can be gained by telling people to act respectfully. If they do not, then they will be *forced* to. This was a large and fundamental error of judgement. In trying to 'secure respect' via threat of censure the state itself is acting disrespectfully. This 'state disrespect' has been disproportionately targeted at certain populations, particularly children and young people, their mothers, street people, even skateboarders.

Is there an alternative?

For the Respect Agenda New Labour took a narrow conception of respect, that it can only be earned – an approach similar to 'appraisal respect' as outlined in the introduction. We all use forms of appraisal respect, as Darwall put it, 'when we speak of someone as meriting or deserving our respect' (1977: 39). The difficulty is when the state bases policy on such appraisal. The population is divided between a majority of respectful citizens and a minority who are disrespectful (and disrespected). And, as noted, the state will then use the threat of censure in an attempt to move citizens from the minority to the majority. A common theme in many of the chapters in this volume has been the 'othering' or 'pathologising' of minority populations; as Peter Squires highlights in Chapter Ten, there is 'a profound preoccupation with the "worth" of individuals at a time when some individuals appear to be "worth" less than others'. The impact of this value judgement has also been noted by Jamieson (2005: 189):

> The vilification inherent in the pejorative rhetoric and punitive emphasis of the 'respect' agenda promotes profoundly negative portrayals of the parents, children and young people targeted.

But a drive to promote a culture of respect does not have to be pejorative, or punitive. Rather than basing policy on respect having to be earned (and following an actuarial risk paradigm where certain groups are identified – and labelled – as potentially anti-social, or as not likely to earn respect), a policy based on a Kantian perspective of respect could be promoted. As Hill (2000: 69) notes, a Kantian perspective is that 'human beings are to be regarded as worthy of respect as human beings, regardless of how their values differ and whether or not we disapprove of what they do'. Such respect is based on inherent human dignity, rather than whether people 'play by the rules' (HM Government, 2008: 17). Some ultimate (criminal) boundaries will have to be maintained, but below that there is scope for more inclusive and understanding discourse and policy, promoting tolerance of difference, promoting cultures of *mutual* respect (see, for example, Chapter Seven by Bannister and Kearns).

Promoting cultures of mutual respect

The notion of mutuality brings the discussion back to the work of Richard Sennett (2003) that helped to inform the Respect Agenda in the first place; however, Sennett's emphasis on mutual respect between the state and its citizens was not so strongly emphasised in the government's work. A need for mutual respect or reciprocity is a theme that repeatedly emerges throughout this volume. For instance, according to Peter Somerville in Chapter Six, mutuality is closely allied to notions of civility, solidarity, sociability and trust. A focus on 'trust' is an important one, and is also explored in Chapter Ten by Peter Squires. Drawing on the work of Halpern (2001), Squires suggests that trust and mutual respect are both closely linked to the development of social capital; that, 'Where social capital is in short supply or where levels of trust and respect are diminished, crime, ASB *and* intolerance appear more prevalent.' Further, Squires claims that:

> It follows that ASB legislation and 'respect' agendas are not solutions for the cultural crisis, but, rather, symptoms of it.

The 'cultural crisis' is the *assumed* loss of respect and civility. Developments in social capital (see Putnam, 2000), based on a trust relationship between the state and its citizens, could lead to developments in truly mutual respect. But, as Somerville points out, this needs to be a balance between formalised codes of behaviour (state control) and 'the informality of everyday processes' (or trusting citizens *to get on with it*). This would seem to be quite a risk, and goes against natural political instincts to be controlling. Nonetheless, the benefits may be worth it. Such trust will certainly demonstrate respect, with the government leading by example.

In the different contributions to this book various models for achieving mutuality are offered. For instance, Somerville suggests a form of co-governance between state and citizen. Bannister and

Kearns recommend what they term 'dynamic' tolerance, or engagement leading to mutual respect and empathy. In my chapter (Chapter Eight) cosmopolitanism is offered as a possible way to nurture mutuality, 'that allows for plurality of behavioural norms and expectations'. I think there is probably some truth in each of these suggestions. From each of the chapters some key ideas are identified that will be important in nurturing a culture of mutual respect, including:

> *Tolerance; trust; engagement; education; citizenship; identity; worth; plurality; empathy; cosmopolitanism; urban performance; and play.*

It seems that *all* these factors could also be important for the formation of a more civil or civilised society. What is missing from the list, but is central to the Respect Agenda, is the idea that respect – or civility – can be enforced, that it can be secured. Put simply, the government needs to learn how to be less controlling.

I shall end with an example of how *less* control could possibly lead to *more* respect. For the past couple of decades the solution to speeding traffic within neighbourhoods has been to introduce speed humps and various chicanes and signs to slow traffic down. This seemed to work, and could have had a significant influence in the decline in British 'joy riding' during the mid to late 1990s (stealing cars becomes less fun if you cannot drive them fast). Yet the current vogue in neighbourhood-level road traffic management is the introduction of 'home zones' (eg Biddulph, 2001; Department for Transport, 2005). It is an idea developed in the Netherlands in the 1970s that, instead of trying to enforce careful and slow driving by physical design, a little chaos is introduced:

> by stripping out all road markings, signs and signals, and injecting uncertainty into the encounters between motorists and pedestrians and cyclists, planners have not only removed the clutter that defaces so many British streets, but reduced accidents as well. (Adams, 2005: 41)

To translate this to the Respect Agenda, a lot of the policy and legislative 'clutter' could be removed. Similarly, some uncertainty could be 'injected' into encounters with 'others'. As noted in Chapter Eight, 'if risk is minimised to the extent that encounters with others unlike ourselves disappear, then the urban experience will be sanitised, and be the lesser for it'. This view may be somewhat utopian, but if citizens are allowed to simply *get on with it*, and there is less state involvement, it is possible that 'accidents', or disrespectful encounters, will be reduced. I am not suggesting that *all* government involvement is removed and that anarchism is the solution to disrespect and anti-social behaviour. Some forms of behaviour will always require state intervention. But a little less control and a little more uncertainty in public spaces, a little chaos, 'a certain anarchy' (see Sennett, 1970: 108) may help. The more we encounter otherness, the more we can tolerate, trust and actively engage difference, and the more we can empathise. Rather than enforcing standards of behaviour, empathy becomes the mark of true mutual respect, of true civility.

References

Adams, J. (2005) 'Streets and the culture of risk aversion', in CABE (ed) *What Are We Scared Of? The Value of Risk in Designing Public Space*, London: Commission for Architecture and the Built Environment, pp 34–43.

Biddulph, M. (2001) Home Zones: A Planning and Design Handbook, Bristol: The Policy Press.

Cameron, D. (2007) 'Civility and civil progress', Speech at the Royal Society, 23 April. Available at: www.conservatives.com/tile.do?def=news.story.page&obj_id=136420.

Cameron, D. (2008) 'Stronger families', Relate Lecture, 9 June. Available at: www.conservatives.com/tile.do?def=news.story.page&obj_id=145186.

Cohen, S. (1972) *Folk Devils and Moral Panics: The Creation of Mods and Rockers*, London: MacGibbon and Kee Ltd.

Darwall, S.L. (1977) 'Two kinds of respect', *Ethics*, 88(1), 36–49.

Department for Transport (2005) *Home Zones: Challenging the Future of Our Streets*, London: Department for Transport.

Etzioni, A. (1993) *The Spirit of Community. The Reinvention of American Society*, New York, NY: Touchstone.

Giddens, A. (1998) *The Third Way: The Renewal of Social Democracy*, Cambridge: Polity Press.

Halpern, D. (2001) 'Moral values, social trust and inequality: can values explain crime?' *British Journal of Criminology*, 41(2), 236–51.

Hill, T.E. (2000) *Respect, Pluralism, and Justice: Kantian Perspectives*, Oxford: Oxford University Press.

HM Government (2008) *Youth Crime Action Plan 2008*, London: COI.

Jamieson, J. (2005) 'New Labour, youth justice and the question of "respect"', *Youth Justice*, 5(3), 180–93.

Millie, A. (2009) *Anti-social Behaviour*, Maidenhead: Open University Press.

Number 10 website (2008) 'Government ready to act on plastic bags – PM', 10 Downing Street Online Newsroom, 29 February. Available at: www.number10.gov.uk/output/Page14779.asp.

Putnam, R. (2000) *Bowling Alone: The Collapse and Revival of American Community*, New York, NY: Simon & Schuster.

Respect Task Force (2006) *Respect Action Plan*, London: Home Office.

Sennett, R. (1970) *The Uses of Disorder: Personal Identity and City Life*, New York, NY: W.W. Norton.

Sennett, R. (2003) *Respect: The Formation of Character in an Age of Inequality*, London: Penguin Books.

Squires, P. (ed) (2008) *ASBO Nation: The Criminalisation of Nuisance*, Bristol: The Policy Press.

Youth Taskforce (2008) *Youth Taskforce Action Plan: Give Respect, Get Respect – Youth Matters*, London: Department for Children, Schools and Families.

Index

Note: The abbreviation ASB has been used for the term anti-social behaviour in some subheadings in the index. Page numbers followed by *n* indicate information is in a note.

A

active citizenship 161*n*, 244
Adams, J. 274
aesthetics and cosmopolitanism 204-7
age discrimination: young people 83, 85
Alibhai-Brown, Y. 202
Althusser, L. 151
altruism 8, 247
Anderson, E. 249-50
anti-social behaviour (ASB) 1-2, 3
   and aesthetics 205-6
   contested meanings 193
   hooligans in Victorian era 41-69
   negative perceptions of young people 75, 85, 188, 267-8
      in public spaces 104, 105, 200-1, 205, 241
   and norms of behaviour 129-30
   and pluralist approach 11, 201
   and policy 1, 4, 13, 29-33
      discourse of respect 243-5
      gendering of ASB 119-35
      intolerance and policy approach 174, 188, 189, 246-9, 269
      subversion and resistance 251
      youth policy and 'culture of respect' 76-7
   and political ideology 25-9
   and Scottish anti-sectarianism policy 224-5, 229-31, 233
   and tolerance 172-3, 174, 188, 189, 246-9, 269
   see also incivility
Anti-Social Behaviour Act (2003) 30, 32, 34, 201
Anti-Social Behaviour Orders (ASBOs) 12, 26, 27, 33, 83
   and criminal sentences 29
   mothers and responsibility 129-30, 131, 132-4
   private sphere limitations 123
   subversion and resistance 251
   victimisation of families 128
Anti-Social Behaviour Unit 30-1, 32
Appiah, K.A. 194, 203
appraisal respect 5, 6, 7, 272

associational solidarity 144-5
Atkinson, R. 152
authority and respect 6-7, 157, 158-60

B

Baden-Powell, Sir Robert 46-7, 53, 55, 56, 58-9, 64-5, 66
Bagnoli, Carla 4, 6, 209
Bagot, Josceline 55-6
Balls, Ed 2, 12, 33
Banksy (graffiti artist) 206
Bannister, J. 13, 151, 181, 199
Barber, A. 99-100
Barnes, J. 154, 155
Baudelaire, Charles 181
Beck, Ulrich 204
behaviour
   and plurality 10-11, 195-7, 201
   politics of 23-37
   in public spaces 9-10
   and public values 1-2
   tolerance and self-awareness 180
   see also anti-social behaviour (ASB); governance of behaviour; norms of behaviour
Bell, J. 249
Berman, Marshall 10, 181
Besant, Walter 50, 51
Binnie, J. 203
Blair, Tony 1
   and anti-social behaviour 26, 30, 31, 32-3, 195, 244
      moralising approach 194, 197, 268-9
   on meaning of respect 31
   moral standpoint 3-4, 5, 23-4
   on tolerance 171
   and youth and Respect Agenda 75, 76
   see also Respect Agenda (New Labour)
Blears, Hazel 33, 34, 194, 203
Blunkett, David 27, 29-30, 31-2, 35-6
BMXers and public open space 106, 205
bonding social capital 242, 251
Booth, Charles 50
Bourdieu, Pierre 140, 143, 249, 252
Bourgois, Philippe 250, 251

boxing clubs and hooliganism 55-6
Boy Scout movement and hooligans 56
Boyd, R. 141-2, 143, 148, 180
Brah, A. 155
Braithwaite, J. 35
Bray, Reginald 42, 43, 47
bridging social capital 242
British Crime Survey 241
British Youth Council 83
'broken society' discourse 35, 241
'broken windows' thesis 30, 199
Brokenshire, James 2
Brown, A. 163*n*
Brown, Gordon 33, 171
  and Respect Agenda 2-3, 9, 24, 77,
    195, 270
Bunting, M. 172, 186
Buonfino, A. 161*n*
Burns, T.R. 140
Burrows, R. 162*n*

C

Cameron, David 2, 9, 35, 241, 271-2
Carr, H. 123
Carvel, John 241
Casey, Louise 30-1, 32, 33, 76, 188, 239
Catholic schools in Scotland 226-7
Cavan, R.S. 175
Celtic Football Club 226, 227, 229
children and young people
  anti-social behaviour 28-9, 186
    negative public perceptions 75, 85,
      105, 188, 200-1, 205, 241, 267-8
    Victorian street life and hooligans
      41-69
  as focus of Respect Agenda 11-12, 33,
    76-7, 225-6
  intergenerational violence 126-7
  and public spaces 97-111, 186, 200-1
  and Scottish anti-sectarianism policy
    225-6
  street culture and respect 249-58, 260
  youth policy and 'culture of respect'
    75-90
  see also anti-social behaviour orders
    (ASBOs)
Children's Plan for England 12, 97, 110
Christian socialism and Blair 3, 24, 268
Christie, N. 246
cities *see* urban living and respect
citizenship 151, 274
  active citizenship 161*n*, 244
  and young people 80, 88, 89, 109
civic absence/presence 150, 159
civic spaces 100, 104-5, 105-6, 109, 205
civil society 24-5, 31-2, 35-6, 37, 247
'civilising offensives' as policy 219, 222,
  223, 225, 229-31, 232-4, 270-1

civility
  and interaction 139, 140, 141-3, 146
    and 'informal social control' 152-5
    and policy to promote respect 158,
      188
    and social inequality 148-9, 154-5
    and Scottish anti-sectarianism policy
      222, 223, 224-35
    Elias's 'civilising process' 219, 220-4,
      229-31, 232-4
    and tolerance 173, 179-80, 181-9
    Victorian morals and manners 37, 41
Clarke, Charles 32
Clinton, Bill 24
co-governance 156, 157, 158, 273
cohesion 155, 156-7, 189
Collins, R. 252
communitarianism 3, 24-5, 31-2, 144,
  197, 247, 268
community
  and ASB policy 29-30, 31-2
  as Blair theme 23, 24
  and 'informal social control' 152-7
  lack of respect for neighbours 27-8
  policies for promoting respect 158-9
  and Respect Agenda 35-6
  see also communitarianism
community associations 156
community safety and victims 128
community solidarity 144-5
Comte, Auguste 8
consumption and respect 184, 197-201,
  204, 208, 209, 267
  and aesthetics 205-7
  'chav' culture 249
  consumption and disrespect 150
  exclusion of 'undesirables' 199-200
contest and cosmopolitanism 193-210
contractual governance 151, 229
cooperative interaction 139-63
cosmopolitanism 142-3, 193-4, 202-7,
  274
  see also multiculturalism
Court of Appeal 120-1, 123, 131-4, 135
Cowan, D. 124
Cramer, H. 124, 125
Crawford, A. 158, 199-200
Cresswell, Tim 199, 205
crime 29, 172
  and gang culture 254-8
  and young people 77, 84, 243-4
    Youth Crime Action Plan 269-70
  see also police

D

Darwall, Stephen 4, 5, 7, 272
Davis, Mike 245
de Swaan, A. 223

Dean, K. 151
deference: decline in 6-7
Dekker, K. 162*n*
democracy and respect 145, 152
democratic schools 89
demonisation 123, 128, 135, 195
Dennis, Norman 28
Dept for Children, Schools and Families 2, 11-12, 33, 77
Deverell, Commander 56
deviancy 123, 196
difficulty and intolerance 242, 243
diffuse civility 180
Dillon, R.S. 78
discipline
  and hooliganism 54
  and resistance 251
  women and ASB 119-35
  young people in custody 85
  see also enforcement
discrimination
  age 83, 85
  ethnicity 84, 86
Dispersal Orders 32, 83, 105, 201
disrespect
  contested meanings 193
  minority/majority division 1-2, 76, 173-4, 194-5, 203, 209, 270, 272
  and social inequality 1, 139, 145, 147-9, 154-5, 248
  violence and respect in street culture 250-1, 252-8
diversity and tolerance 184, 185, 188, 189, 197, 242
  and urban public space 207, 209
Dobson, A. 142-3
domestic open spaces 100
domestic violence and ASB 125-7, 131-2
Douglas, Norman 43-4
Downes, D. 10-11, 196, 246
drunkenness and ASB 30, 201
Durkheim, E. 195
Dwyer Hogg, C. 79
dynamic tolerance 177, 178, 274

E

early intervention policies 77, 85, 248
earning respect 5, 12-13, 36-7, 79-80, 89, 245, 272
  government approach and disrespect 149-50, 248, 270
  and youth culture 78-9
  'street respect' 249-58
Eckbo, G. 99
economic uncertainty 184, 185
education 274
  for citizenship 88, 89

see also schools
Eekelarr, J. 124
Elias, Norbert 219, 220-4, 225, 227, 229, 230, 231, 232, 233, 234
Ellickson, R.C. 185
Ellison, N. 162*n*
empathy 8, 178, 179, 210, 274, 275
employment *see* paid work
enforcement
  ASB policy 29-33, 155-6, 268
    minority/majority approach 194-5, 209, 270, 272
  moral standards 3-4
  Respect Agenda 12-13, 268, 269, 272, 274
engagement 178-9, 181, 184, 204, 274
Ensor, Ernest 58, 59-60, 61
equality and respect 3-4, 4-5, 86
  top-down approach 150, 151, 260
  see also social inequality
established–outsider theory 222-3
Etzioni, Amitai 24-5, 35, 197, 268
EURO 2008: 'Respect' campaign 239-40
Every Child Matters agenda 12, 97
eviction court cases 120-1, 131-4
exclusion
  from public space 199-200
  policy and respect discourse 246-9
  see also othering and Respect Agenda
exercise *see* physical exercise

F

Fairclough, N. 25
false civility 148-9
families
  and ASB policy 30, 77, 123
  family stability and behaviour 27-8, 119-20
    Victorian concerns 42
  and solidarity 145
  see also parental responsibility
Family Intervention Projects (FIPs) 120, 122, 125-30
Field, Frank 27-9
Fixed Penalty Notices (FPNs) 30, 31
Flint, J. 109, 152, 161-2*n*
football
  as remedy for hooliganism 57-66
  Scottish anti-sectarianism policy 227-31, 233
  tolerance and rules of conduct 260*n*
formal civility 141-2
Foucault, Michel 162*n*
Foust, C.R. 199, 208
Fox, Colonel 53, 54, 57
Freeman, Arnold 60, 61-2
Furnivall, J.S. 196

G

Gale, T. 162*n*
games: Victorian street games 43–5
gang culture 254–8, 261–2*n*
Garland, D. 124
Gemeinschaft and *Gesellschaft* 144–5
gender and governance of conduct
    119–35
Giddens, Anthony 25, 196–7, 243, 268
Gilchrist, A. 155
Gill, Tim 109
Goffman, Erving 9–10, 140–1, 152
Goss, Jon 200
governance of behaviour
    'civilising offensives' 219, 221–2, 223,
        225, 229–31, 232–4, 270–1
    contractual governance 151, 229
    problems of plurality 196
    Scottish anti-sectarianism policy
        225–34
    women and ASB 119–35
    see also self-governance/self-regulation
graffiti writing and aesthetics 205–6
Green, Reverend Peter 65
Greenhalgh, L. 99
group relations theory 222–3

H

Habermas, J. 143, 160*n*
Hales, G. 255, 256, 261*n*
Hallsworth, S. 256, 262*n*
Halpern, D. 243–4, 273
Hancock, L 175, 176
'hanging about' of youth 200–1, 241
Hannerz, Ulf 204
Harris, K. 143–4, 145, 153, 158–9, 162*n*
    and Respect Agenda 13, 149, 150, 259
Hart, R. 108
Hayward, K.J. 197–8, 249
health and public open spaces 101
Hendricks, B.E. 108–9
hero worship and Victorian sport 60–1
Heseltine, Michael 198
Hill, Thomas 4, 6, 9, 11, 272–3
Hirschman, A. 160*n*
Home Office 174
    see also Respect Task Force
'home zones' 274
homeless people and exclusion 199, 205
hooligans in Victorian era 48–69
    sport as remedy 53–66
Hope, Arthur 64
Hope, Phil 198–9
Horton, J. 176
Horton, John 196
housing *see* social landlords
Hughes, B. 102

Hughes, Gordon 35
human dignity and respect 4–5, 272–3
Hunter, A. 186
Hurtwood, Lady Allen of 101

I

identity and respect 184, 231, 233, 274
incivility
    'incivil' behaviour 148–9
    increase in bad manners 173
    and Scottish football 229–31, 233
    and urban life 181–9
    see also anti-social behaviour (ASB);
        civility
individualism 6, 28, 184, 197, 204, 242,
    245, 267
inequality *see* social inequality
'informal social control' 139, 151–7, 273
informal support systems 150
Intensive Supervision and Surveillance
    Programmes (ISSPs) 84–5
interculturalism 202–3
intergenerational violence 126–7
internal group opinion 222–3
intervention
    policy and private sphere 123
    and self-governance 153–4, 155, 156
    tolerance as non-intervention 174–5,
        176–7
    see also early intervention policies;
        Family Intervention Projects
intimacy and interaction 139, 141, 145,
    146, 158
    false intimacy 149
    and 'informal social control' 152, 153,
        159
intolerance
    and ASB policy 174, 188, 189, 246–9,
        269
    and discourse of respect 242–3, 246
    and social withdrawal 187, 243

J

Jacobs, Jane 153, 156, 207–8, 209
Jamieson, J. 13, 272
Jeffries, Stuart 9
Jenkins, R. 184
Jones, R.G. 199, 208
Joseph Rowntree Foundation 75,
    183–4, 185

K

Kant, Immanuel 4–5, 79, 195, 203
Karstedt, S. 174
Katz, J. 253, 260
Kelling, G. 30, 199
Keun, Odette 171

Knowles, D. 174
Kooiman, J. 152

L

Landry, C. 202-3
language: discourses of respect 239-62
'Larrikins' 49, 53
Le Corbusier 66
Lefebvre, H. 207
Levine, M. 162*n*
liberty and tolerance 171, 174, 175
licensing and sectarianism 228, 230
local authorities 26, 27, 31, 32
Lofland, Lyn 207
London, Jack 47-8
London Planning Advisory Committee
99
London street life 41-8, 49-50
lone parents *see* single-parent families
low pay for young people 83
Luhmann, N. 140
Lynch, K. 99

M

McCarthy, P. 78, 248, 249, 259
MacDonald, R. 82-3
McGhee, D. 202
Macmillan, James 224
Macmurray, John 24
Madanipour, A. 99
majority/minority approach 1-2, 76,
173-4, 194-5, 203, 209, 270, 272
manners *see* civility
Marsh, J. 82-3
Masterman, Charles 54-5
Matthews, R. 175, 176
Matza, David 10, 196
May, Lord 56
Meath, Lord 55, 56
Mendus, S. 175
mental illness and children 101
meriting respect 5, 12-13, 80, 245
meritocracy and disrespect 147
Middleton, D. 79
migration: effects for tolerance 184
Millie, Andrew 6, 11, 200-1
minority *see* majority/minority
approach
Misztal, B. 141, 142, 143, 145, 153, 157
Mitchell, Don 199, 200, 205
Mizen, P. 81, 82
moral philosophy and respect 4-5
morality
government enforcement 3-4, 194-5,
197, 204, 268-9, 272
dichotomising society 8-9, 10, 194-
5, 203, 209

top-down approach 150, 155-6, 259,
272
parental responsibility and gender 121
pluralist approach 10-11
sport for Victorian hooligans 57
youth policy and 'culture of respect'
75-90
Mulgan, G. 161*n*
Mullins, C.W. 252, 253
Multi Use Games Areas (MUGAs) 103
multiculturalism 184, 202
see also cosmopolitanism
mutual respect
and cooperative interaction 139-63
mutual identification and civility 220,
222, 223
promoting culture of 273-5
and reciprocity 7-8, 36-7, 161*n*
and tolerance 178-9, 193, 209, 242-3,
243-4
and urban performance 208, 209-10
and young people 79, 80, 249
youth policy and 'culture of respect'
76, 89, 90

N

'naming and shaming' policy 30, 147,
150, 247
National Minimum Wage 83, 86
National Union of Students Scotland
226
nationalism and respect 204
and Scottish football 231, 233
neighbourhood open spaces 100
neighbourliness and sociability 143-4
neoliberalism
and consumerism 197-8, 199-201,
208, 267
and plurality 196-7
New Deal for Young People (NDYP)
82
New Labour
urban renewal/regeneration 198
see also Respect Agenda (New Labour)
Newey, G. 175
Newlove, Gary 35
Nicholson, P. 176
night-time economy and ASB 30, 201
Nolan, N. 205
'non-negotiable support' 12
norms of behaviour
and anti-social behaviour 129-30
minority/majority approach 1-2, 76,
173-4, 194-5, 203, 209, 270, 272
women and gender norms 124-5
contested expectations 193, 267
and mutual respect 140
civility and non-conformity 148

government's top-down approach
150, 155-6, 259
and 'informal social control' 152-7
policies to promote respect 157-60
Scottish football and anti-sectarianism
229-31, 233
and tolerance 176, 188, 189, 197
see also anti-social behaviour (ASB);
civility

O

Olds, David 35
open spaces and children and young
people 97-111
see also public space
Opie, Iona and Peter 43, 107
organised sport and hooliganism 53-66
othering and Respect Agenda 8-9, 10,
272
ASB discourse 121-2
dangers of exclusion 35, 36
engagement and cosmopolitanism 204
exclusion from public space 199-200
tolerance and intolerance 185, 186-7,
246-9

P

Pahl, R. 157
paid work and respect 81-3, 147
Parekh, B. 180
parental responsibility 27-9, 30, 34-5
as gendered issue 119-35
and 'informal social control' 154
shift to public patriarchy 124, 269
Parenting Orders 30, 34
participation and young people 86-8
Paterson, Alexander 43, 46, 60, 62
patriarchy: public patriarchy 124, 269
performance
of respect 7-8
urban performance 205, 207-8, 209-
10
Phillips, T. 150-1
Phoenix, A. 123
Physical Deterioration Committee
53-4, 57
physical exercise
children and public open spaces 102
as remedy for hooliganism 53-66
Pilcher, J. 124-5
Planning Policy Guidance 17 100
Platini, Michel 240
play 274
children and public open spaces 102-
3, 106-9
Victorian street games 43-5
Play England 103, 110
play spaces for children 97, 106-9

Playground Association of America 107
plurality and behaviour 10-11, 195-7,
201, 274
Podhoretz, Norman 196
police
enforcement role 29, 30, 31, 32, 156
'extended policing family' 155
perceptions of 'gang-related' crime
256-8
and Victorian street life 44-5, 51-2
politics of behaviour 23-37
power relations
government top-down approach
149-51, 155-6, 259
social inequality and disrespect 147-9,
154-5, 248
prevention policies 12, 35, 77, 85, 248
Prior, D. 36
privacy and public space 187
private sphere 123, 124, 269
proximate civility 179-80
public opinion
and aesthetics 205-6
and 'bad parenting' 34-5
and changes in urban society 183-4
and tolerance 172-4, 175-6, 185, 241
and young people 75, 85, 104, 105,
188, 201, 205, 241, 267-8
public patriarchy 124, 269
public and private sphere and state 123
public schools and organised sport 57-8
public space
and ASB policy 30
exclusion of skateboarders 105-6,
109
and behaviour 9-10
and children and young people 84,
97-111, 186
and consumerism 199-201, 208, 209
exclusion of 'undesirables' 199-200
and incivility 173
tolerance and civility in 181-2, 185,
186
Putnam, R. 143, 242

R

racial degeneration fears 54-5, 59
Rangers Football Club 226, 227,
229-31, 233
Ratner, C. 144
Rawls, John 79, 80
Raz, Joseph 4
'Real Respect Agenda' 2
reciprocity 7-8, 36-7, 143, 156, 161*n*
see also mutual respect
recognition and giving respect 139, 141,
151-2
recognition respect 5, 6, 80-3

redemption and respect discourse 246-9
religion *see* sectarianism in Scotland
remorse in ASB discourse 130, 132-4, 135
Rentoul, John 23-4
reputation 259
  and street culture 252, 253, 255
resistance
  street culture and respect 250-1
  and top-down approach 227, 248
  women and ASB 129-30, 132-4
respect
  definitions and meanings 1, 31, 77-8, 139-40, 240
  policies for promoting respect 157-60
  and tolerance 179
  see also civility; mutual respect
Respect Agenda (New Labour) 1-2, 4, 7, 8, 11-13, 41, 268-72
  discourse of respect 239, 241, 243-5, 247-8, 258-9
  and political ideology 23-37
  resistance and 'street respect' 251
  and Scottish anti-sectarianism policy 224-5, 232-4
'Respect' campaign in EURO 2008 239-40
Respect and Responsibility (White Paper) 29-30, 241, 244
Respect Task Force 33, 239
  'decent people' rhetoric 194, 203, 209
  parenting survey 34
  Respect Action Plan 1-2, 4, 7, 11, 12, 32, 76-8, 81
    and discourse of respect 244-5, 247-8
    government approach and disrespect 139, 149-51
    lack of tolerance in message 173-4, 185-7, 268-9
  see also Youth Taskforce
Respect Zones 195
'respectable' behaviour 147, 149, 150-1, 159
responsibility and respect 3-4, 5, 23-4
  rights and responsibilities discourse 24-5, 244
  youth and citizenship 75-90
retaliation: women and ASB 129-30
revanchism 199
Richardson, L. 162*n*, 163*n*
rights and responsibilities discourse 24-5, 244
'Rights Respecting Schools' initiative 89-90
risk and intolerance 242-3
Roberts, Paul 11
Robins, Kevin 194

Rock, P. 10-11, 196
Rodger, J.J. 223, 241, 242-3, 261*n*
Rogers, Lord 198
role distance and interaction 141, 142
Roman Catholic schools in Scotland 226-7
'rough' behaviour 147
Russell, Charles 57, 60-1, 62-3

S

Sandberg, S. 249-50, 252-3
Sandercock, Leonie 202, 203
Sayer, A. 139-40, 147, 152, 153
Scarman Report 198
School Travel Plans 102
school-to-work transition 81-2
schools
  and ASBO enforcement 30
  and 'culture of respect' 89-90
  decrease in walking to school 102
  public schools and organised sport 57-8
  reduction in playtime 101
  and Scottish anti-sectarianism policy 225-7
  and types of play 102-3
Scotland: anti-sectarianism policy 219, 222, 223, 224-35
Scotson, J.L. 222-3
Scottish Executive 219, 224, 226, 228, 232, 233
Scottish Royal Commission on Physical Training 54, 55
Scottish Social Attitudes Survey 184
scouting as remedy for hooliganism 56
sectarianism in Scotland
  anti-sectarianism policy 219, 222, 223, 225-35
  and Elias's 'civilising process' 220-4, 229-31, 232-4
Secure Training Centres 85
self-governance/self-regulation 119, 121
  group relations and established–outsider theory 222-3
  and mutual respect 139, 151-7, 158
  and Scottish anti-sectarianism policy 228-9, 232, 233
self-respect 5-6, 23, 28, 31, 248, 249
  and tolerance 178
  and youth policy 76, 79-80
  see also worth
Seligman, A.B. 177
Sen, J. 148-9
Sennett, Richard 3, 109, 147, 209, 240, 248, 268
  barriers to respect 179
  mutual respect 7, 8, 36-7, 140, 161*n*, 193, 208, 247, 273

and Respect Agenda 1, 273
and self-respect 81
and stigmatisation 9
and tolerance 187
Sentamu, John, Archbishop of York 7, 8
shame and shaming
   disrespect and social inequality 147
   'naming and shaming' policy 30, 147, 150, 247
   and Scottish anti-sectarianism policy 224, 232
   and social control 221
shopping centres: exclusion 199-200, 208
Short, J.R.F. 250
single-parent families 28
   mothers and governance of conduct 119-35
skateboarding 97, 103-6, 109, 205
Smith, Adam 162*n*
Smith, P. 150-1
sociability and interaction 139, 141, 143-5, 146, 158
   false sociability 149
   and 'informal social control' 152, 153, 154, 155, 156-7, 159
social capital 36, 143, 247, 248-9, 273
   and intolerance 243-4
   'street capital' 249, 250, 251, 252-3, 255-6
   and tolerance 241-3
social causes and policy 31, 35
social control
   adult control of public open space 105, 106-9
   'informal social control' 139, 151-7, 273
   reduction in control 274-5
   resistance and street culture 251
   role of shame 221
social inequality
   and disrespect 1, 139, 145, 147-9, 154-5, 248
   and Scottish anti-sectarianism policy 227-8, 233-4
   and tolerance 181-2, 184
social landlords and ASB 26, 119
   Court of Appeal cases 120-1, 131-4
Social Landlords Crime and Nuisance Group (SLNG) 26
socialisation
   and civilising process 220
   perceptions of young people 241
   withdrawal and intolerance 187, 243
solidarity 142-3, 144-5, 156-7
Somerville, P. 179, 180
spectatorship and Victorian sport 58-62
Spelman, Caroline 35

sport
   as remedy for hooliganism 53-66
   see also football
Squires, Peter 129, 246, 257-8
Staeheli, L.A. 200
status and respect 6-7
   and street culture 257
   young people and recognition 79-83
Stephen, Dawn 129, 246
stereotyping and intolerance 187
stigmatisation 9, 248
   and established–outsider theory 222-3
   and Youth Justice System 84-5, 270
   see also demonisation; shame
Straw, Jack 25-7
street culture and respect 249-58, 260
   'street capital' 249, 250, 251, 252-3, 255-6
street life in Victorian era 42-53, 66
   football games 61-2
   hooligans and fighting 48-53, 55-6
substantive civility 141, 142, 180
surveillance 84, 85, 155
Sutton-Smith, B. 102

T

Tawney, R.H. 24, 245
'teen shelters' 103-4
'thin' and 'thick' civility 142, 143-4, 146, 158
   and informal social control 152-4
   and tolerance 179, 180
Third Way politics 4, 25, 197, 268
Thrift, Nigel 207, 208-9
Titmuss, R.M. 247, 248
'Together' campaign 30-1
tolerance 8, 171-89, 194, 197, 267, 274
   as British trait 171
   definitions 174-5
   and respect discourse 246-9
   and social capital 241-3
Tönnies, F. 144
traffic calming and 'home zones' 274
Truss, Lynne 208
trust 140-1, 157, 158-60, 273, 274
Turner, P. 243

U

UK Youth Parliament 87-8
UN Convention on the Rights of the Child 83, 86
'uncivil' behaviour 148-9, 153
'underclass': lack of voice 122, 128
unemployment and young people 82-3
UNICEF: 'Rights Respecting Schools' 89-90
urban cosmopolitanism 203-4
urban living and respect 193-210

tolerance and intolerance 181-9, 197
  see also public space
urban performance 205, 207-8, 209-10,
  274
urban renaissance policies 198, 199
Urban Task Force 198
Urwick, E.J. 41-2, 55

V

Valverde, M. 124
victimisation
  women and ASB 125-8, 130, 131-2
  of young people 84
Victorian era 37, 41-69
violence
  family violence and ASB 125-7, 131-2
  and respect in street culture 250-1,
    252-8, 260
  street fighting in Victorian era 48-53
  and young people in custody 85
voice
  lack of voice for 'underclass' 122, 128
  and young people's participation 86-8

W

Wacquant, L. 249
Walby, S. 124
Walker, J. 78, 248, 249, 259
Walzer, M. 98-9
Washington, George 179
Watson, S. 186, 188
Watt, P. 162-3*n*
Watts, B. 183-4, 185
Weinstock, Anne 33
welfare benefits 82-3, 248
welfare systems and gender 122-3, 124,
  135
White, Jerry 42-3
Whiteing, R. 57
willingness to intervene 153-4, 155, 156
Wilson, J. 30, 199
women and ASB discourse 119-35
Wood, P. 202-3
work *see* paid work
Worpole, K. 99
worth 3-4, 5, 79, 158, 260, 272-3, 274
  see also self-respect
Wright, T. 205

Y

Yar, M. 249
Young, J. 121-2, 184, 186, 242, 243, 245,
  250
youth *see* children and young people
Youth Crime Action Plan 269-70
youth crime policy focus 77, 270
Youth Justice System 84-5, 86
Youth Offending Teams (YOTs) 30, 33

Youth Parliament 87-8
Youth Taskforce 33, 37, 188, 195
  Youth Taskforce Action Plan 2-3, 11-13,
    77, 248, 269, 270

Z

Zukin, Sharon 205